D0909200

COLLINGWOOD PUBLIC LIBRARY

BANK
HEIST

BANK HEIST

How Our Financial Giants Are Costing You Money

Walter Stewart

A Phyllis Bruce Book
HarperCollins*PublishersLtd*

BANK HEIST: HOW OUR FINANCIAL GIANTS ARE COSTING YOU
MONEY
Copyright © 1997 by Walter Stewart
All rights reserved. No part of this book may be used or reproduced
in any manner whatsoever without prior written permission
except in the case of brief quotations embodied in reviews.
For information address HarperCollins Publishers Ltd,
Suite 2900, Hazelton Lanes, 55 Avenue Road,
Toronto, Canada M5R 3L2.

http://www.harpercollins.com/canada

First edition

Canadian Cataloguing in Publication Data

Stewart, Walter, 1931–
Bank heist : how our financial giants are costing you money

"A Phyllis Bruce book."
Includes bibliographical references and index.
ISBN 0-00-255442-9

1. Banks and banking – Canada   I. Title.

HG2704.S83 1997   332.1'0971   C96-931884-7

---

97 98 99 HC 10 9 8 7 6 5 4 3 2 1

Printed and bound in the United States

For William Krehm, Jordan Grant, Susan Bellan,
Duff Connacher, and all those who devote their energies
to trying to bring our banks to heel

Contents

The Birth of a Notion

Perhaps nowhere in the world can be found so intensive a degree
of close organization as among the bank interests in Canada.

—Gustavus Myers,
A History of Canadian Wealth, 1914

I would strongly suggest that, when we have the opportunity
with journalists, politicians or opinion leaders in the months to
come, each of us remember to underscore that there is a solid
public policy rationale for the government's action to hold the
line on bank powers.

—Mark Daniels,
President of the Canadian Life and Health Insurance Association,
in a letter to his colleagues, 1996

EVERY TEN YEARS, the Bank Act, the legislation that covers the conduct of
our financial leaders, to the extent that it is covered at all, is reviewed
by government, and it is now up for its once-a-decade revision. This
process, which began with salvos of press releases and scurrying lobbyists in the autumn of 1994, will go through in two stages. There will be
some tinkering with the rules in 1997, but the main changes will be proposed in 1998, after a special task force reports back to the government.
This was not the way it was supposed to be; by law, the Bank Act is
amended every ten years, and that's that. However, there was such a

battle about the proposals, and the banks were so angry at the idea that they would lose some of the perks they were demanding this time, such as the right to sell insurance in their branches (rather than merely through their subsidiaries and by mail), the right to swallow most of the car-leasing business, and the right to merge to form fewer and even larger banks, that the whole process was brought to a halt.

Doug Peters, the secretary of state for international financial institutions, and the man responsible for shepherding the revisions through the House of Commons, had prepared a White Paper of proposals for release in March 1996. But the pushing and shoving of the lobbyists on both sides of the banking issues grew so raucous that Peters was concerned that the interests of ordinary Canadian consumers would be lost, and he delayed release of the White Paper. As he noted in a speech to the Canadian Life and Health Insurance Association on May 30, "Unfortunately, in my view, consumer concerns have been all but lost in the consultation process. In this heated environment, it has been hard to reach a consensus on what policies would best serve Canadians as we head into the 21st century."[1]

The minister was immediately attacked for his speech. The government should ignore the lobbyists and just do what it wants done, thundered a number of columnists and editorialists. When I spoke to Peters about this in a private interview, he made it clear that what he was objecting to was not the fact that a great many interests want to contribute to policy debates; rather, his point was that policy was best established, not through the pushing and shoving of lobbies, but through the proper forum for this discussion: specific hearings before parliamentary committees such as the House of Commons Finance Committee, or the Standing Committee on Industry, which has already produced two solid reports on banking.

I reminded Peters that he had referred to the lobby wars earlier in the year, on an open-line radio show in Montreal, when he noted that "[the banks] are not quite in the same class as the Montreal bike gangs, but ..."

I asked, "How did you plan for that sentence to end?"

Peters laughed. "Some of my staff thought I should apologize," he said, "to the bike gangs."[2]

His speech was an attempt—valiant, but possibly in vain—to have the next round of debate on the Bank Act conducted on a higher plane. In June, he released the White Paper, with only minor adjustments, and began the process of setting up the task force, with orders to report "within eighteen months."[3]*

The task force will consider all the major issues in banking today and, if Peters is right, will produce a more thoughtful approach to legislation than we have had in the past. The usual way to deal with these matters has been to give the bankers almost everything they ask for, holding back only one or two items—not unlike a skilful strip-tease—to draw applause in the next round. However, it is the argument of this book that they ought not to get what they want, and, indeed, ought to be relieved of some of the spoils of earlier forays before the Parliament of Canada, while there is still time. It may already be too late. Our banks have become so bloated, so self-satisfied, so full of themselves, and so successful in persuading our politicians of their virtues, that they may be beyond control.

I have been down this road before. In 1982, I wrote a book about the Canadian banks called *Towers of Gold, Feet of Clay*,[4] which sold very well and brought a song to my lips, but not to those of Canadian bankers. They didn't like it much, and would rather I hadn't done it. However, I thought, that's that; I have pointed out the error of their ways, and it remains only for them to go and sin no more.

But the sons of guns are still at it—are, if anything, at it worse than they were before. In the spring of 1995, as part of the runup to the revisions in the Bank Act, when I was summoned to Ottawa to appear before the House of Commons Standing Committee on Industry, in secret session, I found the MPs on the committee seething with discontent. The banks are bigger than ever, they said; they control more than ever; they are meaner than ever; they make more money than ever; and they provide lousy service to their customers, who produce profits, and to small business, which produces jobs. The good news, then, was that at least some MPs were, for the moment anyway, restive enough to take some action against the banks, if only they knew what to do. In fact, they asked me: What should we do? I said I would go away and think about it, and I have thought about it, and this book is the result. To begin the process of deciding what, if anything, should be done with the legislation now before the nation, we need to know a little about our banking system.

---

* It took until December 19, 1996, to get the task force established. Its report is due in September 1998.

The Canadian Banking System

Banks are "deposit-taking institutions," along with trusts, credit unions, provincial savings institutions, and, occasionally, insurance firms. The operative legislation is the Bank Act, which covers the business of banking. And what is the business of banking? It is whatever the banks do. They have never had their occupation defined; instead, the Act says: "bank means a bank to which this Act applies."[5]

Then, under the section titled "Business and Powers of a Bank," we have this: "A bank may engage in and carry on such business as generally appertains to the business of banking."[6]

So, a bank is a firm that does banking, and banking is what a bank does. What could be fairer than that? To operate, a bank needs a charter, and these come in two classes, called "Schedules." (They used to be called "Classes.") Schedule I banks (formerly Class A) are widely held, must be under majority Canadian ownership, and are public companies. That is, they issue shares which are traded on the stock exchanges. By law, no more than 10 per cent of the shares of any Schedule I bank may be held by any one person or group. Schedule II banks (formerly Class B) are nearly all foreign-owned, and can be narrowly held, as, indeed, most of them are. The Canadian Bankers Association (CBA), which likes its little joke, says the latter "have the same powers as Schedule I banks."[7] Not quite. When the law was amended to allow foreigners in, it effectively prohibited any of them from running more than five branches,[8] and limited the total operations of foreign banks to 15 per cent of total commercial lending. In effect, foreigners can never own more than a tiny share of the market, and can never provide any competition to the Big Five (see Table 1 in the Appendix).

There are seven Schedule I and fifty-five Schedule II banks. Besides the Big Five, Schedule I institutions include the National Bank of Canada, which has assets of $49 billion, and the Canadian Western Bank, with assets of $1.3 billion. The most significant of the Schedule II banks, from a Canadian perspective, are the Amex Bank of Canada and the Laurentian Bank of Canada, for quite different reasons.

American Express was handed the right to operate a bank here in late 1988, although it did not meet all the criteria for a foreign bank. In particular, the regulations said that any such institution must be regulated as a bank in its own home country, which American Express is not. This is no minor point in considering whether a bank is backed by a company that is solvent, and properly regulated within its own jurisdiction. The company had been pressing for letters patent for more than two years, but it was blocked by Canadian bureaucrats who kept pointing out that it failed to meet this crucial requirement. Then, on November 21, 1988, the day of a federal election, the Mulroney cabinet overruled the bureaucrats and handed out the prize. Richard Thomson, chairman of the Toronto-Dominion Bank, charged that there appeared to have been a deal made behind the scenes, a charge he later retracted for lack of any proof.[9] In any event, we now have a scattering of Schedule II banks which meet the rules and appear to have little potential for growth, and Amex Bank, which is something else again.

The other significant Schedule II bank is the Laurentian, which is mostly owned by the Desjardins Laurentian Financial Corporation, based in Quebec. It has been gobbling up trust companies—Standard Trust in 1991, La Financière Coopérants prêts-épargne inc. and Guardian Trust Company in 1992, General Trust Corporation and Société Nationale de Fiducie in 1993, and Prenor Trust and twelve branches of Manulife Bank of Canada in 1994.[10] It now has more than $10 billion in assets and 260 branches across Canada.

That, in raw outline, is the system. In the eyes of many, it is not a bad system, compared with the systems of many other nations. But if we look at it from the point of view of the banking sector we need in this country, its central flaw becomes apparent. It is an oligopoly, and oligopolies, by their nature, are economically inefficient, non-competitive, and dangerous. Our banks say this is nonsense; they contend that they are models of productivity and healthy competition, and that we should rejoice in their profits, instead of constantly whining about them.

However, while reasonable profits are indeed essential to any well-run enterprise, the way the Canadian banks are able to rack up ever-larger profits, no matter what is going on in the general economy, suggests that the gains come, not from efficiency, but excessive power.

We get a glimpse into how they use their power, and for whom, in the way they treat their employees, and their executives, respectively. In 1996, the five largest Canadian banks piled up profits of $6.3 billion. In this year, the average wage of a full-time teller was $21,000 per annum, plus a small annual bonus. In Toronto, a family of two with an income below $21,092 is considered to be living in poverty. However, none of the bank executives were in danger of sliding into poverty. Their earnings, including salary and bonuses, were in the millions. John Cleghorn, chairman of the Royal Bank, received $2.28 million in 1995 (the 1996 salaries are not yet public), a jump of 37 per cent over the previous year, while one of his tellers reported getting a hike of six cents an hour.

Richard Thomson, chairman of Toronto-Dominion, did even better than Cleghorn; his total remuneration for the year was $2.8 million. Al Flood, chairman of the Canadian Imperial Bank of Commerce, received $2.9 million; Matthew Barrett, chairman of the Bank of Montreal, $3.9 million; and the top take went to John Hunkin, president of CIBC's stock firm, Wood Gundy, who received $4.9 million.

The banks' explanation is that these matters are determined by "market forces," which apparently decree that hugely profitable firms should lavish millions on the bosses, while the tellers on whom so much depends get about half as much in a year as John Cleghorn earns in a week.

If you find your bank teller a trifle cranky, remember that he or she is probably earning just about enough to keep from sinking, while the bank's executives take home millions—and that they see nothing wrong with that. Some might see it as a sign that the bank managements are a trifle greedy.

Every year, their hold on the economy becomes wider and stronger, and every year, their share of the national wealth goes up. Now they are poised to take another leap, up and out. They are going global, moving beyond our control entirely, and to do this, they want more powers, and weaker regulation. They want to merge, to become fewer in number and wider in reach and even less responsive to the nation that spawned them than they have been in the past.

If the new Bank Act allows this, they will get away with the biggest bank heist of all.

PART ONE

Your Bank Is Not Your Buddy

Banking establishments ... are more to be feared than standing armies.

—Thomas Jefferson,
letter to John Taylor, 1816

CHAPTER 1

Myths and Reality

The proposal of any new law or regulation which comes from this order of society ought always to be listened to with great precaution ... It comes from an order of men whose interest is never exactly the same with that of the public, who have generally an interest to deceive and even oppress the public, and who accordingly have, upon many occasions, both deceived and oppressed it.

—Adam Smith,
The Wealth of Nations, 1776

The bankers are telling us that if, in the future, we want a competitive banking system, which is controlled and headquartered in Canada, then we may have to set aside our instinct that the banks are already too big and be prepared to accept a development that would make one or two of our banks almost twice as big as they are today.

—David Crane,
Economics Editor, *Toronto Star*, 1995

IN SEPTEMBER 1977, Raoul Blanchard, a farmer near Duck Lake, Saskatchewan, borrowed $37,000 from the Bank of Montreal on a promissory note, with interest "payable monthly at the rate of 10.75% per annum," secured by a mortgage on his home and farm, which was co-signed by his wife, Shirley.[1] He already had two other loans, to finance the operations of the farm, and all three were paid automatically out of an account at the local branch, where he had dealt for years. From time to time, he received statements detailing the dollar amounts that were charged to this account, but never stating what rate of interest he was actually being charged. That was a pity, because, five years after he had made this arrangement, the local bank manager, who was leaving his job, mentioned in casual conversation that Blanchard was not paying 10.75 per cent, as he had assumed; he was being charged the Prime Rate plus 2.75 per cent. This was considerably higher than he had contracted for; at one point, he was actually paying just under 24 per cent, or more than twice what he and the bank had signed as the deal. Blanchard pointed out that there must be some mistake, and the bank manager promised to check into it to make sure, but, apparently, he just forgot.

When a new bank manager took over, and Blanchard discovered that he was indeed paying a floating rate, he told the manager to "go to hell" and stormed out of the bank. Within a few days, he received a letter demanding immediate payment of $63,340.14, for everything owed—the two operating loans and the third, mortgage-backed loan. This was followed by a letter from the bank's solicitors, demanding immediate payment again, on the basis of a promissory note which did not exist, and never had existed, for Prime plus 2.75 per cent. The letter ended: "You will understand that if legal proceedings are commenced, you will ultimately bear these costs. Please govern yourself accordingly."

Blanchard, a fifty-three-year-old man with a Grade Nine education, was thoroughly spooked, particularly when his own lawyer indicated that it looked to him as if the Blanchard farm could, and would, be seized. So, Blanchard borrowed from a credit union and paid off the entire amount claimed.

But, after a while, he got to thinking, No, dammit, that wasn't right, and launched a lawsuit against the bank for the extra interest he had been forced to pay—$11,246.54. The bank, in its defence, did not claim that there was a note for Prime plus 2.75 per cent. Rather, its case was that the normal demand loan was on a floating rate; that the plaintiff did not complain within thirty days of receiving the statements (which he did not understand), and that "the interest rate inserted was the interest rate prevailing at the time the notes were given and was subject to change ... as understood and agreed to between the parties."

The bank asked the court to change the note, now, to reflect what it had done years before.

The court declined, seven years later, when the matter finally came to trial. Mr. Justice Batten of the Saskatchewan Court of Queen's Bench found that "the bank was in a fiduciary arrangement with the plaintiffs; the plaintiffs relied on the bank for advice in regard to their financial dealings." It could not, therefore, simply rearrange things and say the Blanchards ought to have complained about changes they knew nothing of, and which, if they were real and legitimate, the bank had a duty to tell them about. The judge said that, "although the bank was 'arbitrary' and 'high-handed' in its treatment of the plaintiffs' loan, negligent in its practices, and in breach of its fiduciary duty to the plaintiffs to keep them informed, its actions were made in the bona fide belief that it was entitled to the interest charges it demanded and were not so wilful and wanton as to warrant the granting of exemplary damages."

He therefore socked the bank merely the $11,246.54 in extra interest it had collected, plus interest going back to the beginning, and costs of the trial.

Just about the time Blanchard was discovering that he had been docked far too much money, a Toronto man closed out his account at a Toronto-Dominion bank in Toronto and was given $600 too much. When he hung onto it, the bank had him charged with theft. County Court judge Lloyd Graham dismissed the charge, and rapped the bank for not simply taking the man to civil court to collect, rather than trying to make a criminal out of him. The bank was not very contrite. Its lawyer explained that TD doesn't just use the criminal courts to collect its money; usually, it sues as well.[2]

I think the banks have been getting away with multiple repetitions of the Blanchard case because of the wide gap between the myths they promulgate about themselves and the reality of banking today. If we can explode these myths, there is a chance, over the next two years or so, to institute a real reform of the financial sector, rather than merely giving the bankers more of what they want. The process must begin, then, with a look at what the banks say, and what they actually do.

The Myth

Canadian banks are safe places to put our money.

The Reality

Canadian banks are not as stable as we have been led to believe. They are no longer required to hold reserves with the Bank of Canada. This change slid through almost entirely unobserved in 1991, in amendments that triggered a series of moves that lowered the requirements at three-month intervals, until they are now gone entirely. Only two other advanced nations on earth allow their banks to create money without reserves—the United Kingdom and Switzerland—because it means there is no real control over the rascals. In *Towers of Gold, Feet of Clay*, I suggested this was what the banks were aiming for, but I never thought they would actually get away with it. The implications are huge. First, there is no effective curb on the amount of money a bank can conjure up in the bowels of a computer, with a few keystrokes, and if that isn't dangerous, I don't know what is. There is an apparent curb, in the capital ratios set up by the Bank for International Settlements—that is, the banks themselves—and there is a regulatory curb, overseen by the Office of the Superintendent of Financial Institutions. But the superintendent believes—unbelievably—that if a bank is sliding towards failure, the proper course is to let it crash, and have the government (in reality, the taxpayer) pick up the pieces, through deposit insurance.

Second, there is no longer any effective instrument, other than jacking up interest rates, that the government can use to control inflation. In the past, when the economy got too hot, the government could instruct the Bank of Canada to raise the reserve requirements, which meant the banks had to put more cash into the vault to match the money it created as loans. That's gone now, which is why you hear only about interest rates as an inflation curb; and it is not a curb, it is a club. We cool off inflation by battering the economy into unconsciousness, and then wonder where the jobs went.

However, by far the greatest threat to the safety and stability of the banking system is the way our banks have used the money freed by the end of reserves to go plunging into derivatives trading, the most volatile trading in the world, as we will see in Chapter 8.

The Myth

Banking is one of the most regulated industries in Canada.[3]

The Reality

This is the line the lads lay out for public consumption. When a banker is talking to his own kind, another theory emerges: "The reality today is that globalization has made effective regulation by a single nation difficult, if not impossible."[4] This is the Bank of Montreal, the most interesting of the Big Five* Canadian banks, talking to the troops in its 1995 annual report. Of course, when the insiders say that no single nation can control banks, they don't mean that a *gang* of nations can, or will. They mean there is no control. No, they mean that the control is exercised by "re-regulation." Thus:

> In a world of such unpredictable flux, it is reassuring that the appropriate response has been forthcoming from global regulators: the emerging concept of re-regulation. Re-regulation recognizes that the international marketplace represents a greater force for constructive self-governance than any national regulatory body, and in conjunction with the framework provided by international market-watchers such as the Group of 30, seeks to ensure that the discipline of an efficient marketplace is the discipline that regulates best.[5]

Re-regulation is not what you or I would consider to be regulation. Rather, international market-watchers, a.k.a. other bankers, look on to

---

* We will meet the Big Five often. They are, in alphabetical order, the Bank of Montreal, the Canadian Imperial Bank of Commerce, the Royal Bank of Canada, Scotiabank (legally, it retains its former name, the Bank of Nova Scotia), and the Toronto-Dominion Bank.

make sure that "an efficient marketplace" is imposing discipline by, well, being a marketplace. Before 1929, when the Great Crash and a subsequent worldwide financial meltdown persuaded governments that there was a need for something more robust in the regulatory line, it was the marketplace that monitored the stock exchanges. What the banks are doing today is placing their industry in the same position the stockbrokers in 1928 were in. And boasting about it.

The fact that no nation can regulate the banks, however, doesn't mean that the nation has no role to play. Its role is to stand by with an open wallet in case of trouble. When the bank goes belly up, the nation pays off the depositors, and then conducts a post mortem to prove that everything that needed to be done had been done before the crash, and nobody is to blame.

The Myth

The bank is on *your* side. Or, as the Toronto-Dominion Bank puts it, "Your Bank. Your Way." Honest. "We're here to help make it easier ... We cannot deliver to shareholders if we do not deliver to customers."[6]

The Reality

This is the same Toronto-Dominion Bank that helped out a customer named Lorne Seier, president of a Winnipeg firm, Vita Health Co. (1985) Ltd., which manufactures nutritional products. Seier had been burned in a bankruptcy to the tune of $20,000, and the manager of the TD bank with which he had dealt for the past forty years told him that he should have asked for a credit inquiry on the company that keeled over before shipping to it. Later, when Seier noticed that his largest account receivable, General Nutrition Centre Ltd., of Montreal, seemed to be in trouble, he ordered a series of credit reports on the company. In March 1989, he got a report that indicated all was well. A month later, the bank stopped payment on two cheques from GNC, which had exceeded its line of credit by $214,000. That action was followed by a second credit report, in June, which indicated that the account was still not in danger;

the words later used in court were that a bank official "considered the account satisfactory and that it should not be at risk." In August, there was another report, suggesting that the company was experiencing cash-flow problems, but that these were due to the "time of year." Seier continued to ship products based on these assurances. When GNC went into limbo shortly thereafter, and he could not collect, Seier sued the bank for negligent misrepresentation and breach of fiduciary duty. If it had been "His Bank. His Way" he ought to have received a cheque and an apology, instead of which he had to go to court. After the usual long court hassle, The Manitoba Court of Appeal found that the bank was liable on the grounds of breach of fiduciary duty. (The earlier reports had just left a few things out.) The court found that the bank benefitted from the fact that Seier's firm continued to shop products long after GNC was in trouble—because the bank's security was based, in part, on goods in inventory—but there was no finding that it gave the faulty reports for the *purpose* of improving the value of its security. Seier eventually collected $399,349.60.[7]

The Myth

Banks are efficient.

The Reality

In the 1970s and early 1980s, Canadian banks piled into the resources business, especially in the United States, lending out a lot of money to a great number of people who wanted to play in the oil patch but didn't want to use their own funds for the purpose. A depressing number of these loans went sour. The banks wrote off the losses and promised to be more careful next time. Then they piled into real estate loans, and watched billions of dollars evaporate because they were lent out in circumstances that, to say the least, lacked prudence. At one point, when Olympia & York Ltd., the giant Canadian developer, was sliding towards oblivion, it asked a group of Canadian banks for another $250 million (U.S.) in walking-around money. By this time, the banks were hearing rumours that not all was well at O & Y, so they asked for some numbers. The developer then produced, at its head office in downtown Toronto, a looseleaf notebook containing revenue-flow numbers, which was strapped to a table. The bankers could look at the numbers, and make notes, but no copying. On this basis, most of the lending banks agreed to advance the money. When O & Y toppled off the pier at Canary Wharf, in London, and went into bankruptcy protection in Canada, the United States, and England at the same time, the banks lost billions. Upon which, the CIBC, which had led the charge to lend to O & Y (and whose chairman, Paul Reichmann, was for years on the CIBC board), announced that it was going to institute a tough new lending standard.[8] When the banks got that mess cleared up, they plunged into more huge loans in Mexico.

In the spring of 1996, one of those tip-of-the-iceberg stories broke that throws some light on the rigour of our financial institutions, which, while they may insist on dissecting your income tax return before lending you enough to pay what you owe on it, are not so tough with some of their corporate clients. Eight financial institutions from around the world, including the Bank of Montreal's U.S. subsidiary, were taken for $441 million in a fraud which one reporter called "a cartoon quality caper."[9] It was dubbed "Project Star," and involved a syndicate of banks who thought they were putting up money for a research project for the tobacco giant Philip Morris Companies Inc. in 1993. The lenders were told that the company was studying "future cigarette alternatives," now that everyone was objecting to the way cigarettes tended to kill people. Project Star was surrounded by secrecy, and all dealings went through one contact, a man named Edward Reiners. After a few hundred millions had been plopped into the pool, some smart alec at Long Term Credit Bank in Japan thought it might be a good idea to check with Philip Morris, to ensure that Reiners had the power to sign contracts on behalf of the firm. It turned out he had been fired from Philip Morris in 1992. When the Bank of Montreal—which had dropped $120 million (covered, the bank hastened to note, by fraud insurance)—was asked who was responsible for checking this kind of elementary stuff, the bank, in effect, replied that it was none of the public's business.

The Myth

When they make money, we make money, or, as Richard Thomson, chairman of the Toronto-Dominion Bank, put it, "My message is that the bank's profits are yours."[10]

The Reality

Try to cash that statement at your local branch, and see where it gets you, although it seems now to be the party line among all the bankers. When, in the spring of 1996, the Bank of Montreal and Scotiabank announced, yet again, record profits for the first quarter, Robert Chisholm, vice-chairman of Scotia, declared that this should please us all, because "most Canadians are shareholders of banks but they may not realize it."[11] The bank profits are given back to the shareholders, and most pension plans and mutual funds own bank shares; *ergo*, more for the banks means more for the Registered Retirement Savings Plans that hold bank shares, and which many Canadians own.

If you look at Table 2 in the Appendix, you will see three lines that bear on this claim. For each of the Big Five Canadian banks, I have shown the Earnings per Share, the Dividends Paid per Share, and the Dividend-Payout Ratio, for a five-year period. You will see that what the banks earn has only a distant relationship with what they give the shareholders. For example, the Bank of Montreal, in 1995, earned $3.45 per share and declared, in dividends, $1.29, or 38.2 per cent of the take. Scotiabank earned $3.38 per share, of which $1.24, or 36.7 per cent, was paid out. And if you look across the five-year performance of the banks, you will see that the dividends do not, in fact, go up and down in proportion to the earnings, at all.

Well, then, what happens to the rest of the money? Most of it goes to pay salaries and bonuses to a select few. For example, Scotiabank profits went up from $210 million to $249 million in the quarter ending January 31, 1996—a jump of $39 million. But pay for bond and equity department salaries went from $349 million to $426 million—an increase of $77 million.[12] Similarly, the Bank of Montreal earned $68 million more in the first quarter, and paid $50 million more in salaries and bonuses in its trading departments.[13]

The Myth

The banks are "aggressive competitors."[14]

The Reality

Banks buy and sell money. As we shall see, they make up most of the money they sell, manufacture it right on the premises, but it is still the essential product of all these institutions. And, as any Canadian can see by looking at the newspaper or Table 3, they buy and sell it, almost all the time, at the same price. It used to be that the trust companies would pay you more, but the banks own most of the trust companies now, so even that option is gone. Similarly, the amount a bank will charge you for borrowing is exactly the same for all banks.

The whole notion of the Prime Rate is the perfect symbol of how little our banks compete; it is a rate that floats about one and a half percentage points above the Bank Rate, and *it is exactly the same at every bank, trust company, and credit union in the land, and, as soon as one changes it, they all follow suit.* Suppose we had a Prime Rib Rate. Every week or so, the packing plants would tell us what the cattle were fetching on the market, and the cost of a pound of prime rib would be set two dollars above that, and it would be the same in every meat counter in the country. Would you think of the packers and butchers as fierce competitors?

Canadian banks are an oligopoly; that is, the market is controlled by a few dominant firms which set the prices for all of the goods they buy and sell. The Big Five, which aspire to become the Big Two or Three, hold more than 90 per cent of all the assets in banking in this country, and they reap huge profits, decade in, decade out, by selling their goods at exactly the same price, which, as we will see, they have been raising steadily, in lock-step, over the years.

They compete, as other oligopolies compete, mainly in the array of services they offer, and the gimmicks they proffer. TD will give you five dollars if you have to stand in line for more than five minutes, but when you get to the counter, you will be treated to exactly the same brief, harried smile and pretty much the same interest rates as at other banks. The Big Five banks have 180,811 employees, and more slogans, advertising tags, and gimmicks than we know what to do with, but I defy any Canadian, once he or she is inside a bank, to tell what distinguishes it from any other bank. The slogans differ, the tellers change, as does the degree of cheer or surliness on the other side of the counter, but these vary from branch to branch, not from bank to bank. They are a factor of local management, not of competition.

The Myth

"The banks meet the country's credit needs by making funds available to individuals and businesses seeking loans."[15]

The Reality

It is precisely the banks' unwillingness to lend money to Canadian small businesses that has led to the current concern among MPs. The Big Five have done such a poor job serving small and medium-sized businesses that governments have had to create their own instruments such as the Federal Business Development Bank to take up the slack. Canadian banks are merely maintaining tradition; Canada's early economic development was markedly slowed by the unwillingness of the banks to allow venture capital to seep out to the frontiers, where it was needed.

Max Ward, one of the nation's most innovative and energetic businessmen, described his relationship with the banks, in the formative years of Wardair, this way:

> Raising money for a jet wasn't going to be easy for a man who, when he went through the front door of a bank, saw the bankers all piling out the back. I remember once during this period, an official with the Canadian Imperial Bank of Commerce told me he would never lend me any more because "You don't care about money, you just use it." I was astounded. Apparently, you were supposed to accumulate the stuff in ever-higher piles. Then, and only then, would the banks give you some more.[16]

The Myth

"Bank services continue to evolve to meet customers' changing demands."[17]

The Reality

We have 7,744 bank branches and 15,000 Automatic Banking Machines (ABMs),[18] which makes us the most over-banked nation in the world, except for Japan, but the service is still lousy. The ABMs and the direct-deposit cards, and the so-called smart cards, are, in fact, huge profit centres. It costs banks less to lift our money through a machine than through a person. Thus, we have the Bank of Montreal explaining that it was able to jack up its income from operating service fees "due to an increase in the number of FirstBank Plan fee programs used by customers to manage their service charge costs."[19] When you buy the FirstBank Plan, for which you pay a monthly fee, you do so because you expect to save money; indeed, that's what the bank sells you on.* But, the more people who do this, the more the bank makes. Similarly, we have CIBC explaining to the shareholders that it cleaned up an extra $15 million in 1995 in large part due to "the CIBC Menu Account, introduced in 1994."[20] The Menu Account is the one where the CIBC suddenly began to charge customers for *not* using its services.

The Myth

"The banks are committed to employment equity."[21]

---

* Every bank now has its version of these "savings" to be made by opting for a monthly fee instead of individual charges. Some customers, who have a great deal of activity in their accounts, will save money by paying, say, $12 a month for a package of services. But I have never met one on which I would save money, and, it is clear from this statement in the Bank of Montreal's annual report that the bank believes it makes more money by signing customers on to the monthly tab—much more money. That can only mean that the customer loses.

The Reality

This is part of a larger, general myth that the banks are good corporate citizens, which is not so easy to attack. In some ways, they are; they are generous contributors to charity. However, it is not hard to examine their claim to treating the "gals," as we like to call them in banking circles, just like the guys. In Table 4, you will see that the Big Five banks have 205 directors, of whom 23 are women, and 319 officers, of whom 22 are women. Women represent more than 50 per cent of bank customers and have, for more than two decades, represented more than 50 per cent of bank employees. They represent 11 per cent of directors and 7 per cent of bank officers.

The Myth

"Most banks have a code of ethics, which details not only what is legal but what is *right*. The code typically stresses integrity, respect for the customer and the bank, confidentiality, fair dealings and how to avoid conflicts of interest and other compromising situations."[22]

The Reality

Historically, the banks have made up their boards of directors by conveniently appointing the presidents of the largest firms with which they do business. As far back as 1978, the Royal Commission on Concentration pointed out the danger to the banks:

> The boards of our major lending institutions are composed almost entirely of individuals who have an additional relationship to the bank, usually as the chief officer of a borrower. Inevitably this creates the possibility of a conflict of interest, collective as well as individual, where the directors' obligation may clash with their duties elsewhere.[23]

The banks paid absolutely no attention to this warning.

There is another constant conflict when the banks move, as they have in the past decade, into the trust, brokerage, and mortgage businesses. They are handing out advice on what shares to buy, or where to invest. Information, tips, contacts, and commissions pass back and forth among the various arms of banking, and when you buy a mortgage or a RRIF, or a mutual fund, at your local branch, if you think you are getting arm's-length, independent advice, you are kidding yourself.

The Myth

"The banks' net interest margin is so tight that a cut of less than 1% in all loan interest rates would more than wipe out net earnings."[24]

The Reality

Banks make their profit from loans out of what is called "the spread," the difference between what they pay us for our money and what they sell it for. There are two points to be made about the particular brand of nonsense we are being served here. The first is that it is simply not true. You will see, in Table 5, what the real spreads are, and how they have risen over the past years, on the most important sector of bank lending. Indeed, the Canadian Bankers Association's own booklet contains a table that shows that all the Canadian chartered banks had a wider spread in 1992 than in 1989.[25] But the banks say, No, that's not what we mean. We mean the margin is narrow on *all* our money, all over the world, which we are not going to show you, because you would only get rude about it. Take it from us, when you add up the loans on which we make very little, over there in Dar es Salaam, and those back home, the spread is less than a point.

However, some of the banks do show enough detail to prove how wrong the myth is. The Bank of Montreal's 1995 annual report clearly shows a "Total Bank Spread on Average Assets" of 2.56 per cent, but none of the Big Five shows the spread on deposit accounts. In 1982, I complained that they had widened the spread to as much as 4.5 per cent on a standard chequing account. They were paying depositors 12 per cent, and charging 16.5 per cent for secured loans. In early 1996, they were paying 0.25 per cent and charging 7.5 per cent; the spread is 7.25 per cent.

A Profit, Not a Killing

The Canadian banks would have us believe that they are safe, fair, ethical, efficient, equitable, and responsive only to our needs. But fewer and fewer Canadians believe this, particularly when they see news reports of astounding profits being piled up by the banks while other sectors of the economy are in dire straits. And when, as consumers, we see every day that they grow richer while we grow poorer, we are inclined to consign the chummy mythology of the CBA to the ashcan.

Canadian banks are no worse than the banks of other nations—but they are no better, either. They are large, aggressive, profit-seeking corporations driven by exactly the same mixture of greed, ambition, zeal, and impatience with regulation as other large corporations. We can hardly fault them for trying to make as much money as they can, to avoid as much interference from government as they can, to provide as little service as they can get away with, at the highest possible cost—that is the nature of the corporation, which has no soul to save or backside to kick. What we can and must do, however, is to persuade, bend, and if necessary force them to behave in a way that is consonant with the public purpose, as well as the bottom line. We want them to make a profit, but not a killing, and, to that end, we need now to bring them to heel. If we succeed, it will be for the first time in Canadian history, as we will begin to see in Part Two.

A Brief History of a Rogue's Game

Here lies old twenty-five per cent.
The more he had, the more he lent.
The more he had, the more he craved.
Great God, can this poor soul be saved?

—Anon.

CHAPTER 2

The Invention of a Useful Fraud

bank n (ME, fr. *banc* MF or OIt; MF *banque*, fr. OIt *banca*, lit., bench, of Gmc origin; akin to OE *benc*) ... an establishment for the custody, loan, exchange, or issue of money, for the extension of credit, and for facilitating the transmission of funds.

—*Webster's*

Bankers have done more injury to the religion, morality, tranquillity, prosperity, and even wealth of the nation than they can have done or ever will do good.

—John Adams,
letter to John Taylor, 1819

THERE IS SOME DOUBT about when banking began, which turns on what we mean by "banking." In ancient Egypt, grain was a common medium of exchange,[1] and people paid their taxes in this commodity, which was stored in depositories run by the state. Under the definition in the first epigraph to this chapter, these were banks. In many early civilizations, the royal palace and the temple were both centres of distribution and storage facilities for crops used as money. The landholder would deposit his grain and get back a receipt, which allowed him to withdraw what he needed, when he needed it. The owner presented his receipt and was given the grain. It was not much of a step from this to a note directing the priests in charge to deliver the grain to another party. The cheque was born.

However, modern banking owes its start to the goldsmiths of the Renaissance period, who controlled most of the specie—gold, silver, and bullion—and whose presence was essential to the operations of the fairs that were the major marketplaces of Europe for centuries. Like modern goldsmiths, they worked in precious metals, but they did much more than that. They knew the value of the dizzying array of coins that had been put into circulation by dozens of states, kings, and even private merchants, because they could measure the value of the metal in the coins. At the trade fairs, they were on hand to change money, advance funds, and accept deposits. Because coins weighed so much, were so hard to carry from town to town, and were so attractive to the element that preferred to take out loans with the aid of a dirk, it became simpler for merchants to have current accounts with the goldsmiths as they moved from fair to fair, and to pay in notes which were demands on the goldsmiths' vaults. These became clearing-houses, and transactions were accomplished through "policies (later bills) of exchange," the first paper money.

As the economy grew, it became necessary to increase the money supply faster than gold and silver could be mined and turned into coin by government. The invention of paper money, then, was crucial to the expansion of trade; but in allowing private goldsmiths to become the source of paper funds, governments gave away an important economic tool. Could the supply of currency have been increased in any other way? Yes. Governments, which had been the sole issuers of coins, could have provided all the bank notes needed for expansion.[2] That they did not, but allowed private merchants to do so, is one of those accidents of fate that sound so small and loom so large. The most important part of finance, the creation of money, was left mainly in the hands of private entrepreneurs rather than government. As we will see later, it still is.

Sometime early in the seventeenth century, the goldsmiths made a marvellous discovery, the discovery that leads the standard texts to refer to "the beginning of fractional reserve banking."[3] What they found was that, when someone deposited money with them, they could lend it out again, at interest, in the form of notes, several times over. A merchant—we will call him Olaf—would deposit a sackful of cash with a goldsmith, and get back a note that said, in effect, "Olaf has 5,000 kroner on deposit with me." Then the goldsmith would give out another note, representing all or part of Olaf's deposit, to another merchant, and charge him interest on it. In return, he would receive a promissory note from the second merchant, stipulating the interest to be paid and the time for repayment.

Olaf could spend his note, which would eventually come back to the goldsmith for redemption. The other merchant could also spend his note. As long as all the notes issued were not presented at one time for conversion into coin, goldsmiths could dispense notes for far more than the value of the coin they held. As one scholar noted, "The goldsmith assumed the role of the modern commercial banker who, through his lending operations, creates money out of his customers' promises to pay."[4]

The miracle of banking was the discovery that it was rare for a customer to ask for all of his money back at once, and even rarer for all customers to demand cash at the same time. So long as they kept a sufficient supply on hand, the goldsmiths could lend out the same money over and over again. It was exactly as if a landlord discovered that he could rent the same house to half a dozen families at the same time, and charge them all rent for the whole place, or a hostler found he could sell the same horse to a dozen different customers, and not get hanged. It was even better, because the landlord at least owned the house, and the hostler, the horse, while the goldsmith or banker was able to rent out money that wasn't even his in the first place, and charge interest on it. The money men could make up their product on the premises, and sell it in multiples, just so long as the innocent customers didn't enquire too closely into what they were doing. It remained for future generations to sanctify this hokum with complex economic theories.

Today, it is becoming imperative for our bankers to deny that this is the basis of their craft, for reasons we will meet later. A new mythology is being developed in which, it is claimed, the banks merely borrow money from some customers and lend it to others; they do not create cash out of thin air. But they do, and until recently, never bothered to deny it. "Fractional reserve banking" is merely a way of saying that a bank can survive and prosper by keeping on reserve in its vaults only a fraction of the money it circulates by way of notes. As John Kenneth Galbraith, the eminent economist, has noted wryly, "The process by which the banks create money is so simple that the mind is repelled. Where something so important is involved, a deeper mystery seems only decent."[5]

The other side of the coin, of course, is that if you make up out of thin air several times more money than you can actually produce in your vaults, and the folks want to see it all at once, you have an embarrassment. A number of goldsmith-bankers discovered this when, in 1667, a Dutch fleet destroyed a British fleet off Chatham. Panicky English depositors did what depositors have done ever since; they hustled down to convert their paper notes into clinking cash as fast as possible. Since there was only a fraction of specie on hand, compared with the notes outstanding, dozens of goldsmiths were forced to declare bankruptcy, and thousands of their customers followed them into ruin.[6] The First Law of Banking might be stated as follows: A banking panic occurs when the customers want to take out of the institution all the money they put into it, thus exposing the underlying fraud.

The Bank of England

The advantage of multiplying money became clear to the British after the establishment of the Bank of England, late in the seventeenth century. It was a private bank (and remained so until 1946), founded by an interesting rogue named William Paterson, who, like so many bankers—and so many rogues—was a Scot. He was an adventurer and promoter who had travelled a great deal, made a lot of money out of a scheme for supplying water to the city of London,[7] and had in mind an even greater idea, which was to establish a colony on the Isthmus of Panama. The "Darien Scheme," as it was called, was not attracting many investors. What was required was a needful royal, and fate produced the very man, William III, William of Orange, up to his peel in debt. What with a war against France, and a civil commotion in Scotland, and another in Ireland, William was running out of money to meet his army payroll; even a giant lottery and a raid on the finances of the London-based Orphans' Fund left His Majesty short, when Paterson, and a group of fellow investors, came up with the solution.

They would create a national bank, into which they would put capital of £1.2 million, and which would immediately lend the money to the

Crown, at 8 per cent per annum, plus a management fee—a rather rich management fee—of £100,000 annually. Then the Crown would allow the bank to issue paper currency, again paying 8 per cent per annum to the general public, based on the same £1.2 million. This would instantly double the money—chicken feed, by modern standards, but a miracle at the time—and the notes would be accepted because they had the backing of the Crown. Paterson and his group planned to keep about £200,000 or £300,000 on hand, to meet demands for specie based on these notes, and use the rest as often as possible. There was no provision in the law that established the bank for any level of reserve.

What made the scheme even more brilliant was that the original capital that launched the process came from a deal called the Tonnage Act, which authorized the bank to levy a tax on British ships. The promise of this forthcoming money allowed the bank to advance credit to the king, with a promissory note as its only security. Then the bank printed notes, backed by the royal promise, and these notes were lent out, at interest, to merchants who used them as we would use any bank note (it is only in recent times that bank notes ceased to command interest). Had the king slapped a straight tax on shipping, he would have had a political battle on his hands; instead, he gave up that right to the new bank, got a loan in return, put up a piece of paper to secure the loan, and the bank issued notes based on this paper.[8] The king got money, the bank got money, the public got loans, and the entire scheme was floated on the basis of revenues that might or might not ever be collected under the Tonnage Act. The Bank of England, which was to become to banking what Westminster Abbey is to the Anglican Church, not only hoisted itself by its own bootstraps, it invented the bootstraps by which it was elevated.

The effect of this series of frauds was to create a new supply of money, which gave the economy an immediate, and badly needed, boost. Paterson[9] put it this way: "This bank will be in effect as nine hundred thousand pounds or a million pounds of fresh money brought into the nation."*

The bank project was opposed by some of the more old-fashioned nobles, who believed that banks were republican by nature, and to be avoided,[10] but the king's need overcame their scruples and, on July 27,

---

* Depending on whether the bank kept in reserve £200,000 or £300,000.

1694, the bank's charter was sealed at Powis House, Lincoln's Inn Fields, London. It opened for business a few days later at Mercer's Hall in Cheapside, with a staff of seventeen clerks and two doorkeepers.[11] In the bank's museum today, in its new (1732) headquarters on Threadneedle Street, not far from the original site, there is a nice bronze bust of Paterson, and the modest explanation that "Paterson was, for a brief period, a Director."

In point of fact, he ceased to be a director when it was discovered that he was promoting a rival institution, called the Orphans' Fund Bank, and he was invited to depart.[12] He returned to his native Scotland, where his new renown enabled him to raise the funds for the Darien Scheme. Wily Scots emptied their sporrans to invest in the rich mixture of mosquitoes, malaria, and malarkey in far-off Central America, until it all sank in the swamps. Most of the 1,200 colonists, including Paterson's wife and child, lost their lives, and he barely survived. Returned to England, he became an elder statesman of finance, frequently consulted for his wise counsel, and beginning the long precedent by which scoundrels with friends in high places achieved nobility.

The bank he launched narrowly escaped becoming involved in the South Sea Bubble disaster in 1720, more by good luck than by good management. The South Sea Company proved more skilful at suborning and bribing members of Parliament than the Bank of England had been, and so obtained the necessary parliamentary charter to launch the scam that led the way to ruin for so many. The B of E lent a good deal of the seed money for this noisome venture, but did not own the shares, and got out before the bubble burst.[13] It went on to become in fact, if not in form, a government bank, raising the funds to fight the Napoleonic Wars, keeping the accounts of most government departments, and managing the national debt. By 1781, it had become so resolutely respectable that the prime minister, Lord North, described it as "from long habit and usage of many years ... a part of the Constitution."[14]

Another National Bank

When the time came to create a national bank in France, it was another Scot, John Law, who brought it off. Law, the son of a jeweller, had fled his native country after he killed a man in a duel, and went to live in Amsterdam, where he gambled, whored, and studied finance.[15] His gambling led to a meeting with Philippe, Duc d'Orléans, himself an inveterate gambler, and his studying to the writing of an essay, *Money and Trade Considered*, published in 1705, in which he proposed the founding of a national bank whose notes would be secured, not by anything as ephemeral as a tonnage tax, but by the value of land itself, most of which belonged to the Crown. This notion was far too radical for most economists, but appealed greatly to Law's old friend the Duc d'Orléans, who became, in 1715, Regent to King Louis XV, then a boy of five. Louis XIV had left the nation on the verge of bankruptcy, and Law argued that an expansion of credit would restore prosperity. He turned out to be absolutely correct.

In 1716, Law was given a charter to form the Banque Générale, with capital of 6 million livres and the right to issue notes as currency based on the state's landholdings. Most of these notes were lent back to the government, which used them to pay off its debt, and in turn accepted them as legal tender for the payment of taxes. This hocus-pocus created mountains of new money; trade prospered, prices rose, and employment increased. In 1718, the bank became a national institution, and was renamed the Banque Royale.

The next year, Law had another bright idea. He would form a company to exploit the riches of the French colonies overseas, and finance it through the Banque Royale. He would give the regent some of the money from the sale of stocks in his new venture, and keep only a fortune or two for himself. The regent gave him a monopoly on trade into the Mississippi region of North America, much of what is today the central United States. With that in hand, Law launched a furious campaign to flog stock in his Mississippi Company, backed by the bank. Prices shot through the ceiling, as bright-eyed Frenchmen counted the worth of untold supplies of gold along the Mississippi, until reality set in, and stock prices plummeted again. When holders of the bank notes tried to redeem them for specie, the money had vanished (most of it, as a matter of fact, had been lent to the government to cover running expenses; almost none was spent in North America). During a run on the bank in 1720, fifteen people were crushed to death.[16] After the bank collapsed, Law made a living as a gambler, and died ten years later.

We now have the Second Law of Banking: When things look dodgy, take whatever money is left, and run.

The French experience showed how easy it is to abuse public trust in any enterprise that shows initial signs of success, and how rapidly that trust can be shredded. Between them, Law and Paterson had also shown how a bank can be used as an arm of state policy, how, indeed, the creation of money out of thin air can work miracles for a national economy. It is a lesson that has been driven home many times since. The French Revolution was won on the back of paper money whose value went up and down as swiftly as the blade of a guillotine. The American Revolution was also financed on hope and ignorance, in about equal amounts;[17] paper money was issued, which had no backing except the promises of a government that might or might not be around the next year, but it was accepted, and kept the armies of discontent going. The U.S. Civil War produced another outpouring of paper that retained its value on the winning side and turned into a derisive phrase—Confederate notes—on the other side. In turn, the Russian Revolution was financed on dreams and wood pulp, just as Canada financed its economy through two world wars by having its banks invent enough money to keep the national engine oiled.

Over the past two centuries, great state banks have sprung up to stand beside the private institutions, and to invent the money on behalf of the nation, rather than the stockholders; central banks have developed to spread the process around the globe; and a number of dodges have been devised that would have excited even the flamboyant John Law, such as debit cards and derivatives. But, by the time of Law's death in 1729, the basis of modern banking was in place: the creation of paper money to replace grain, hides, or coins so large that it took six men to carry them; the establishment of credit and interest; and the evolution of a simple barter system carried out at local fairs into a system of international trade financed, in the main, by little bits of paper representing promises to pay, moving from hand to hand. It would take some time to discover that, if private banks could manufacture money on the premises, for the benefit of their owners, a government bank could do the same for the benefit of its owners—the general public.

CHAPTER 3

Maple Leaf Rogues

The most efficacious and the most immediate means which the Canadians have to protect themselves against the fury of their enemies, is to attack them in their dearest parts—their pockets—in their strongest entrenchments—the banks.

—Louis-Joseph Papineau,
Montreal Gazette, December 11, 1834

There is no God but money, and Canada, with its unparalleled natural resources, is the most God-fearing country in the world.

—Carleton W. Stanley,
educator, in *Hibbert jour*, 1922

TRADITIONAL HISTORIES of the Canadian banking system are so reassuring; our bankers were always men of probity, our banks were always bastions of stability. The reality of our banking history is that it has little to do with that tradition. Our early bankers were rogues and rascals, almost to a man; our banks were sinkholes of corruption until comparatively recently. As for stability, there was little of that until a few banks gained such a stranglehold on the system that it became well-nigh impossible for them to fail, and when, as in the 1980s, some of the smaller banks collapsed amid evidence of, at the very least, appalling ignorance and creative accounting, the broken shards were simply absorbed into the remaining banks, at public expense, with little public anguish.

Nothing our bankers have done is more impressive than the image they have planted in our minds of their own virtues. In large part, this myth has been created by a manipulation of the facts; our bankers prudently ensured that banking history was written mainly by themselves, or by what two of their rare and regrettable critics called "Bankers' Toadies."*

The real history of our banking past is far more colourful than the pap we have been fed, and it began, as all banking history does, with the invention of money, the stuff that makes the whole system go. In North America, money came, at first, entirely from abroad, from England, Spain, France, Holland, or other trading and conquering countries. There was no opportunity to have banks of our own, in any meaningful sense, until we in North America had money of our own.

The Massachusetts Bay Colony began to print "colonial notes" in 1690, to spur local commerce. These were money made up on the spot, in the same way that the Bank of England would function four years later, with the important difference that the beneficiary was the colony itself, not a clutch of private entrepreneurs. Pennsylvania followed with its own notes in 1723, and lent them at interest, which made taxes largely unnecessary.[1] The commonwealth created £45,000 worth of notes—a lot of money—and, to safeguard them, counterfeiters were to have their ears cut off, or be fined and "sold into servitude."[2] The result was a remarkable revival of the economy, and Pennsylvania continued to create its own money up to the time of the Declaration of Independence, with great success.

The well-known Canadian economist William Henry Pope notes an irony of banking history:

> It is our great misfortune that while the American colonies were proving that governments could issue paper money efficiently—without causing inflation, and profitably for the people—with interest accruing to the government in lieu of taxes—England set up the Bank of England in 1694 as a

---

* "My child, you should never say hard or unkind things about Bankers' Toadies. God made Bankers' Toadies, just as He made snakes, slugs, snails, and other treacherous and poisonous things." The authors were G.P. Powell and J.L. Unwin, in a pamphlet produced in Edmonton in 1938.

private, profit-making institution and the world subsequently followed England's lead.[3]

The excellent example provided by the Americans went unheeded at our end of the continent, where money began, and mostly remained, a private creation. In Canada's early days, under the French regime, skins were currency, and barter the usual method of trade. With the Indians, of course, booze was also turned into money. It filled the traditional three functions—as a medium of exchange; a measure of value; and, until it was consumed, a store of value. Such coins as arrived from France rapidly returned there to buy imports, since what we now call our balance of trade was perpetually and purposefully tilted against the colonies. Exports from New France were worth about 30 per cent of imports, and to make up the difference, and finance purchases from the homeland, a supply of coins was shipped across annually and released by the authorities as required.[4]

Playing Cards Become Money

In 1685, the annual coin shipment failed to appear, and the Intendant, who had grasped the most important thing about banking—if you don't have it, make it up—simply created his own money by cutting up playing cards, and turning them into "fungible" notes—money—by signing them. "Fungible" means interchangeable with other notes at a standard rate. The bits of card were not legal tender, but "promise to pay" notes, and, as long as they were accepted, worked well. Bits of playing cards represented denominations of four francs, forty sols, and fifteen sols. The soldiers were paid with these[5] and colonists were ordered to treat them as cash, which would be redeemed in goods and coin when the fleet eventually arrived. The scheme worked so well that thereafter France made no attempt to ship over specie in advance; cards would do as well. Off and on, cards were used as cash until Wolfe's victory at Quebec in 1759; they were exchanged for drafts on the French treasury, or for coins.

After the Conquest, the British used Mexican coins, Portuguese and Spanish money, anything that would pass as currency, to pay their troops, and this combination became, along with trade goods, the coin of the realm. Banks capable of issuing their own notes were non-existent in British North America—although, as we have seen, some colonies did this—until the Bank of North America of Philadelphia was established in 1781.[6] A year later, Montreal merchants moved to establish their own institution, the Canada Banking Company.[7] The Bank of Montreal always refers to itself as the "First Canadian Bank," but the honour actually belongs to the Canada Banking Company, which also goes unmentioned in the Canadian Bankers Association's potted history, *Bank Facts*, possibly because it failed in short order, as did two other attempts, one in 1807, in Quebec City, and another in 1808, a joint Montreal–Quebec venture.

The outbreak of the War of 1812 brought about a pressing need for more money to augment the collection of coins and papers of various nations that served as currency. The governor was therefore authorized by the colonial office to issue "Army bills" with which to pay the local conscripts, in denominations ranging from $100 down to $4. Notes between $25 and $100 were really like the Treasury bills of today; they bore interest, and could be exchanged for specie, government bills of exchange drawn on London, or more Army bills.[8] Lower denominations paid no interest. The money was readily accepted and proved a great boon, not only to help finance the war, but to aid commerce, which had been struggling by with its mongrel currency. New issues of Army bills, all of which were eventually redeemed in full, helped to re-establish paper money as a safe currency, and clear the way for creation of our own banks.

These early ventures were all joint-stock banks, private institutions with limited liability, owned by a handful of men, as opposed to the major banks of today, which are still private, but widely owned, institutions, with shares traded daily on stock exchanges. The first of these joint-stock operations was, indeed, the Bank of Montreal, which opened its doors for business in August 1817.[9]

Canada was now launched into the era of bank-creation, land frauds, and railway speculation that made our nineteenth century so rich and ripe. Enos Collins, a Nova Scotian who became a privateer during the Napoleonic Wars, added to his booty during the War of 1812, and used some of his money to finance other privateers. Then he started the Halifax Banking Company in 1825, and died the richest man of his time in British North America; he is saluted in a suitably flattering plaque on the Halifax waterfront today, near the site of his bank. The narrow line between piracy and finance was also trodden by many of our other banking pioneers.

The Family Compact

The Bank of Upper Canada was controlled by the same men who made up the Family Compact, and they hit on the simple device of having the legislature refuse banking charters to any group that looked as if it might be able to compete with them in the trading businesses which they also owned. This proved profitable for the bankers, but constraining for the rest of the community. The Compact members had little interest in promoting any industry that might cut into their markets. When the Bank of Upper Canada became the mortgagee of the first machinery works in the nation in 1836, it instantly foreclosed on the mortgage, broke up the foundry, and disposed of the pieces at a sheriff's sale.[10] People went back to buying their machinery in England, as God, and the Family Compact, intended. Complaints of this sort provided part of the ferment for the Rebellion of 1837.[11]

The year of the rebellion also brought a business panic, and a run on some of the privately owned banks. One history of the time notes that "the private bank of Trustcott, Green & Co., known as the Agricultural Bank, failed, the partners leaving the country."[12]

In point of fact, the more bankers that left, the better off Canadians should have been. To collect on the notes issued by a bank, you had to present them to the bank itself, if you could find it. In Montreal, a sign above a doorway proclaimed the presence of the Merchants' Bank, which issued a great many notes, but behind the doorway was only an empty office, smelling of dust, disuse, and mice. In the same way, the St. Lawrence Bank circulated notes in Buffalo, but kept the real money at La Malbaie, high up the St. Lawrence River, in the reasonable hope that few would make the journey to collect what was owed in hard cash.[13]

Over the next few decades, Canadian banking threw up such figures as Samuel Zimmerman, a palpable rogue who founded his own bank to finance crooked railway schemes, and Sir Francis Hincks, an even greater rogue, who went into politics, with the backing of the business interests he represented, and became Prime Minister of the United

Province of Canada. He used that post to manipulate the stock of the railway companies, whose major financing came from government. He was a land speculator, a con man (who pushed through a swindle on the City of Toronto with the help of the city's mayor), and the cheerful recipient of numerous bribes.[14] He received his knighthood in 1869, the same year he became Sir John A. Macdonald's minister of finance, a post he used to sell off fishing rights for personal gain and to raise more money for railway speculation. It was Hincks who arranged for the Canadian Pacific contract that led to the Pacific Scandal and the fall of the Macdonald government.

The defeat of the Conservatives on this issue allowed Hincks more leisure time, so he put together two shaky banks, the City Bank and the Royal Canadian Bank, into one really shaky bank, the Consolidated, of which he became president, and which proceeded to spend a lot more money than it had. In essence, it was a pyramid scheme, sucking in money to invest by paying high interest rates to depositors and, when the time came to pay off, borrowing more to meet the payments, and doing it all over again. These busy activities were covered by a series of fake books that made it look as if the bank had a lot of money that it did not. When the scheme came crashing down in 1880, it took with it the fortunes of a great many investors, but not that of Hincks. He had already unloaded nearly all his shares at a fat profit. In the furore that followed, Hincks was charged with filing false annual returns to the federal government, under a law that he himself had drafted.

Despite the parade of witnesses who came to testify on his behalf—including the general manager of the Bank of Montreal, who testified that Hincks's manipulations, while illegal, were common banking practice—he was found guilty of fraud by a jury. The minimum sentence for this was two years in prison, but it was never carried out. As Adam Shortt (yes, another banker) wrote in his *History of Canadian Currency and Banking, 1600–1800*, "The public were amply satisfied with the fact that a striking warning had been given."[15]

Then there was Sir Hugh Allan, who founded another Merchants' Bank in 1861, and became one of the central figures in the Pacific Scandal, as a wholesale briber of legislators; Peter McGill, who combined the roles of head of the Bank of Montreal and a leading role in the British American Land Company, a notorious scam in which he was joined by Sir Alexander Galt, the finance minister. Galt also started the Eastern Townships Bank, which he used to divert more public funds to his private use.[16]

George Stephen's Great Bank Caper

The Bank of Montreal seemed to turn out scalawags as fast as it did loans; another of the early presidents was George Stephen, who siphoned $8 million out of the coffers without bothering to tell the board of directors, for investment in the St. Paul and Minneapolis Railway. Stephen managed to get the St. Paul at a knockdown price by having an American accountant prepare a fraudulent report which showed that it was close to bankruptcy, when it wasn't. This report was sent to the major stockholders in Holland, who unloaded their shares at a discount, as soon as the Montreal banker made an offer. Then the accountant sued Stephen, claiming that he was entitled to part of the loot, but a court threw out the claim when the judge declined to decide "how plunder should be divided among different members of a gang."[17] Stephen made so much on the railway that he was able to smuggle the $8 million back into the bank vaults, continued to rule the bank, and was first knighted, and then ennobled, as Lord Mount Stephen, in 1892.

Those were the days when a banker could spread his wings without a lot of nosey reporters or querulous stockholders raising a fuss. One of the best dodges available to the politicians, who were also, in the main, the bankers, was to found a bank, give it a parliamentary charter, and then have the government deposit a lot of public funds in it, interest free. The Bank of Montreal prospered this way, as did the Bank of Ontario and the Montreal and District Savings Bank.

The Molsons Bank, put together by a group of Montreal notables and MPs, including William and John Molson, the brewers, caused the American social critic Gustavus Myers to complain:

> Politicians in the United States have long since so well appraised the value of bank charters that as early as the years 1799, 1805, 1811 and 1824 bribery had been used to wrest from the legislators charters for the Manhattan, Mercantile,

Merchants' and other New York City banks. But in Canada, with many of the bank incorporators themselves leaders in legislative councils, bribery was, in general, superfluous.[18]

After the union of Upper and Lower Canada in 1841, Lord Sydenham, the first governor general, proposed the foundation of a new bank, to be called "the Bank of the Province of Canada," which alone would have the power to issue bank notes. Sydenham's argument was that the plethora of colourful, but dubious, notes issued by the commercial banks led to instability. No doubt about that, but it also led to prosperity for the issuing banks, and the proposal died a-borning.[19] Instead, the banks agreed to buy government debentures—bonds payable either on demand or at some future date, some of which bore interest, and some of which did not. This "laid the foundation for a permanent element of government paper in the currency of the country,"[20] a very peculiar way of describing the fact that governments began to feel that they had at least as much right to issue notes as did private banks. There was still no "government bank of issue," but the idea had been planted.

In 1866, the Provincial Notes Act was finally passed, on the heels of the collapse of the Bank of Upper Canada and the suspension of conversion of their bank notes into specie by the American banks during the Civil War—two circumstances that left a great many people holding what they thought were bank notes, but which turned out to be wallpaper.[21] The government of Canada was authorized to issue up to $8 million in notes, redeemable in gold. The banks still objected to the government invading their domain, so the authorities agreed to hold off actually issuing notes if the banks would lend them $5 million, and, when they declined, the first government notes were issued. The banks, however, except the Bank of Montreal (which had become the government bank in 1864), ignored the provision in the Act which made it illegal for them to issue notes, and went on printing pretty bits of paper that became money. However, they began to accumulate small amounts of the government notes, because these were convertible into specie—hard cash—while the banks' papers were not; holding a store of government paper provided some reassurance to the public that there was at least some backing for the bank notes. In the second half of the nineteenth century, more than 100 Canadian banks issued their own currency, in notes such as the

Molsons Bank's $6 bill, the Bank of the People's $8 one, the Farmers' Bank of Canada's $25 note, and $3 bills from a handful of institutions.[22] One little stunt the bankers pulled was to circulate a rumour that a competitor's currency wasn't worth the paper it was printed on, and soon a run would overwhelm the rival, whether it was indeed in trouble, or was one of the comparatively few comparatively honest institutions around.

After Confederation—by which time, the crush of freelance institutions was reduced to thirty-four chartered banks in Canada, of various degrees of stability[23]—the Dominion Notes Act of 1870 restricted the chartered banks to issuing notes of $5 or more, and gave the government a monopoly on lower-denomination bills. The Act required the government to hold a gold reserve against these notes, which eventually rose to 85 per cent. "Dominion notes," writes H.H. Binhammer, "had practically become gold certificates."[24]

The First Bank Act

The first federal legislation governing the banks was the Bank Act of 1871, whose offspring is amended every decade. It provided that all new banks were to be chartered by Parliament, and that the Act would be renewed every ten years. The banks were, and still are, required to have paid-up capital of at least $100,000, and could issue notes only up to the amount of that capital. They were limited to issuing notes of $4 and upwards, with the notes of lower value again held as a government monopoly.

The Act was drafted, essentially, by the Bank of Montreal, which was the government's bank, and then amended by a "joint committee of Parliament and banks."[25] Bank directors and presidents, some of whom were also MPs and senators, sat together to make sure the law did the right things, as, for example, bringing all the Maritime banks under Ottawa's control, and opening the region to the larger institutions of central Canada. The establishment of the Canadian Bankers Association in 1891, and the appointment of an official lobbyist, Z.A. Lash, ensured that any rough places would be made smooth. Sir Edmund Walker, president of the Bank of Commerce, noted that, when some "objectionable clauses" were introduced in 1894, "the attention of the proper authorities being called by Mr. Lash to these features, they were removed."[26] Walker once boasted that every change in the Bank Act between 1871 and 1913 had been initiated by the bankers themselves.[27]

Continuing bank failures led to a number of changes over the years, including a provision that bank notes were to be a first charge against a bank's assets in the case of bankruptcy; that is, before anything could be paid over to the institution's creditors, it would have to make good on its notes. This process was supported by another legal provision to establish a bank circulation redemption fund, into which the banks had to deposit 5 per cent of their annual average circulation, and which was a sort of mutual insurance fund in case of failures, because it was required to replace the sunken notes of a fallen bank with good, that is, fungible, ones. This came about because, in one spectacular case, while a bank was going down, its agents fanned out to trade its notes for those of other banks, leaving a great many Canadians, some of them bankers, with their hands full of dud paper.

In return, the banks were given the right to operate a clearing system,[28] through which credits and debits among the banks could be balanced against each other and reconciled by passing money back and forth until the books were balanced—that is, "cleared." The banks were also given the right to a veto on the issuance of bank charters. Then, in 1913, they received the right to issue notes beyond their capital base, provided that they were backed, dollar for dollar, with gold or Dominion notes in a central gold reserve. This lasted for just over one year; with the First World War looming, the convertibility of Dominion notes and bank notes into gold was temporarily suspended, to allow more money to be created to fight the war. (Canada went permanently off the gold standard in 1931.) The Finance Act of 1914 made the Department of Finance into a pseudo-central bank, issuing notes to the chartered banks to back their own issues, and this system remained in place until the establishment of the Bank of Canada in 1935.

Canadian Conservatism, American Expansion

Although they had some common characteristics—chiefly, the rascality of their founders—in common, the Canadian and American banking systems developed quite differently. Thomas Naylor, the economic historian, puts this down to the fact that "Canadian banking was a branch plant of English commercial banking,"[29] while the American system, after the unpleasantness of the American Revolutionary War, grew up beyond the sheltering shade of the Mother Country. Canada's economy was based on staple crops, which would be shipped back to England to be turned into finished goods, which the colony would buy back later, at higher prices. Money was provided to move resources to market, but not to promote Canadian entrepreneurs. "It was," Naylor writes, "the model least suited to promoting industrial development in the colony."[30]

The great virtue of a banking system that consisted of a few large companies, each with many branches across the country, was supposed to be that the funds would be transferred readily from areas of surplus to the regions where they were needed for development. It did not work out that way. In one Maritime town, by 1912, the ratio of deposits to loans was running at twenty to one—that is, for every dollar collected locally, only a nickel was lent locally, the surplus being transferred to central Canada. When the Maritimers complained, the head of the Bank of Montreal dismissed their grousing as "local grievances against what we regard as the interests of the country as a whole."[31]

In the West, too, complaints about the sacking of local funds to build up central Canada were dismissed with scorn. The Bank of Vancouver, established in 1911, foundered for lack of resources. At the same time, agitation for provincial banks in Alberta and Saskatchewan began, but came to naught. It was easy to see why the Westerners were upset. Grain farmers were faced with a banking system designed to force them to dump their crops onto the market for whatever it would bear. When they went to borrow money, the notes were dated to come due just before harvest-time. If their crops didn't sell, they could lose everything, but, if they did, they had to take whatever was offered in a market crowded by other farmers doing the same thing. Requests for loan extensions to await a price rise were rudely and routinely rejected.[32] In addition, loans for farm machinery and other improvements were rare; what the banks wanted was to finance crops in such a way that, when they came to be sold, prices would be low in the Eastern markets. To get around this, the Westerners tried to found their own institutions, but the Canadian Bankers Association exercised its right to veto new charters to kill a Western bank.[33]

To make things worse, the Eastern banks got around a legal limit on interest rates—7 per cent per annum—by discounting loans in advance. A farmer who borrowed $5,000 would get only $4,400, although he paid interest on the full $5,000—in effect, doubling the interest charge. There was a meeting in Winnipeg every year to fix this discount rate, which all the big Eastern banks attended. Naylor notes that "the Bank of Commerce seemed to win the prize for extortion and usury."[34]

Having made it impossible for regional banks to succeed, the banking establishment explained the failure this way: "There is no doubt at all that if local and regional institutions had been well adapted to the conditions of Canadian life they would have survived, and the fact that they did not survive was an indicator of the needs of the country."[35]

In the United States, banks developed quite differently. There, the banking system, equally marked by rascality, was at least their own. Banks were, from the start, fiercely competitive, regionally oriented, and happy to plunge into the venture-capital financing that our banks eschewed as if it were a social disease. American banks, like ours, found themselves in a basic conflict as the nation began to develop. Eastern banks preferred stable prices and gradual expansion, while the people of the West needed, and demanded, such rapid expansion that it was bound to cause inflation.[36] In effect, the American system split itself into two, as John Kenneth Galbraith, the Canadian-born American economist, has shown. Western banks were expansionist and venturesome, while those in the East followed much more conservative policies. The Americans had the best of both worlds at the time of their greatest need for expansion, while the centralized Canadian system remained tied to policies that stultified development, but made a lot of money for the bankers. Over time, we shook off the British colonial ties, only to replace them with ties attached at the business end to bank counters in Montreal and Toronto.

What made the process richly comic, unless you happened to be a victim of it, was that our repressive approach was sanctioned on the grounds of the rectitude of our bankers, and by the stability of the system, attributes which were non-existent. The period from Confederation to 1923 was punctuated by bank failures, usually accompanied by the sudden disappearance of both the cash and the principal officers of the institutions.

The Teller Left, with the Cash

The collapse of the Banque Ville Marie was typical. It was formed by a group of Quebec businessmen, and was in trouble as early as 1876.[37] The bank began to manipulate its own stock to raise money, and, when the federal officials discovered this illegal action, they recommended that, at the least, government deposits sitting, interest free, in the vaults should be rescued, but nothing was done. The bank struggled on until 1899, when a teller departed with $58,000, and, when word leaked out, there was a run on the bank by anxious depositors, who discovered that, sure enough, the cupboard was bare. The bank's charter was suspended, and a subsequent investigation produced evidence that the president had siphoned $300,000 from the till by means of promissory notes on firms that were in bankruptcy at the time, and that an accountant had blown $173,000 in depositors' funds on stock gambles. He was charged with theft, but no one would testify against him, so no further action was taken.

Between 1867 and 1914, seventy-two banks received charters in Canada, and twenty-six of them failed. That failure rate, 36 per cent, was a good deal higher than the U.S. rate—22 per cent—and, in dollar terms, Canadian losses to shareholders were much higher than those in the United States.[38] Bank failures were much more common than bankruptcies in other areas of commerce, and the level of criminality was much higher—of the twenty-six failures, nineteen involved criminal conduct on the part of bank officers and/or employees. Naylor concludes: "The record of stability of the Canadian banking system is alarming, and the myth of stability sheer propaganda."[39]

Because they were so busy looting the till, Canadian bankers developed a reluctance to submit to the ministrations of bank inspectors, and they even had a rationale for it. Inspection systems might cut the number of failures, they said, and that would impede the efficient operation of the banking system by interfering with the survival of the fittest. It was God's will that some banks should go under, and who were mere mortals to trifle with the intentions of the Divine?[40]

The Sinking of the Home Bank

However, the national mood changed after the failure of the Home Bank in 1923. Established in Toronto, in 1903, the bank went through twenty years of graft, manipulation, and mismanagement, all carefully concealed from the public. Though the bank was effectively bankrupt in 1914, the federal government refused to act because it didn't want to put a bank under during wartime. It struggled on for nine more years, but, when the general manager died, the bank's shortage of funds became a matter of public knowledge. The subsequent investigation followed the usual path; it showed that the president, general manager, five directors, the accountant, and the auditor had all been cooking the books.[41] All but the president, who died before his case could come to trial, were convicted. The convictions were overturned on appeal, but the federal government was forced to repay some of the missing funds to depositors, because it had been so negligent.

The Home Bank case, in combination with a number of other visible blunders, helped spur the demand for a central bank. In 1920, for example, during an inflationary boom, the banks abruptly cut back on credit to control rising prices, bringing on a ruinous recession.

Nine years later, when the Great Depression began to devastate Canada, the banks raised interest rates and cut back on credit again.[42] As they foreclosed on farms and businesses throughout the land, their behaviour promoted the idea of a national bank, such as existed already in other countries, which would be "independent" of the financiers. Canadian bankers were happy to accept the new idea, in part because they could see that the Federal Reserve System in the United States, put in place to respond to the numerous failures of American banks, was rapidly and completely taken over by private bankers; instead of being the hindrance they had feared, it was a great help to commercial banks, especially in calming the fears of depositors. As economic historian William F. Hixson notes: "[The Federal Reserve System's] management and operation were handed over to bankers; and thus to speak of it as being independent of them is absurd. The only group the Fed was indeed independent of was debtors."[43]

We will be looking at that national bank again, in Chapter 6; for now, the point to note is that it began, and mainly continued, not as the adversary of the banks, but as their servant.

However, the Bank of Canada, as it was called, did take on two important functions, hitherto in the hands of the chartered banks. The first was responsibility for control of the money supply, through reserve requirements that were clearly spelled out. The second was responsibility for the issuance of bank notes. In time, the central bank became the sole issuer of these notes, while the private banks dominated the creation of all other forms of money, which turned out to be more than 95 per cent of the stuff.

The Canadian banking system continued to evolve as a branch-banking system, unlike the "free" banks of the United States (where, by and large, each branch was a separate bank). There were, and are, both advantages and disadvantages for Canadians in this system. Money could be pooled through the branches much more rapidly than was the case across the border, for investment elsewhere, and the size of the banks that survived gave them, at last, a stability not enjoyed south of the border. The disadvantages have already been alluded to; there was very little competition among the large institutions, and the nation's economic policy was held in thrall by a handful of men at the centre of the nation. Private, regional, and savings banks were run out of business, often by extending, and suddenly withdrawing, credit, or simply by using the Bank Act provisions to close them down.

In 1880, Canada had forty-four chartered banks, with 295 branches, and, that year, seven of them failed.[44] In 1968, we were down to nine,* with 5,922 branches, and none had gone broke since the collapse of the Home Bank, a quarter of a century earlier. One way to look at this is that our banking system had achieved a marvellous equilibrium, where failure was unlikely; another, that it had become an oligopoly, where failure is nearly impossible.

In many ways, the banks of seventy years ago, when the Home Bank was still perking along, were not all that different from our own, except that they were smaller, and few had the national reach of the multi-branch system we have now. They had individual and commercial accounts; both men and women could maintain and use accounts (although married women were considered to be under the control of their husbands, legally); and there were deposits, withdrawals, cheques, and

---

* Today, as we saw in the Introduction, we have sixty-two banks, but only five that really count.

books through which customers could keep track of their accounts. Of course, cash was used much more than cheques, and the joys of the credit card and debit card were far in the future, but if you read Stephen Leacock's immortal "My Financial Career," written in 1910, you will see that the surroundings he describes are not that different from the typical Canadian bank of a couple of years ago. Now, however, everything is changing, almost faster than the eye can follow, as the banks stride into the new global environment, which means, for them, digital banking through computers, a blend of services in a single bank—everything from financial planning to insurance—and an end, if they can work it, to the comforting business of handing over your account book to a person, and maybe even exchanging hellos. Although they are too polite to say so out loud, the banks apparently want us to avoid their premises, unless we have really big business to transact, and deal with them on the telephone, through a computer, or even through the Internet.

The banks want to leave the narrow confines of the nation behind, and become truly international. The Bank of Montreal, for example, is shedding that trusty old name, and turning itself into something called m̲banx. I guess if you spell your name in lower case, underline a letter, and end with an "x," it proves either that you are very, very modern, or that you don't know how to spell. The new moniker also distances the bank from attachment to a single city, Montreal, within a single country, Canada, and lets us know that the corporation is ready to leap over all boundaries into the brave new world of deregulation.

In the end, if there was anything we could learn from our history, it was that the banks were not to be trusted to regulate themselves, and that the most dangerous situation we could have was to allow bankers to venture into other businesses, where they could, and would, use the funds left with them by depositors, and those they manufactured on site, to gamble in areas of the economy where they had clout without competence.

It took us a while to forget these lessons, which had been burned into the national psyche at considerable expense, but, by virtue of innate stupidity or stubborn persistence, and with the help of the myth-makers of the Canadian Bankers Association, we managed to do so. The next chapter traces this exercise in national amnesia, and examines some of its consequences.

CHAPTER 4

Pulverizing the Pillars

The oligopolistic position of the Canadian chartered banks results in higher interest rates than are justified, a more conservative lending attitude, and less flexibility.

—Statement of the Premiers
Western Opportunities Conference, Calgary, 1973

Just you wait, they're going to take over the whole damn shooting match.

—Carne Bray,
Association of Canadian Financial Corporations, 1981

DURING THEIR FIRST CENTURY of operation, from 1867 to 1967, Canadian chartered banks became larger, richer, more centralized, and fewer in number, year by year. They did not become more competitive, nor did they intend to—the notion that there is nothing the boys like better than rolling up their sleeves and going at each other has been one of the industry's little jokes. What the banks have always wanted is what they are openly campaigning for today—fewer, larger institutions, and less competition, although it is never put that way. Instead, we hear of the need for our banks to merge in order to come to grips with "the global marketplace."[1] This is simply the latest slant on a habit of doing away with competition that has been in place for more than a century.

The tone was set by Thomas Fysche, a leading banker of the 1890s, who declared that the only reason any element of competition appeared in banking was because of "the lack of proper organization. When the latter is achieved we may regard the rapid disappearance of competition with comparative equanimity."[2] Competition in price, the only thing that matters to consumers, had effectively disappeared when the series of mergers of the 1950s and early 1960s reduced the system to eight banks,* five of which held more than 90 per cent of the assets. The same five dominate the system still.

The banks shared control of not only their own industry, but many others as well, through the cross-directorships that have always been such an interesting part of our banking practice. That is, the bank directors and officers were, and are, directors of other companies in business with the banks, and the presidents of the companies that are the financial firms' main customers, in return for being named to the bank boards, invite bankers onto their boards, until they are coupled together in ways that would make mating octopi blush. In one of the few detailed studies of this phenomenon, the Department of Consumer and Corporate Affairs noted in 1971 that "bank directors serve as official communications links between other companies."[3] The study looked at Canada's 260 largest corporations and discovered that banks were the linchpin of a system of interlocking directorships that joined them on most policy issues. For example:

> The Bank of Montreal has interlocks with 73 other companies, and the Bank of Nova Scotia has interlocks with 38 companies. Thus any industrial company which has directors on both these bank boards, of which there are 22 such companies, has access to directors who sit on a total of 89 other companies in Canada.[4]

---

* Bank of Montreal, Canadian Imperial Bank of Commerce, Bank of Nova Scotia (which now also calls itself Scotiabank), Royal Bank of Canada, Toronto-Dominion, Banque Canadienne Nationale, Banque Provinciale du Canada, and Mercantile. The last three later became the National in 1985. In all, the Bank of Montreal swallowed seven other banks; the Bank of Commerce swallowed six, and then merged with the Imperial, itself the result of two other mergers; the Royal took over five others; and the Toronto-Dominion was the final amalgamation of another series of mergers, culminating in the joining of the Bank of Toronto and the Dominion Bank in 1955.

Everyone agreed that this was shocking, and that something should be done about it, so it was; a resolution was taken, and kept, never to study this subject in such detail again.

You might have thought the banks would be happy with their lot—they were big, fat, and powerful—but they were not. The financial world was still dominated by what were known as "The Four Pillars": banks, securities dealers, trust companies, and insurance firms. Banks felt they were being restricted by old-fashioned, out-of-date policies, which kept them out of commercial lending, mortgages, trust activities, stock sales, and insurance. They were, in the main, "financial intermediaries," whose principal function was to attract funds from savers, through interest paid on their deposits, and lend it out again to investors, in a formula that became known as "three–six–three"—pay depositors 3 per cent, charge borrowers 6 per cent, and get out to the golf-course by 3:00 P.M. There were other deposit-taking institutions, the so-called near-banks—trusts, co-operatives, and credit unions—but they specialized in their own areas, just as the banks did, with very little cross-over.

The main reason for this separation of financial institutions, besides the obvious one that oligopolies are a bad thing and lead to higher prices, was the danger of conflicts of interest if any of the sectors was allowed to swallow any of the others. The banks, the only one of the pillars that already operated as an oligopoly, was the sector most in need of restraint. Take the position of a small-business person who has an outstanding demand loan at the bank—that is, the bank has the right to call the poor sap in at any time and demand payment forthwith of the entire amount owing—and wants to buy some insurance. If the bank were in the insurance racket, he or she might well feel compelled to buy insurance there or find that loan called. In the same way, an executor or executrix of a large estate dealing with a bank in the trust business might feel compelled to use the trust services of the bank, for fear of something drastic happening on the loan front. Or, the bank, having access to the customer's financial statistics, might put on the pressure to buy stocks, insurance, a car lease, whatever.

Worse still, how can you ensure caution and impartiality in lending when deposit-taking institutions are allowed to use the savings of their customers to support companies affiliated with themselves? Obviously a loans committee faced with having to decide between backing Seek and Ye Shall Find Finance, a wholly owned subsidiary of its own institution, and Rock Solid Inc., owned by strangers, will be more inclined to support the former. It was bad enough having overlapping directorships; if we had overlapping ownerships as well, the whole notion of independent evaluation would go out the window.

No one was saying the banks were corrupt; it was just common sense to assume that if you put them in the position of being able to pressure customers, and invade the privacy of customers by passing on information from the banking sector to other sectors, they would do so; so the law very sensibly removed the temptation by establishing safeguards to ensure that each of the four financial pillars stood on its own.

The Four Pillars

Banks and trusts could not sell securities; banks and insurers were blocked from offering trust services; banks and trusts could not sell insurance; and trusts and insurers did not have the lending power of banks. Moreover, banks were elbowed out of the mortgage business—the bread-and-butter of mortgage, trust, and insurance companies—in two ways. The first was a legal provision that they could back only mortgages which were guaranteed under the National Housing Assistance Act; the second was a limit of 6 per cent on the interest rate banks could charge. This limit also kept banks out of commercial lending, because they couldn't make money financing TV sets, cars, and stoves at that rate. Finally, they were not allowed to own a brokerage, because of the obvious danger of conflicts of interest. You say you have your widow's mite to invest, Mrs. Smith? Well, now, our very own in-house brokerage, Grabbit and Run Finance, has a wonderful deal in Hidden Valley Oil shares, which we will be happy to finance at our usual terms.

The Four Pillars were our bulwark against oligopoly, conflicts of interest, and bank domination until Centennial Year, 1967. Pierre Elliott Trudeau was prime minister, the nation was in a celebratory mood, and the banks wanted to expand their influence, so we said, Why not? And away they went. The Bank Act revisions had been slipping back, what with one thing and another—mainly, a string of minority governments that had trouble getting legislation through on time—so the overhaul that ought to have taken place in 1961 was still to be done.

The process didn't really get under way until 1964, with an inquiry into the operations of the banks, called the Porter Commission, officially the Royal Commission on Banking and Finance. This august body said, in a mild and understated manner, that there were some problems with the banks, that they clung together in ways that led to higher costs for their customers, and that the nation needed "a more open and competitive banking system."[5] To this end, the commission wanted to withdraw the right of the Canadian Bankers Association to operate the cheque-clearing system, through which the banks balanced their accounts with one another. It also wanted to allow foreign banks into Canada, and to provide, at last, a legal definition of banking as a way of keeping the banks from straying into other areas and making competition even more limited than it already was.

Not surprisingly, none of these recommendations had the support of the banking community, and none was followed, but a number of changes which the bankers *did* want were turned into law, in what the minister of finance, Mitchell Sharp, called, without a trace of irony, "A Blueprint for Competition."

First, the legal limit of 6 per cent on the interest banks could charge was lifted temporarily in 1967, and permanently in 1968, and the banks creamed the finance companies. This was presented as a good thing for Canadians generally, because the banks would save us from the exactions of firms that were charging as much as 12 per cent per annum for loans. But before long, the banks were charging 24 per cent for the same loans.[6] Now, incidentally, the only legal limit is a provision in the Criminal Code, which outlaws a "criminal interest rate," defined as interest above 60 per cent per annum.[7]

However, the finance companies were not one of the Four Pillars, so that was all right.

The 1967 revisions also allowed the banks into the mortgage-loan field in a major way, for the first time, by removing their limitation to mortgages guaranteed under the National Housing Act. Lifting the 6 per cent interest barrier helped here, too. Prior to 1967, when mortgage loans went above 6 per cent, the banks dumped their portfolios and used the money elsewhere. The new Bank Act allowed them free access to conventional mortgages with only one restraint: they were not allowed to hold mortgage loans amounting to more than 10 per cent of their deposits, plus debentures (that is, the total of all the deposits they were holding, combined with the total of all the debenture bonds they had issued). And to make the pot richer, a provision that the banks had to hold reserves against their own debentures was scrubbed. In addition, there was no limit on the mortgages that could be held by a mortgage company which was a subsidiary of a bank.[8]

The banks swarmed into the mortgage market, multiplying their portfolio twenty-two-fold between 1967 and 1980, from $825 million to $18.6 billion.[9] The traditional mortgage holders—insurance firms, mortgage companies, and trust corporations—became minor players in this rich market.

However, the mortgage companies were not one of the Four Pillars, so that was all right, too.

There were some who worried, because of the trend, and because mortgages were a substantial part of the trust and insurance businesses, but no one paid much attention to them. However, the banks did not get everything their way in 1967. To uphold the Four Pillars, and because the banks were buying into the trust companies at an alarming rate, the law provided that no bank could own more than 10 per cent of a trust. The banks also got another mild knock. Until that time, it had been common practice for the bankers to meet together to discuss the setting of rates. This was done quite openly; although it smacked of collusion, it was legal. The 1967 revisions barred this practice. Not that it made much difference; the rates remain virtually identical. Apparently, the banks work by ESP, so that they all change rates at once, like birds wheeling in flight at some unseen signal from the skies.

The revisions also required the banks to provide more information to customers about the cost of their loans, and to give the inspector general of banks, their watchdog, more information about their activities.[10] Reserve ratios were raised, too, but wound up being lower, because the law distinguished between time deposits, which can be withdrawn only after giving notice, and demand deposits, which can be pulled out anytime. The old law called on the banks to have 8 per cent of their deposits in reserve (for every $100 the bank lent, or held on deposit, it had to have, on deposit with the Bank of Canada, $8 in cash or notes that could be immediately redeemed for cash); under the revision, demand deposits—more likely to be called for in haste—required a 12 per cent reserve, and time deposits 4 per cent. That worked out to an average ratio of 6.5 per cent, given the mix of time and demand deposits, so the banks were ahead of the game as billions came floating out of reserve.

The Birth of Deposit Insurance

The ripest plum of all for the banks was the provision, for the first time, of deposit insurance in banks and near-banks, guaranteeing each account up to $20,000 in the case of failure of the institution. Provincially chartered institutions, such as credit unions and trust companies, gradually came under the same protection from provincial governments. This provision did not affect competition, since all players wound up in the same place, but it did provide reassurance to depositors. The money came from a small charge on all deposits, which was paid to the Canada Deposit Insurance Corporation (CDIC), formed for the purpose; beyond this, it was, and is, backed by the public purse. Ordinary Canadians stood to benefit from this change—copied from similar legislation in the United States—because it meant that, if any member bank or trust company went down, there would be cash to pay back the depositors. But the biggest benefactors were the banks, because, except for catastrophe dreadful to contemplate, the danger of a run on any Canadian bank was now over. The risk had been transferred to the CDIC and, in the end, to the taxpayer, because when the CDIC gets into trouble, it borrows on the guarantee of the federal government that the money will be repaid.

The major banks, however, did not favour deposit insurance, and still do not; they regard it as an interference in the working of the free market, which it would be if there were any free market in finance. Without deposit insurance, every prudent saver would transfer his or her money out of any financial institution against which there was even a rumour of trouble, and nothing would be left standing but the Big Five. It took until 1996 for the banks to make a serious dint in this insurance system, as we shall see in Chapter 10.

Before the 1977 banking revisions, which were really the 1971 revisions pushed back, could be written into law, a certain amount of restiveness developed in the political world. The banks seemed to be making more and more money while everyone else made less, and some folks resented it.

One issue was the attempt to found a Bank of British Columbia, which would be 20 per cent owned by the province itself. It was not to be. First, the Senate Banking Committee, which, at that time, consisted almost entirely of bank directors, blocked the charter while the 1967 Bank Act revisions were being drafted, and then added a provision that prohibited any government owning voting shares in a chartered bank. This garroted the provincial bank. When the Bank of British Columbia finally got off the ground, it was strictly a private institution, and it struggled along for a few years, foundered, and was folded into another bank; the remnants are now part of the Hongkong Bank of Canada.

The Western premiers were sore as a boil at the interference and, at the Western Economic Opportunities Conference in Calgary in June 1973, issued a joint statement that complained: "The branch banking system, characterized by the five major chartered banks with branches coast-to-coast and head offices in Central Canada, has not been adequately responsive to Western needs."[11] To add to the furore, another royal commission, this one on corporate concentration, reported in 1978 that, "in Canadian markets, the major banks compete against each other as oligopolists ... We have been able to discover no economies of scale in banking that necessitate the current large size of banks and the oligopolistic structure of the industry."[12]

You might have expected that, in the circumstances, the new Bank Act would have come down on the boys like a ton of bricks. However, it was written by the same coalition of Finance Department bureaucrats, Bank of Canada wizards, CBA lobbyists, and the Senate Banking Committee that composes all revisions. While the banks did not get everything they wanted, they were able to derail proposals that might have done them real harm, and load in a few more goodies.

More Assets, More Profit

Between 1967 and 1977, the banks multiplied their assets threefold and their profits fourfold, but it was not enough, and the banks whined that they were being hampered, discriminated against, and not appreciated. They hated the fact that they had to hold reserves in the vaults of the Bank of Canada, on which they received no interest, while the near-banks were free of reserve requirements. The fact that the Government of Canada socked $100 million into each of the Big Five to cover the clearing of government cheques was not mentioned in any of the whining that accompanied the anti-reserve campaign. Another major controversy in this revision was the banks' complaint that they couldn't get into the car-leasing business, which was turning a very nice dollar, essentially for companies who borrowed from the banks to finance the leases. The CBA also objected to the argument that bank employees should not be allowed to be directors of other companies, because it was such a clear conflict. Shoals of lobbyists swarmed Parliament Hill on behalf of the banks to defeat this idea.

When the Department of Finance produced a White Paper in 1976,[13] Allen Lambert, the former head of the Toronto-Dominion Bank, purred, "There were not many surprises. The paper followed closely the recommendations of the Canadian Bankers Association."[14] Sure enough, the White Paper said the near-banks would have to hold reserves, and the real banks would be able to go into the leasing business—cars, airplanes, whatever. However, for the first time, there was an effective counter-lobby operating in Ottawa, and the CBA did not cover itself with glory. The association's chief spokesman, Robert MacIntosh, a former Bank of Nova Scotia vice-president who had the voice of a bassoon and the subtlety of a Sherman tank, managed to anger many of the MPs who were called in to struggle with various parts of the bill as it dragged on, and on, and on, through three parliaments.

When it finally emerged in 1981, the banks had both won and lost on the reserves issue; the near-banks were not required to keep reserves, but reserves on the banks themselves were cut sharply, freeing more billions. The banks' complaint that the reserves were a discriminatory tax on them, because the trust companies, their rivals, did not have to pay them, was contradicted by the fact that most of the trust companies were barely scraping by, while the banks were rolling in cash. They were allowed to go into leasing, with the exception of car leasing, after MacIntosh told a House of Commons committee that the auto-leasing companies were "Cry babies—all they're afraid of is a little competition."[15] Ben Turpin, an Ottawa car dealer, replied, calmly, that the banks would lease the cars and then dump them back on dealers like himself for repairs. Leasing prices might go down, as the bankers claimed, but as soon as competition had been driven out, they would go back up again. The MPs, more impressed by Turpin than by MacIntosh, slipped through an amendment that banks could lease only vehicles weighing more than 46,000 pounds.[16] Not your average car.

This was the first time the House of Commons really involved itself with Bank Act amendments, which had always been left to the clubby atmosphere of the Senate Banking Committee. This committee made short work of the proposal that bankers should be barred from other company directorships. The whole idea of worrying about conflicts of interest on the part of a banker smacked of sacrilege.

> SENATOR COOK: It is only fair to say it is a criticism made by those who are not bankers.

> SENATOR BEAUBIEN: Is it not fair to say that over the past fifty years Canadian banks have behaved better and turned in better performances than many other institutions? If that is the case, why put in regulations when they have done so well?[17]

This kind of guff from senators who were also bank directors effectively did in the provision, which was turned into a regulation that a bank director could not be a director of another company whose board was already more than 20 per cent composed of bankers—something that rarely, if ever, happened. Still, the CBA did not have things entirely its own way. The law also established a Canadian Payments Association, technically independent of the CBA, to handle cheque-clearing; this meant that the near-banks did not have to operate entirely at the mercy of a bank-controlled clearing system. Their complaint was not that they were losing because of the way the banks operated the system, but that they wanted some say in such policy matters as where the clearing centres would be located.

And, as we have already seen, to meet all the grousing about a lack of competition among our own institutions, foreign banks were allowed into Canada for the first time, but within such sharp limits that it was a wasted exercise. In total, all foreign banks could grow until they were, collectively, about one-sixth the size of the Royal.[18] How they could provide competition under these rules was not explained.

However, the Four Pillars were still in place, so that was all right.

The banks didn't like it, and made no secret of the fact that they thought they should be allowed to do whatever they damn pleased— which, they said, would benefit Canadians, because they were such smart chaps that prices would come down and customers would bene- fit—but nobody believed them. Canadians thought the banks should stick to banking.

Deregulation, the Cure-All

Then Ronald Reagan bit into his first White House jelly-bean, and an- nounced to the world his discovery of the new elixir—deregulation: cures economies, asthma, whooping-cough, and unsightly blemishes. Under the aegis of the new remedy, the banks were turned loose. As the world was wrapped in a theory that deregulation and globalization were the waves of the future, regulation was systematically dismantled. No one ever ad- vanced an argument to offset the concern about the dangers of conflicts of interest, oligopoly, and inefficiency, which were the reasons for supporting the Four Pillars concept. Globalization was bound to mean the erection of a small number of huge corporations, the very set of oligopolies we had been rejecting all these years. Advocates claimed that this was more com- petitive, an Orwellian word-switch that nobody seemed to notice. Big government was bad and inefficient; big unions were bad and inefficient; big anything was bad, except big business, which was good.

To put this philosophy in place in Canada, the Conservative govern- ment of Brian Mulroney, steeped in globalism, reared on the milk of multinational corporations, moved quickly to tear down "barriers to com- petition," beginning with the Four Pillars. This was accomplished with stunning speed, in the next set of Bank Act revisions, enacted in 1987.

The process began, according to Michael Babad and Catherine Mulroney,[19] at a meeting at the Château Montebello, not far from Ottawa, on October 16, 1986. There, a gaggle of bankers tackled the fi- nance minister, Michael Wilson, over the foie gras and a cold bottle, and turned him into Samson, the man who would bring down the Four

Pillars, even if he brought down the building as well. Bob MacIntosh, the CBA lobbyist, wrote the memo to Wilson that set up the meeting, which saw the chairman of each of the big banks, along with at least three top officers, chewing over the canapés and the nation's financial system with Wilson and his deputy, Stanley Hartt, in a private dining room. By the time coffee was served, the deal was done.

You may think it strange that such momentous changes could be wrought so swiftly behind closed doors by such a biased group, but bear in mind the arrogance of the financiers, who knew what was best for Canada and acted accordingly. The stage had already been set by the series of moves to deregulate then sweeping across the world.

In the United States, the savings and loan associations had been turned loose, and had come crashing down with a series of frauds, bankruptcies, and defalcations that, in the end, will cost American taxpayers more than a trillion dollars. This failure was blamed, unbelievably, on excessive regulation.[20] In Canada, at about the same time, there had been a series of spectacular scandals, usually involving the self-dealing of a handful of financiers, or wild gambling on dubious ventures, which led to the collapse of a number of trust companies and banks (see Chapter 9). This proved to the wise folks who make these decisions that we ought to place more faith in the financiers.

In the fall of 1986, the British government, under Iron Lady Margaret Thatcher, set off the "Big Bang," which was to eliminate barriers that hampered the efficiency of financial institutions, allowing the banks into the securities game, and, in the United States, regulatory bodies were discarding rules daily. Sears, the department store, set up its own financial house, and was soon dealing socks and stocks over the counter from coast to coast. This was seen as the herald of "one-stop financial shopping," which would make everyone rich, starting with the companies that got the business. Actually, it turned out that stores set up to sell socks are not so hot with stocks.

In Canada, we went through our federal–provincial gavotte; that is, every time a province, or Ottawa, seemed in a mood to maintain a modicum of common sense, the financial institutions involved would threaten to move their business elsewhere, and government would give way. As the provinces regulate the securities industry, and Ottawa regulates the banks, this proved a particularly effective tactic.

Jacques Parizeau, later to become the leader of the Parti Québécois, was the provincial finance minister in a Liberal government in Quebec, and he argued that loosening the reins would allow francophones to grab business from the wicked anglos.[21] Before you could say "*Zut, alors,*" provincially chartered deposit-taking institutions were allowed to buy into the brokerages, beginning with the Laurentian Group, which set up financial boutiques in its downtown Montreal headquarters, to flog insurance, stocks, and banking services under one roof. However, they still felt cramped, because they needed access to the Toronto Stock Exchange, which would not allow such goings-on. In Ontario, no other player could own more than 10 per cent of a brokerage.

This rule went out the window under the threat of losing business to Quebec, and, before long, the Ontario Securities Commission called a rare public hearing to pave the way for the establishment of the first bank-owned broker in the province.[22] This was the Toronto-Dominion Bank's Green Line service, which was still not allowed to sell stocks directly, but could steer customers to a broker.

By late 1985, the public had been re-educated—some might call it brainwashed—by an outpouring of articles in the business media pointing out that all the old worries about conflicts of interest and self-dealing were merely the carping of timid souls afraid to meet the challenge of global competition. This performance on the part of the media was particularly impressive when you consider that the reassuring noises were being made as firms were collapsing after being looted by self-dealing executives and owners.

When, in that same year, Quebec allowed the Bank of Nova Scotia to set up a full-service financial subsidiary, and the gang over at the Toronto Stock Exchange could see their commissions piling into trucks and pulling out onto the Macdonald–Cartier Freeway, it was all over. The securities dealers simply told their provincial regulators in Toronto that, if they couldn't sell their companies to the banks—with nice fat bonuses and stock options all around—they would relocate in Quebec, and *then* sell out.[23]

Destroying the Safeguards

The crucial issue remained unresolved. If a bank owned a broker, how could it deal at arm's length with the broker who was borrowing money to float a new share issue, or with customers who were borrowing money to buy stocks, or, indeed, with any part of the equation? It became a race to see which level of government could destroy the safeguards that had been in place for 120 years faster and more thoroughly.

The subsequent new legislation, which came into place in June 1987, removed the restrictions on other firms owning the securities operators. Ottawa would supervise the banks, and any in-house securities transactions, while the provinces would continue to regulate the brokers. A new federal office was created, the Office of the Superintendent of Financial Institutions (OSFI), which would have general overseeing powers.

The change in law led to what Babad and Mulroney call "a frenzy of bidding," as the Royal Bank bought Dominion Securities for $1.4 billion, the Bank of Montreal bought Nesbitt Thomson, the Bank of Nova Scotia swallowed McLeod Young Weir, and the National Bank grabbed the largest francophone brokerage, Lévesque-Beaubien. By the time the dust settled, every large bank had its own securities firm, but no securities firm had a bank. The brokerage business had become an offshoot of banking.

However, there were still three financial pillars, so that was okay.

The same process was repeated in a new set of amendments to the Bank Act that were speeded up, for once, and passed in 1991. There was a lot of talk about the need to meet global competition, and a heavy lobbying effort in Ottawa and the provincial capitals, and a barrage of media coverage of the inevitability of one-stop financial shopping. The result was the removal of the rules that kept the banks from majority ownership of trust companies, and out of the insurance game. They still couldn't sell insurance over the bank counter, but they could buy insurance subsidiaries. On paper, the new law merely made it possible for any of the players to own any of the others, and there were some occasions where this happened. Manulife Financial, for example, created a small Schedule II bank by merging three trust companies. However, the overwhelming effect was that the banks quickly gained control of the trust business, and expanded rapidly in the insurance business.

Tables 6 and 7 in the Appendix will give you a quick thumbnail sketch of the change. In 1987, the Big Five banks owned among them 132 Canadian subsidiaries; now, they own 408. Their holdings embrace mortgage companies, leasing firms, trusts, securities companies, investment counselling firms, insurance companies, aviation corporations, energy conglomerates, and holding companies that hold other companies that hold still other companies, whose activities are a mystery, as far as the public record is concerned. They have even begun to sprout numbered companies, such as 133317 Canada Limited, one of twenty-four numbered companies Statistics Canada[24] discovered among the holdings of the Bank of Montreal, but which do not appear anywhere in the bank's annual report.

In this Bank Act revision, banks and other federally regulated institutions were still barred from owning car-leasing firms, and naturally the banks still groused about that. However, the Act was given a five-year "sunset clause," which meant that it would be reviewed again in 1997—five years after the revisions came into force—to see if there was anything left to give the banks. It is this clause that has the bankers back at the trough today demanding to be able to bring to car leasing and the insurance industry the same appetite that prompted the digestion of the mortgage industry, the trust business, personal finance companies, and the securities firms.

The Four Pillars were now reduced to rubble: the banks dominated every field of finance but the insurance industry, and the Big Five all owned subsidiaries in that business against the glad day when the last vestige of independence disappeared under the onslaught of their lobby.

How times have changed. When Tom Hockin, the junior finance minister, tabled his Blue Paper on financial reform in 1986, he said that, "to protect against harmful concentration ... large financial institutions will not be allowed to acquire other large financial institutions."[25] But when, on September 1, 1993, the Royal Bank, the nation's largest bank, which also owned the nation's largest securities firm, swallowed Royal Trust, one of the two largest trust companies in the land, no one of any consequence anywhere in our regulatory authority said a word, although the same government was still in charge.*

Throughout this long-drawn-out takeover process, the public could see, from time to time, examples of why it is a bad idea to have cross-ownership among the various segments of the financial world.

---

* See Chapter 9 for details of the takeover.

- It was the trust companies that pushed the banks into better hours, daily interest accounts, split-level mortgages, and cashable Guaranteed Investment Certificates. The trusts also provided price competition for the banks. Today, there are only two trust companies of any size that are not subsidiaries of the banks—Canada Trust and National Trust—and, here's a funny thing: the interest rates paid by, and charged by, the trusts today are virtually the same as those charged by their owners, the banks. On average, at the time I wrote *Towers of Gold, Feet of Clay,* loans were about half a percentage point cheaper, and certificates of deposit half a percentage point higher, at the trusts. Today, they are identical with the rates offered by the banks.

- Paul Reichmann, chairman of Olympia & York, the giant developer, sat on the board of the CIBC when it ladled hundreds of millions of dollars into his firm, which not long afterwards went into bankruptcy protection.

- Two banks, the Canadian Commercial Bank and the Northland Bank, collapsed in 1985 and 1986 and, as we will see in Chapter 9, they represented almost textbook cases of the dangers of loose regulation. Their absorption into other banks brought to an end the prospect of a regional bank anywhere in the country.

- In early 1993, Wood Gundy, a wholly owned subsidiary of the CIBC, was one of the two major underwriters on almost $1 billion of John Labatt Ltd. stock when the Hees–Edper group, which was banking at the CIBC, decided to sell its controlling stake in the brewing company. This raised an issue common to a score of such deals every month that was questioned by Babad and Mulroney: "While there is no suggestion of impropriety here, one has to ask how the securities firm could hope to appear independent by being involved in a stock sale whose proceeds could be used to pay down debts owed to its parent bank?"[26]

- There is already a potential for conflict when a securities dealer is underwriting stock and providing advice to its customers on what stocks to buy; add the banking dimension and the danger doubles. This was made clear when a securities analyst named Douglas Cunningham quit First Boston Canada because the bank would not publish his negative report on Rogers Communications, a company the bank was helping to finance.[27] The banks get around the concern about conflicts of interest by promoting the notion that there are "Chinese walls" which divide the savings area of the bank, where Mrs. Smith has her account, from the sucker-sluicing, or investment, section. The thing to note about these Chinese walls is that they are made of paper.

- Banks went from having no ownership in investment dealers to owning 70 per cent of the industry.[28] This was followed, in 1995, by the announcement that all but one of the Big Five (the exception was the TD) had cut off access to subordinated loans to any broker not owned by a bank. This was a crucial source of capital which remained available to the banks' own brokerage subsidiaries.[29] The Investment Dealers Association struck back in 1996 with a regulation banning their members from accepting these standby loans from their owner-banks, which left everybody scrambling for capital.[30] To anyone who could read, it was clear that the banks, not surprisingly, would clobber the competition any time they could.

- Among themselves, the banks actually admit that the notion that Chinese walls divide one section of their activities from another is a fairy tale. *Canadian Banker Magazine* runs inspirational articles on the advantages of one-stop shopping, like the one featuring Wes Nelson, a commission salesman for the Bank of Montreal, who "works in association with 16 bank branches, which often tip him off to potential clients. He receives a straight commission on RRIF [Registered Retirement Income Fund] sales; the rate depends on whether they're bank-generated referrals or if he drummed up the business himself."[31]

Or listen to Coral Tarasio, an independent mortgage seller:

> My card says CIBC, and I feel like I have a desk at every branch. We're a source of business for the branches, a big

source of business. Whenever I bring in a mortgage applicant, I always introduce them to other products: overdraft protection, credit approval ... something. I plant the
seed for the branch.[32]

It would be astonishing if bank employees, or, in this case,
sales staff on commission, did not take advantage of their access to bank information to make a pitch, and their access to
customers to steer them to the bank, but ask yourself whatever happened to the notion of privacy in the bank business?
And, how would you, as one of the bank's few remaining
competitors, like to try to sell any other financial product to
a customer who is being swarmed over this way?

- In 1994, TD Capital Group Ltd., a wholly owned subsidiary of
  the Toronto-Dominion Bank, lent about $35 million to MLG
  Ventures Ltd., a company owned by grocery tycoon Steve
  Stavro, to help him take over Maple Leaf Gardens Ltd. in
  Toronto, for $34 a share. At the same time, the bank invested
  about $10 million itself for an indirect stake in the hockey fran-
  chise. Stavro was also an executor of the will of Harold Ballard,
  the man who built the Gardens, and who had also left provisions in his will that would give a lot of money to charities. The
  way it worked, whatever was left after debts were cleared
  would go to the charities. Before the deal went through, TD
  vice-chairman William Brock wrote a memo to bank chairman
  Richard Thomson noting that this arrangement would "leave
  only $1 or $2 million in the estate after debts and expenses."[33]

  A question was raised that these shares were probably worth
  a good deal more than $34, along with an allegation that the
  bank had confidential information on this point.[34] The
  Ontario Public Trustee sued a number of parties, including the
  bank, on behalf of the charities, and, after lengthy legal proceedings, wrested another $23.5 million out of the process for
  the charities from Stavro and his company, MLG Ventures.
  Then, the TD Bank issued a press statement to say, correctly,
  that "the bank and TD Capital Group Ltd. at all times acted
  in a completely legal and proper manner."[35]

The bank's position was that it had no "inside information" when it entered into these transactions, that indications shares were worth more than $34 were based on Steve Stavro's "opinion" about potential revenue from broadcasting revenues, and that this opinion came before the broadcasting contracts, on which it depended, were renegotiated. In the end, the bank said, the value of the shares turned out to be lower than Stavro's estimates.

We have established a financial climate in which the banks can be on several sides of almost any deal, and the concerns this raises are met by your friendly banker-broker-mortgagee-estate manager-insurance financial agent with two words: Trust me.

On what grounds?

The notion of the Four Pillars was a good one, and history has proven its case, but that has not mattered a tinker's dam in the rush to provide our banks, by far the largest and most concentrated system in any of the Group of Seven industrial countries,[36] with more anti-competitive tricks to play in the name of competition.

However, the bank's largest coup in the 1991 revisions remained almost a state secret for three years: the ending of the requirement that they keep reserves on tap at the Bank of Canada, without interest. To follow what happened, and how it happened, we need to probe a little deeper into the process by which the banks manufacture money.

PART THREE

Money in the Bank

Once a nation parts with control of its currency and credit, it matters not who makes that nation's laws. Usury, once in control, will wreck any nation. Until the control of currency and credit is restored to government and recognized as its most conspicuous and sacred responsibility, all talk of the sovereignty of Parliament and of democracy is idle and futile.

—William Lyon Mackenzie King,
Radio address, August 2, 1935

CHAPTER 5

Multiplying Money

After all, the easiest way to get money is to earn it.

—Peter McArthur, *To Be Taken with Salt*, 1903

It is still largely a system wherein not the federal government but private banks control the money-creation process. It remains today a preposterous system, and the trouble it can cause is far from at an end.

—William F. Hixson,
Triumph of the Bankers, 1993

IF YOU ASK CANADIANS who actually has the right to create money in our economy, nine out of ten will reply, "The Government of Canada." The tenth, who took Economics 101, will reply, "The banks make about ninety-five out of every hundred dollars created in Canada, and the government, through the Bank of Canada, makes the rest." The tenth is right. The money sponsored by the government is called "legal tender," which is what it says on the face of any bill. If you owe someone $20, and you give him or her two tens, the debt is cancelled. But he or she doesn't have to accept your cheque, even if certified, because that is not legal tender. It is "promise to pay" tender, or "transaction money," or "bank money." It is as real as any other money for every purpose except that of dealing with some hardhead who insists on legal tender. When your bank sends you a credit card in the mail, with a little note that says that your credit is good up to $5,000, it is creating that money, as well. You can spend it by using your card, but nobody actually printed it. If you are able to borrow a really substantial amount of money—let us say, $100,000—the bank will set you up with a nice account and, after you have surrendered title to your house, car, and first-born child as collateral, deposit $100,000 into the account. But this will not be done by pouring 100,000 one-dollar bills out of a sack; a teller will punch a one and five zeroes into the computer, and, presto! money is created that you can spend.

For many purposes, bank money is more convenient than legal tender. A cheque is more convenient than a sheaf of notes when you are paying off your mortgage; even more convenient is signing a piece of paper that allows the bank to take the money straight out of your account, every month.

Those who create money, like other priests who preside over the inner temples, prefer the process to sound mysterious, with a dash of magic to it, and so most explanations of money-creation by the banks were obscure.

Thus, W.T.G. Hackett, an economist with the Bank of Montreal, in a text published by the Canadian Bankers Association in 1945, pontificated: "When the government borrows by selling securities to the central bank there is made possible an expansion of chartered bank deposits equivalent to about ten times the value of the bonds thus sold, which would bring an approximately tenfold addition to the money supply."[1]

As noted earlier, in Chapter 2, the multiplying process was called "fractional reserve banking," to salute the fact that the money created was limited by government reserve requirements, which established what fraction of legal tender the bank was required to keep in reserve as a proportion of its deposits. In 1945, the banks were required to leave with the Bank of Canada $1 in reserves for every $10 of deposits, which is why the multiple was ten. Today, it is much higher.[2] Note, too, that the process began with the government selling securities to the central bank. It still does; all that has changed is the nature of the reserve system. If the government does not start things off, no money can be created, but once the government sets the machinery in motion, the bank can multiply what the government issues by anything from fifty to a hundred times.

Over time, the banking system has hugely expanded its leverage, so that for every $1 it was able to conjure out of the ether in 1945, it can now invent anything between $5 and $10, depending on what it thinks it has to have on hand to meet sudden demands. Not bad, if you happen to be a bank.

The Magical Multiplier

Let's look at how the government floats money out into circulation, and what the banks do with it. Because the math is easier to follow, I am going to use a reserve ratio of 1:50, meaning that $2 in the Bank of Canada vault are required for every $100 in the system.*

The Bank of Canada, as the government's custodian of the monetary process, decides that the economy needs the infusion of $100 million in new money. To accomplish this, it buys $2 million worth of Government of Canada bonds from the government, and issues a cheque or bank draft drawn on itself to pay for these. Then it prints new bank notes in the amount of the debt, and deposits these in a commercial bank account, let us say in Bank 1. The Government of Canada, which issued the bonds, pays the interest on them to the Bank of Canada, which now owns them, and, at the end of the year, the Bank of Canada pays that interest back to the government as part of its annual profits. Bank 1 now has $2 million more in deposits than it had before, and, since it wants to make every dollar work, it will lend the new cash out as quickly as possible. Keeping on hand the necessary 2 per cent reserve, it can create $1,960,000 in loans (assets), which will show up as new bank deposits, and which will be spent by cheques drawn on these accounts. The $1,960,000 now flows out to Bank 2, as that bank turns the cheques into cash (keeping it simple, we assume all the cheques are drawn there), leaving Bank 1 with new reserves of $40,000, and $1,960,000 in new assets (loans). Now Bank 2, with a new $1,960,000, sets aside a 2 per cent reserve and lends out $1,920,800, which is drawn out by cheques on Bank 3. Again, bank notes to cover this flow to 3, leaving 2 with new cash reserves of $39,200 (2 per cent of $1,960,000) and new assets (loans) of $1,920,800. Bank 3 works the same multiple, as do 4 and 5, and back to

---

* The model I am following is that used in two books already cited, Campbell R. McConnell, Stanley L. Bruce, and William Henry Pope's *Economics: Principles, Problems and Policies*, 5th Can. ed., and H.H. Binhammer's *Money, Banking & the Canadian Financial System*.

1. If all the banks lend to their maximum, and they will, the original $2 million created by the central bank will soon have multiplied to $100 million in assets. Remember that it cannot just keep multiplying forever, so long as there is a reserve ratio, because that sets the upper limit of multiplication at each stage of the operation.*

Note in passing that out of the projected $100 million, the commercial banks will get the interest on $98 million, and the government, through the Bank of Canada, interest on only $2 million—the interest on the bonds that began the process. Thus, the greater the multiple, the greater the return for the commercial banks.

Because the multiple increased so much in recent times the whole process became somewhat reckless. Here were the banks telling us to pull in our belts, while they were multiplying their multiplier almost endlessly. There was another problem. As banks shoved their interest rates higher and higher during the late 1970s, which, they kept telling us, was to make us curb our excessive spending, they justified the increases by explaining that they did not benefit from higher rates, because they had to lay out more themselves to get the money to lend us. They were, as we saw in Chapter 4, acting as "financial intermediaries." In these circumstances, if they went from borrowing at 5 per cent—that is, paying 5 per cent interest on savings accounts—and lending at 8 per cent, to borrowing at 15 per cent and lending at 18, they didn't gain a thing. The spread was still 3 per cent. Rowland Frazee, then chairman of the Royal Bank, noted in his annual message for 1980 that "banks don't like high interest rates ... [They] are better off on the whole with lower, stable rates." He described 1980 as "frankly, a difficult year." That was the year in which the Royal's profit soared 21 per cent, which Frazee blamed on the public, who kept on borrowing money even though the bank charged more for it. "This growth cannot continue indefinitely at this rate," he noted. Nor could it; the Prime Rate hit 22.75 per cent the

---

* The point was made with elegant simplicity in an exchange before a parliamentary committee in 1939. Graham Towers, first Governor of the Bank of Canada, was asked, "When the government delivers a $1,000 bond to the bank, what does the bank use to purchase it with? Is it the creation of additional money?" He replied, "It is the creation of additional money." See William Krehm, *A Power Unto Itself* (Toronto: Stoddart, 1993), p. 57.

next year, and the Royal's profit jumped 50.4 per cent over 1980, to $651 million.[3]

However, anyone could see, and many people did see, that the banks were telling a tale. If most of their money was created on the premises, it was all gravy. At 8 per cent, the gravy was 8 per cent, and at 18, it was 18. It still is. While the banks were telling us that high interest rates were a regrettable necessity and hurt them more than they did us, their money multiplier was providing them with free cash on which they could charge us stupendous rates and make mammoth profits.

By one of those wonderful coincidences that seem to attend high finance in this country, just about the time people were beginning to sit up and take note of what I think can fairly be described as an unconscionable ripoff, the banks discovered that there was no magic multiplier after all. The whole thing was one of those regrettable misunderstandings. What was really happening, you see, was that people were creating debt by borrowing from the banks, and it was the debt that brought about the new money. J.A. Galbraith, director of economic research for the Royal Bank of Canada, wrote a book in 1979 which, after running us through the standard explanation of the process of money-creation, then waved the cape:

> It is this way of bringing deposits into existence, or of adding to deposits, that has led to the view that bank deposits are created and that, since bank deposits are money, banks create money ... While many support this money creation view of bank deposits, it is not the most useful view for understanding how banks operate. For this reason, a growing body of professional opinion now supports the contrary view that bank deposits represent amounts borrowed by banks from depositors. The argument for this view is that the manner in which deposits come into existence is only a matter of technique and that no matter how deposits arise they are in legal and accounting terms debts of the banks.[4]

I have read this passage seven times, and I think I begin to get a glimmer. You thought banks created money when they set up loans by creating deposits, but no, the most useful way of looking at the thing is that the bank borrows money from the depositor. See how much better that makes it? I tried this one out on the loans officer of my bank, who was getting a little shirty about money owing on a car loan. This is really, I told her, a debt you owe me, in legal and accounting terms, so pay up. All I got was a wintry smile.

The New Truth

The New Truth of banking—banks only borrow the stuff, they don't make it—has some other wonderful collateral benefits for the banks. If they are not creating any new money, it doesn't really matter what the reserve ratio is, as long as they keep enough on hand to meet immediate demand. Indeed, there is not much sense in a reserve, in these circumstances. Not only that, the money in the vaults, all of it, is theirs, because they bought it, in effect, so it doesn't seem right to make them put up reserves with the Bank of Canada, and not get interest on these reserves. The banks began to speak of their reserve requirements as a "tax," rather than as what might be called a user's fee for the privilege of multiplying money.

And guess what? Not only have the banks embraced the New Truth, so has the governor of the Bank of Canada. In an illuminating exchange before the Standing Committee on Public Accounts on December 12, 1995, Liberal MP Marc Assad was trying to persuade Gordon Thiessen, the Bank governor, that the Bank of Canada should make "very substantial loans to the federal government at very low interest rates," to get the economy moving again.[5] Thiessen demurred. This would only cause inflation. No, it wouldn't, Assad replied, not if the reserve requirements on the commercial banks were raised to offset the increase in funds, and that seemed only right, since the banks were able to multiply their deposits. Thiessen shot back:

> No, Sir, it doesn't work that way. The chartered banks, basically, have got to attract both borrowers and depositors. There is no magic multiple. The notion that some of us learned in our economics textbooks way back when that there is this wonderfully miraculous money multiplier ... You

> put in $10 and it suddenly transforms itself into $1,000. No, it doesn't work that way.

Yes it does; not at once, but through a series of bank transactions, over time, not in one bank, but in the banking system. As economist William Henry Pope puts it, "The Governor is wrong in denying that the money multiplier exists. Nor is there anything 'wonderfully miraculous' about it."[6] It is simply the way the system works. As he sprang to the banks' defence, Thiessen said it would also be wrong to use reserve requirements as an anti-inflationary tool because "reserve requirements are essentially a form of tax."[7]

Imagine the senior naval officer of the nation suddenly announcing that all his ships are going to remain tied to their docks henceforth, because he has just discovered that metal is heavier than water, so they'll sink if they are moved. Some textbooks may talk of a wonderfully miraculous flotation system, but, No, Sir, it doesn't work that way. And no fair looking out to sea.

A number of observers have looked out to sea, in the banking world, and found many ships floating there. One of these was William Hixson, an American businessman turned economist, who has written several books and hundreds of essays on banking. The same argument about magic multiples had arisen in the United States, and Hixson approached it by examining the activities of the Federal Reserve System and the U.S. banks. If, indeed, the banks are mere financial intermediaries, borrowing from Peter to lend to Paul, then the banks' assets* will increase at roughly the same time and by just about the same amount as the legal tender available in the system. Customers will put legal tender into the banks, and the banks will lend it out again. Since there is no magic multiple, the two amounts will be roughly the same. It should be easy to test the theory, which will prove that the new loans were made possible by deposits, not government money puffed up by the banks.

What Hixson found was that customers withdraw far, far more from American banks than they deposit, and American banks lend out nearly twenty times as much as the government creates. The loans could

---

* In banking, loans are assets, because they are money owed to the bank, and deposits are liabilities, because this money is owed to depositors.

not be coming from deposits, but had to come from within the banks themselves; they had to be made-up money. Between 1950 and 1990, the amount of legal tender in the hands of Americans increased by $228 billion,[8] but bank loans increased by about $2,200 billion. During this same period of time, the Federal Reserve System created $276 billion in legal tender and used it to purchase government bonds and other securities. The $276 billion was deposited with the banks; $228 billion, as noted above, was withdrawn as legal tender by the public, and the other $48 billion remained in the banks, as reserves. On the basis of these reserves, the banks created $2,200 billion worth of loans, about $46 in new assets for every dollar increase in reserves. Hixson observes:

> Every last cent of the net increase in [the banking system's] capacity to make loans came from the Fed. Not an iota of it came from deposits of legal tender by the public. The banks increased their loans by creating deposits in borrowers' names and thus the deposits increased in step with the increase in loans. But note that it was the increase in loans that brought about the increase in deposits, not vice versa ... Deposits increased because banks created money in the process of making loans.[9]

This observation was in perfect accord with the theory that had been current for fifty years, until our banking admirals discovered that boats don't float. William Henry Pope performed the same calculation for Canadian loans, and came up with an even higher multiplier. Using figures from the *Bank of Canada Review* that track Canadian legal tender and bank loans, Pope found that, between 1969 and 1994, legal tender outside the banks increased by $21,065.3 million. In the same quarter-century, the Bank of Canada purchased $21,018.2 million in Government of Canada bonds and Treasury bills, and increased its other assets by just over $4 billion. It paid for the total with its own bank notes, depositing $25,038.7 million in the chartered banks. The public, as in the United States, took out far more from the banks than it put in, increasing legal tender in circulation by $21,065.3 million. The banks retained the other $3,817.5 million, and: "It was on the basis of this $3,817.5 million increase in its cash reserves that the banking system increased its general and residential mortgage loans by $358,251 million."[10] This produces a multiplier of 93.84, which, Pope argues, becomes larger when loans on non-residential mortgages and leasing receivables are added in. "The multiplier is even greater, probably close to 100."[11]

As in the United States, the huge increase in bank assets could not have come from deposits, if the public was taking more out of the system than it was putting in. And when these deposits are made in the form of cheques, rather than cash, they provide no increase, since the cheques are drawn on the banks, and the net result is a wash; for every dollar that goes in, one comes out. As Pope notes, "For every $100 Government of Canada bond that the Bank of Canada buys, the banking system can—and does—increase its loans, and therefore our deposits and money supply, by approximately $10,000."[12]

Interest on the Made-Up Money

It is not surprising that the banks are unduly modest about their capacity to manufacture money on the premises. For one thing, they are collecting interest on the made-up stuff, as well as on legal tender, and if the general public got onto this, the banks would be even more unpopular than they are today with some folks. There is also the matter of safety. If money can be multiplied dozens of times when it is created, the same leverage will work in reverse when money is destroyed. When a bank calls in a loan (or the government retires securities), assuming it is working on a fractional reserve of 2 per cent, the same multiplier will go to work on the way down, and the final result will be a contraction of fifty times the amount involved.

Economist Henry Simons wrote that "our circulating medium is now at the mercy of loan transactions of banks and our thousands of checking banks are, in effect, so many private mints ... Such a system is dangerous to depositors, dangerous to banks, and dangerous to the general public."[13]

When W.T.G. Hackett wrote his official explanation of money multiplication for the banks in 1945, he was dealing with a tenfold increase. Now it is up to somewhere between 50 and 100. The money on hand in reserves, in case anything goes wrong, was 10 per cent; now it is less than 2 per cent. Isn't that a rather thin thread from which to hang the entire system? The banks hesitate to point this out to us, not only because they are edging farther and farther out onto a limb, but because they are making more and more money with every wriggle. If they had a 100 per cent reserve, as once they did, then they would have to keep on deposit with the Bank of Canada one dollar for every dollar they lent out. The only money created would be what the central bank brought into being, and the interest on this would come to the Bank of Canada, and, through it, to the general public. (I do not favour a 100 per cent reserve, although some do; it would contract the money supply with a crash, and the economy with it; I put the case only to underline how the system works.)

If the reserve is at 10 per cent, the banks can create, and charge interest on, ten dollars for every dollar the Bank of Canada creates; if it is 2 per cent, fifty dollars; it is not hard to see why the banks prefer to get interest on fifty dollars, rather than on ten, but the general public, if it knew about it, would be bound to ask, Where does that leave us? What makes the cheese more binding is that the government having, in effect, privatized the money-creation system by turning it over to the banks, then borrows the new money they manufacture back from them at a high rate of interest.

Ruben C. Bellan, Professor of Economics (Emeritus) at the University of Manitoba, has investigated the matter. He points out that, during 1995, the Bank of Canada held, on average, $25 billion worth of Government of Canada bonds and received $1.7 billion in interest from the government on these. This was the Bank's only income. Its operating expenses amounted to $200 million, and it turned over $1.5 billion in profits to the receiver general at the end of the year. The cost to the government of borrowing from the Bank of Canada was $200 million, that is, the cost of operating the Bank. On $25 billion worth of borrowing, this works out to an interest rate of 0.8 per cent.[14]

On the other hand, the government is paying the commercial banks rates of 5 and 6 and 7 per cent to borrow from them the money they can create only as a result of government deposits. William F. Hixson writes that "a government borrowing money it permits banks to create presents about the silliest spectacle imaginable."[15] But even sillier would be the spectacle of a government allowing banks to create money, or destroy money, without some mechanism in place to control the process. We have such a mechanism, which it is now time to examine. We call it the Bank of Canada.

CHAPTER 6

The Buck Starts Here: The Bank of Canada

It is desirable to establish a central bank in Canada to regulate credit and currency in the best interests of the economic life of the nation, to control and protect the external value of the national monetary unit and to mitigate by its influence fluctuations in the general level of production, trade, prices and employment, so far as may be possible within the scope of monetary action, and generally to promote the economic and financial welfare of the Dominion.

—From the preamble to the Bank of Canada Act, 1934

Central bankers and commercial bankers meet in the same clubs. They lunch together. Almost inevitably they come to see things the same way. This explains—but does not excuse—the policies followed by the Governors of the Bank of Canada for the past several decades. Without question these policies have been good for the commercial banks. Without question these policies have been disastrous for Canada.

—William Henry Pope,
All You MUST Know about Economics, 1996

THE BANK OF CANADA BUILDING towers over the Sparks Street Mall in downtown Ottawa, filling the block between Bank and Kent, from

Sparks Street to Wellington, a thrusting, green marble–sided temple, ruled by the high priests of monetarism. On the ground floor is a museum where, for two and a half bucks, you can pick up a surprising amount of assorted lore about the history of money and banking. The museum is fronted by little ponds and puddles, overhung by greenery, reminiscent of a jungle bereft of beasts. Beyond, where you and I may not go unless one of the priest-bureaucrats has given us the nod, are the smooth plains of the foyer and the throng of elevators that will whirl us up to the offices, with their acres of windows through which the priests can look down and observe the earthlings below.

The Bank of Canada is ours, by the way. We own it. We built it, nurtured it, watched over it as it grew. Now it will have nothing to do with us; it has grown beyond us; it wishes us to leave it alone to manage things by itself. It wants to, has wanted for some time to, confine itself to a single task—imposing monetary stability on the nation, even if it throttles the economy. Zero inflation or bust. The chartered banks love it, because the way to zero inflation is through high interest rates, which they are forced, much against their will, to impose on the rest of us. In 1991, the Bank tried to get the law changed so that it would have no other task than establishing monetary stability, and that task would be written into the Constitution, along with a clause guaranteeing the Bank's independence, so that no busybodies up on Parliament Hill could interfere every time it held the economy down and dosed it with strong medicine.[1] The attempt to change the law very nearly succeeded, but it was blocked, in the end, by a combination of circumstances.

One was the onset of the most severe recession—many called it a depression—since the 1930s, whose roots could be traced directly to the Bank's high-interest–rate policies. MPs, who were feeling the heat from constituents who had been cleaned out, disemployed, or rendered bankrupt as part of the Grand Scheme to cure the economy, were getting restive. Then, there was the attitude of the governor, John Crow, who looked down his long nose at the parliamentarians as if he were the Duke of Wellington, and they mere cannon-fodder. Finally, there was a spirited attack by economists and other academics, backed by a gathering of outraged business men and women called the Bank of Canada for Canadians Coalition, and egged on by the Liberals, which stalled the Bank's plan until the 1993 change of government sent it into limbo.

Then the Chrétien Liberals quietly tipped the coalition on how, and where, and through whom they should mount a lobby to get rid of John Crow, whose seven-year term was coming to an end, and whose reappointment was high on the list of desirable objects in the bank boardrooms and editorial offices of the nation. Cabinet ministers would telephone members of the coalition and tell them where to call to solicit opinions knocking the governor. And they did. They convened confabs, held luncheons, sent out press releases, sponsored petitions, and created a strong backwash to wipe out all the favourable publicity that the Bank had created to help Crow to a new appointment.

On the suggestion of a senior staffer in the Department of Finance, Jordan Grant, chair of the coalition, wrote a letter to Professor Paul A. Samuelson, Institute Professor of Economics at the Massachusetts Institute of Technology, a Nobel Prize winner, and the grand guru of economists all over the world. Grant told Samuelson that the Bank's campaign to achieve zero inflation had resulted in unemployment of over 11 per cent, and begged him to "have pity on us" by weighing in with a comment on the central banking system.[2] Samuelson replied with a pithy analysis attacking "the extremist view" that price-level stability should be the sole goal of any central bank. Such a view, Samuelson wrote, "is dangerous dogma and will ultimately jeopardize the viability of central bank independence."[3] He finished with an anecdote about running into "an eminent Canadian professor" and chatting with him about the federal election, "the debacle that wiped out the Conservative Party of Canada":

> Innocently, I said, "I suppose the dogmatic hard-money policies of the Bank of Canada will be one of the first things to be re-examined." To my surprise, he said, "Oh no. The gnomes of Zurich would be displeased if the Governor of the Bank of Canada were in any way influenced to alter *his* [the professor's word!] policy. Expect no change."
>
> I returned home with a heavy heart, recalling George Santayana's bitter words: "Those who ignore history are condemned to repeat it."[4]

Faster than you could say Xerox, Grant had copies of the Samuelson letter flying around the country, producing a headline in the *Financial*

Post that read: "Nobel economist takes Crow to task."[5] The *Globe and Mail* began to run tough editorials wondering whether it was a good idea to ram monetary stability down our throats at the price of economic strangulation. Then the Liberals were able to say that John Crow no longer had the confidence of the business community, and he was allowed to depart, with a nice jingle in his jeans, and after a series of posh send-off parties.

A New Acolyte

Still, on the way out the door, and in return for pretending that he was happy to go, Crow was able to cut a deal with Finance Minister Paul Martin, the darling of corporate Canada, through which his successor would be Gordon Thiessen, a Bank-bred bureaucrat, one of the priesthood. The coalition had been plumping for anyone but one of the priests, and had mounted a spirited side-campaign to bring Matthew Barrett, the colourful chairman of the Bank of Montreal, into the job. This strategy died when one of Barrett's aides telephoned Jordan Grant, the chair of the coalition, and pointed out that the boss was making in the neighbourhood of $2 million annually, while the Bank was paying a bit more than one-eighth of that.[6]

Thus, while the Bank managed to replace Crow with an acolyte, you couldn't blame the new governor for being a trifle shy. We heard a lot less, in Thiessen's early speeches, of the need to hammer inflation into the ground, and a lot more about the need to give the economy a boost, even, if necessary, by lowering interest rates. In fact, within sixteen months, the Bank of Canada lowered the Bank Rate,* from which all other interest rates depend, sixteen times, and the economy responded, as anyone could predict it would, by rebounding. Despite this temporary setback, zero inflation, the ultimate in price stability, hovers out there in the study papers and minds of the priesthood, a Holy Grail, once glimpsed, never forgotten. The Bank's current policy is to confine the

---

* The Bank Rate is the rate at which the chartered banks borrow money from the Bank of Canada; it is, as much as anything else, an indicator of what monetary policy is to be pursued.

economy to an "inflation range" of 1 to 3 per cent, officially, but there is a strong move within the institution to lower this to 0 to 2 per cent.[7]

The Bank's 1995 annual report, under the heading "What the Bank Does," makes no mention whatever of its legal duty to "promote the economic and financial welfare of the Dominion," and instead says this: "The Bank's primary function and most important responsibility is monetary policy. Monetary policy is concerned with managing the rate of monetary expansion in a way that is consistent with preserving the value of money."[8] This section goes on to describe the institution's role in cheque clearing, issuing bank notes, and acting as fiscal agent for the government. When I raised with Doug Peters, the secretary of state for international financial institutions, the fact that the Bank was ploughing ahead exactly as if the constitutional amendment it wanted had in fact been passed, he said that he was "aware of the statement in the report."[9] That was that.

And when I asked him whether, as the co-author of a book, *The Monetarist Counter-Revolution*, which had fiercely attacked the very position the Bank was still advancing, he was happy with the Bank's current behaviour, he replied: "You must know that in my current position I have to say Yes to that question."[10] That sounds as if the gang over on Sparks Street are going to run their own monetary policy, but Peters sees the matter quite differently. He notes that Thiessen's lowering of the Bank Rate shows that the new governor "appears to have quite a different approach to the job."

I replied that Thiessen could read the papers, too, and saw what happened to Crow; that didn't mean he had a different approach, only that he was smart enough to move cautiously.

The process by which the Bank became converted from the servant of Parliament and the people to the confidante of the commercial banking system is wearyingly familiar. It is the same process by which regulatory bodies always seem to take on the colour, flavour, and goals of the bodies they are supposed to regulate, whether they are stock watchdogs, better business bureaus, or central banks.

The Founding of the Bank of Canada

We have already seen that the Bank of Canada was founded in the midst of the Depression in response to the inability of the chartered banks to do anything but run around shouting "Cut spending!" when what was needed was more spending, and more money-creation. The government tried to stimulate the economy in 1932 by unloading $35 million in Treasury bills to the banks, the process which, as we saw in Chapter 5, should have multiplied money in the general economy. But the financial wizards, instead of lending the new currency out, used it to pay down previous advances, and the money simply circled out of one hole in the Treasury, fluttered around, and disappeared into another. There had already been some agitation for the creation of a central bank, such as a number of other nations had, and this performance increased the pressure; a royal commission was established to investigate the notion in March 1933.

Properly, a royal commission ought to take a year or so reading its mandate and hiring staff, another couple of years receiving evidence, and another year writing a report, which recommends further study and an expanded budget. But the Macmillan Commission, named for Lord Macmillan, who had been chairman of a similar commission in England, was back in a mere six months with a short, simple report that said, Just do it. We are shocked but not surprised to read contemporary accounts that show that the fix was in.[11] Clifford Clark, the deputy minister of finance and Prime Minister R.B. Bennett's economic adviser, had convinced the boss that a central bank was essential for any modern nation. Lord Macmillan, who agreed, rushed through the necessary hearings and returned with the required favourable verdict on September 27, 1933.[12] Two of the five commissioners dissented; they were bankers. The banks' objection was the straightforward one that they were making about $2 million a year on the issuing of notes, a function that would undoubtedly be taken over by the central bank.[13]

No one was disposed to pay much attention to such self-serving arguments, and the Bank of Canada Act was announced a week after the Macmillan report landed on Bennett's desk, and received Royal Assent on July 3, 1934.[14] The Bank opened for business on March 11, 1935. Besides the obvious tasks of operating as the government's bank, regulating monetary, but not fiscal, policy (the currency supply, but not taxes), and managing the public debt, it was given the right of banknote issue (although it would take fifteen years for all the chartered banks' notes to be withdrawn) and the broad mandate to promote the economic welfare of the nation.

The Act also imposed the hated reserves on the chartered banks, requiring them to keep in its vaults a minimum of 5 per cent of their deposits, without interest. However, the Bank was private, not government-owned. A share offering of $5 million, which was oversubscribed, was bought up by a fairly wide section of the monied populace, and it turned out, horror of horrors, that 37 per cent of the stocks were owned by women. This caused the *Financial Post* to worry about the possibility that members of the fair sex could end up with the deciding vote in the Bank: "This is a possible development that was not discussed by the wise men of Parliament when control of the bank was being debated. The bank may eventually have a 'governess.'"[15] Not to worry. The Canadian Chamber of Commerce stepped into the breach, nominating a board of directors composed entirely of male business leaders, and they were duly elected. This created a situation in which a central bank, a government creation, was privately owned and promised to be directed on behalf of commercial, rather than political, policy. This was not unique; the same situation obtained in England, but it was unusual.

This hybrid was passed off on the basis of an ideology which persists to this day, and which holds that a central bank should be "independent," and free to pursue policies free of "political interference." In other words, it should be in the pocket of the private sector, whose interference is untainted by politics, unless you count self-interest, and the pursuit of private profit over public good, as politics.

The Liberals, then in opposition, argued for public control of the bank. Mackenzie King, normally the master of obfuscation, set out the central argument in a radio broadcast during the 1935 election, quoted as the epigraph to Part Three. If the government did not control currency and credit, there was not much point in voting. The Liberals won that election, and moved, slowly, to capture ownership of the Bank, finally buying all the shares in 1938.

The Canadian Bankers Association, which opposed the creation of the Bank, and then its nationalization, adapted. Jackson Dodds, the association's president, acknowledged: "In Canada, for better or worse, we are now to have a Bank of Canada set up. Bankers are realists; they are ready to make the best possible use of the materials at their hands."[16] And so they did; plans were soon under way for regular meetings between the Bank and the chartered banks "to discuss general as well as specific problems."[17]

The Reign of Graham Towers

Graham Towers, the first governor, was one of their own; he had been a banker all his working life; there was nothing he liked better than to jump on the train and dash off to Toronto or Montreal to talk things over with the boys. With him, as with every governor except James Coyne, the banks were able to maintain cordial, and even cozy, relationships.

Towers was an odd bird. He was only thirty-seven when approached to leave his position as assistant general manager of the Royal Bank to take over the central bank. He was a long, lean man, fond of dogs (the fact that he and his wife, Molly, allowed their Airedale, Teddy, inside the house was seen as a possible reflection of a liberal outlook), even fonder of women; he had, in the kindly euphemism of his day, a number of "flirtations" with prominent Ottawa ladies.[18] He was arrogant, intelligent, and liked to tell dirty jokes at parties, which may have led to the breakup of a long friendship with Lester Pearson.[19]

Like many other governors, Towers was strong for austerity on the part of the rest of the nation, but not necessarily for himself. He demanded and got a salary higher than anyone else on the government payroll and, throughout the Depression, kept four maids on staff at his mansion in Rockcliffe to see to the needs of himself and Molly, and, of course, Teddy.[20]

When the Liberals under Mackenzie King came to power, Towers was in an awkward position; he did not want the Bank to be nationalized, and argued that it would be perceived to be an arm of the government. Since that was precisely what King had in mind, the prime minister refused to budge, and Towers backed down. For the moment, at least, it was clear that major policy matters were the responsibility of the government, not the Bank. The government then issued more shares, which it purchased, giving it control of the Bank in 1935; then it named a new board, including a farmer and an economics professor; and, finally, it bought up all the private shares and created a wholly owned government institution just in time to meet the financial demands brought on by the Second World War.

The role of the Bank in financing that conflict was nothing short of brilliant. To begin with, it raised more than $500 million by buying government securities, the interest on which went back to the government. The result was a virtually interest-free loan of what was then a staggering amount of money. During the war, the Bank financed annual deficits that amounted to about one-quarter of the Gross Domestic Product at interest rates ranging from 0.37 to 2.5 per cent.[21] The monetary base of the nation was multiplied eightfold. Essentially, the Bank was creating new money by printing it, and yet was able to do this without causing inflation, which ran at 0.5 per cent in 1944 and 1945, while unemployment was at 1.5 per cent.[22] Of course, the Bank had wage and price controls to help confine inflation, and foreign-exchange controls to guard the value of the Canadian dollar, a fact that helped to plunge the amount of public debt held outside the country from about 25 per cent to under 7 per cent between 1940 and 1946.

The Bank was active, interventionist, and nationalist in its policies. It was also, as it happened, intelligent; when money was needed, it pumped the dollars out, until it held more than one-quarter of all the public debt within its own portfolio—much of it in the form of long-term bonds sold to the public on the instalment plan, as War Bonds. Then, as the war wound down, the Bank began to sell securities, drying up some of the money sloshing around the economy. Still, the Bank pursued, in general, an easy-money policy, and Towers cut the Bank Rate from 2.5 to 1.5 per cent to finance the huge growth that would be needed to provide jobs for 2 million returning service personnel, as well as to finance the new and expansionary social policies that came flooding out of Europe and England at the war's end. In addition, the maximum interest rate permitted to the banks was capped at 6 per cent, where it stayed until 1967.

Canada experienced a short, sharp blast of inflation when price controls were ended, and foreign-exchange controls eased. Towers's response was to "suggest" to the commercial banks that they cut back on lending, which they did. When another blast occurred in 1950, at the outbreak of the Korean War, he raised the Bank Rate again, from 1.5 to 2.0 per cent, and left it there. The Bank was performing its intended function of serving as the regulator of the national economy, expanding when necessary, and retracting when necessary. It did not do this by jacking around with the Bank Rate, but by moral suasion exercised over the chartered banks.

The government was content to let Towers get on with it, and to take credit when his policies worked, but the overall responsibility was clearly in the hands of the administration. As Professor Thomas K. Rymes put it: "While the Bank of Canada was responsible for the day-to-day implementation of policy, responsibility for monetary policy rested with the Minister of Finance and the Government."[23] This was the only approach that made sense. Monetary policy affects almost every aspect of civil life, from job-creation to housing, business credit, and inflation. The difficulty is that, when a change in policy begins to rile the voters, any administration becomes anxious to shed the burden of responsibility. That is precisely what happened when James Coyne, the deputy governor, succeeded Towers in 1955. Coyne was a man so aloof that his staff once proposed to give him an icicle wrapped in a blue balloon for Christmas, but they lost their nerve.[24] He was convinced that inflation would be the ruin of us all, and that, to combat it, what the nation needed was a new, tough, interest-rate regime.

The economy, at the time Coyne took over, was in rather shaky condition, but the governor hiked the Bank Rate three times in short order, and then held a private meeting with the nation's top bankers at which he told them to cut back on loans. He also told them he wanted to impose a secondary reserve on them, which would boost their total reserve requirements to 15 per cent.[25] The bankers hated it, but there was little they could do. These demands took place behind closed doors, but the results were, before long, all too apparently public. The Prime interest rate moved to 5.75 per cent in August 1957, then to 6.41 per cent a year later—higher than the law allowed the banks to charge; their loans disappeared. The economy was collapsing.

Walter Harris, the Liberal finance minister, under attack in the House of Commons, declared that it was the Bank of Canada that was responsible for monetary policy, so don't blame him. At the same time he made it clear that he did not agree with the policy being pursued.[26] At one point, Prime Minister Louis St. Laurent suggested that Parliament had no business considering monetary policy at all.[27]

The Coyne Controversy

The government position, then, was that the Bank of Canada could run whatever monetary policy it liked, and elected politicians could do nothing about it, even though the entire nation was put at risk. Just in time—it seems to be a characteristic—the Liberals were defeated in the

June 1957 election, and left the Conservatives under John Diefenbaker to deal with the recession provoked by the new tight-money economy.

Diefenbaker, who, when he was in opposition, had attacked Coyne, hesitated to do anything about him once he became prime minister, because that would be seen as political interference with the Bank, which presumably was acting for the public good. His finance minister, Donald Fleming, said exactly what Harris had said to the House: Don't blame me, boys, I only work here. In response to a question in the Commons, he stated flatly, "The Bank of Canada is not responsible to the Government."[28] Fleming produced two deficit budgets, designed to stimulate a flagging economy, but Coyne's high interest rates rendered them null and void. Still, the finance minister did nothing, as rates climbed, jobs evaporated, and the provincial premiers—many of whose job-creating programs were strangled by the simple fact that the banks could no longer lend them money at current rates—raged.

There was another problem. Coyne was an unabashed nationalist, and made a series of speeches in the fall of 1959 directly attacking the policies of the federal government, which, he claimed, was selling out the nation's birthright to the United States. These speeches thoroughly alarmed the banking community, which was making a very nice dollar out of the Yankees, and it began to put on pressure to do something about the maverick central banker.

Finally, Diefenbaker's advisers convinced him that he faced the fate worse than death—viz., electoral defeat—if he didn't act, so Fleming asked Coyne to resign. Coyne refused, leaving the Conservatives in an awkward position.

To avoid the charge of indecision, Diefenbaker staged a long, silly, and hypocritical attempt to have Coyne fired because he had not vetoed an increase in his own pension, which had been passed by the Bank's board. Coyne was, possibly, the most frugal banker in the land, and, whatever his faults, they did not include a lack of integrity. This personal attack made him more determined than ever not to budge. Grant Dexter of the *Winnipeg Free Press* called it "the most squalid political conspiracy in our history—which is taking in a lot of territory."[29]

The government muscled a piece of legislation through the House of Commons declaring vacant the position of governor of the Bank of Canada. The reason given was "lack of good behaviour," which should have given the MPs something to ponder—since it was a charge that might have emptied the House of Commons, leaving no one to legislate but the sergeant-at-arms. When this legislation reached the Senate, dominated by Liberals, Coyne was called before a committee of that august body, and defended himself in an emotional speech in which he said he was defying the government's attempts to replace him, not for personal reasons, but because it was an "attack on the integrity of the Governor of the Bank of Canada, whoever the holder of that office might be."[30] The Senate rejected the bill, and Coyne, vindicated, resigned.

His successor, Louis Rasminsky, who, like every governor we have ever had (except Towers), was a deputy governor kissed into a prince, refused to take the job until this business of responsibility could be sorted out. Rasminsky, like other governors, had a rather odd idea of what constituted political interference. When he attacked Gordon Churchill, Diefenbaker's right-hand man, and gave him a dressing-down in front of Donald Fleming, that was not political interference, any more than when he scolded Lester Pearson, then the leader of the official opposition, because he refused to support the government during a monetary crisis in 1962;[31] it was interference only when politicians tried to tell the Bank what to do.

Rasminsky's lordly style had the Tories thoroughly cowed; besides, they dared not go through another battle. The result was a public declaration by Donald Fleming, which became part of the Bank Act in 1967, and is still the law, though it makes no sense whatever.* It says that the finance minister and the governor will consult regularly on monetary policy, but the Bank is in charge unless and until there is a "difference of opinion," upon which the cabinet may issue a specific written directive, which the Bank will then follow. If the governor doesn't like it, he can resign.*

---

* The exact wording:

14.   (1) The Minister and the Governor shall consult regularly on monetary policy and on its relation to general economic policy.

    (2) If, notwithstanding the consultations provided for in subsection (1), there should emerge a difference of opinion between the Minister and the Bank concerning the monetary policy to be followed, the Minister may, after consultation with the Governor and with the approval of the Governor in Council, give to the Governor a written directive concerning monetary policy, in specific terms and applicable for a specified period and the Bank shall comply with such directive.

To find a parallel, we must imagine that the chief of defence staff has the right to conduct whatever military policy he likes, unless he picks a fight with a nation the government happens to like, in which case the government will ask him to back off. It is the mystique of money that allows such a bizarre abdication of responsibility to remain in place.

Needless to say, no directive has ever been issued to the Bank, which, since Coyne, has had absolute control of monetary policy in this country. Instead of the government being able to advise and consent on this vital issue, if it doesn't agree with what the Bank is doing, it has to issue a directive; the Bank is not required to defend its policies; the onus is on the minister of finance to prove the Bank wrong. As Thomas K. Rymes notes: "The Directive has therefore strengthened the independence of the Bank of Canada in a manner inconsistent with the idea of a responsible democratic electorate."[32] If the government cannot decide matters of public policy, but can only attack what has been done by its minions by way of a huge, open, politically charged debate, the notion of democratic control is gone.

The brief-lived government of Joe Clark did, in fact, contemplate issuing a directive in 1979, because the Tories had been so violent, in opposition, in their attacks on the high-interest-rate policy of Governor Gerald Bouey, but, when push came to shove, it was the government that crawled down; Bouey, and his policies, sailed on undisturbed.[33] John Crosbie, Clark's minister of finance, who had described Bouey's policies as "viciously damaging," later explained: "The power rested with Bouey and no amount of opposition from either politicians or a screaming public, was going to talk him out of what he was doing. Someone should have brought him into line, yet no one did."[34]

The question of accountability became crucial when central bankers all over the world got caught up in monetarism, the new religion, and proceeded to impose its absurd precepts on the global economy.

The Triumph of Monetarism

Monetarism, which grew out of the monetarist school at the University of Chicago in the 1970s, holds that the key to determining economic activity is the supply and velocity of money—that is, the amount of money, and the speed at which it moves through the economy; the number of times the same dollar is spent within a given time.[35] Markets, this theory holds, are very competitive, a circumstance that provides the economy with a high level of stability. All you need to keep things humming along is to prevent the government from interfering with the markets, reduce the public sector to the smallest possible size, and keep a curb on the money supply, which is the single most important factor in determining the levels of output, employment, and prices. Inflation will be defeated.

Not coincidentally, monetarism was a product of what was then the New Right (now, the fairly old and dog-eared Right), and its attack on all things governmental. The prevailing economic philosophy, neo-Keynesianism, had developed out of the ideas first initiated by British economist John Maynard Keynes, especially his *The General Theory of Employment, Interest and Money*, published in 1936. This was an attack on the view then held by virtually every economist that the capitalist system, left to itself, would automatically tend towards full employment. Don't interfere, the argument went, as the factories shut and the bread-lines grow and poverty stalks the land; don't interfere, you will only make things worse. The system will soon restore itself to equilibrium.

Keynes said, in so many words, "Equilibrium is blither,"[36] and his book, drawing, as it did, on the Great Depression, seemed to have a point. However, we had not had a really good depression for the next forty years, not one where you could actually witness the arrival of food banks and vagrants and thousands of homeless sleeping in the ditches, and the New Right seemed to think it a pity. At least, they thought we were spending far more than was good for us on government interference in the economy, by way of welfare, unemployment insurance, medicare, and all the other things that are anathema to so many of the rich and righteous. Stop succouring the poor, monetarism advised, you will only spoil them. Government spending was the root cause of inflation, the New Right argued—with scant evidence; the huge jump in prices that launched monetarism was based mainly on a sudden, rapid increase in the price of a number of international commodities, especially energy.[37] But what the theory lacked in fact it more than made up for in enthusiasm, and it swept through academic and bureaucratic circles. The new word was that open markets create jobs, and all that was needed for endless prosperity was to let them do it by keeping a handle on the money supply.

Those who do not believe that markets are open and competitive—those who buy gasoline, beer, or major appliances; those who purchase a car or own a bank account—have some trouble with the first part of the theory, because it is so obvious that we have a system of managed prices, controlled by clusters of giant firms. The second part is even more difficult because, as we have already seen, nobody knows what money is any more. It can be created out of thin air, and it can be whisked around the world through international banking facilities which are established for the sole purpose of evading any form of regulation. As William Henry Pope puts it:

> This proliferation of fictitious money that can be transferred to any part of the world instantaneously has reduced the basic premise of monetarist dogma to absurdity: that the price level can be stabilized by controlling the money supply. Nobody today can remotely say what the money supply really is, let alone regulate it.[38]

However, these are matters of faith, not reason, and the monetarists were resolved to prove their worth by giving the dogma a good try. The Bank of Canada was one of the very first to announce its conversion to monetarism in a speech delivered by Governor Bouey, at a meeting of the Canadian Chamber of Commerce (they ate it up) on September 22, 1975, in Saskatoon.[39] He said that previous attempts to bolster the economy had all ended up "turning economic recovery into an inflationary boom." So we would have no more of that. The way to long-term prosperity lay in monetarism; money-supply rates were officially adopted as the instruments for lowering inflation. Tom Courchene, an economist and monetarist at Queen's University, later noted that, "in thought and word, the Bank of Canada probably qualifies for the designation of the world's most monetarist central bank."[40]

Canada was followed into the breach in October 1979, when Paul Volcker, the newly appointed chairman of the U.S. Federal Reserve System, initiated what came to be called "Volcker's Saturday Night Special," a reaction to what he conceived, incorrectly, to have been a sudden jump in monetary growth.[41] From here on, Volcker announced, the Fed would concentrate on controlling the supply of money, and let the chips fall where they may. The advantage of this was that, since everyone knew that the money supply was under control, inflationary expectations would be dashed; prices would fall, and we would have stability, as advertised. Another advantage was that the government could slide out of any blame when things went wrong, because it was Science that was calling the shots, not mere man. To start things off, there was a swift hike in the discount rate (the U.S. equivalent, roughly, of our Bank Rate), and special reserve requirements were placed on commercial time deposits, the instruments many large corporations used to park funds not required for immediate use. But Volcker and his officials soon discovered that there was no longer any accurate measure of money, and what they thought was a new flood of cash was merely a minor change in the velocity of spending (i.e., the number of times the same dollar turned over).[42] The result was to slam on the brakes just as the economy was beginning to move forward, or as William Greider, an American journalist who wrote a book about the Fed, comments: "For the struggling economy, it was as though the Fed had watched until the bull was staggering to its feet, then hit the beast with another hard blow and knocked it to its knees."[43]

The United States, followed by Canada and most of the Western world, plunged into an instant recession, and inflation, instead of declining, rushed ahead. It turned out that part of the cost of goods and services is the money it takes to finance them, and when you make money cost more, prices rise, instead of falling. Then you have to jack up the rates even more, and create a full-fledged crash, to bring inflation to heel. So that was done. What it proved to the monetarists was that the theory worked after all, if you only kept at it. What it proved to most people was that the monetarists were crazy.

However, the monetarists were in control at the central banks, and if the government didn't agree with their policies, it didn't matter, because no one had to pay attention any more to government. They ignored the fact that there have never been stable prices, in this century, except in periods of deep depression. They acknowledge that there will be some temporary difficulty, as the cuts throw people out of work, but this is a sacrifice they should be prepared to make—let us call it "short-term pain for long-term gain." In the meantime, people who have a lot of money will do well, because the high interest rates will boost their incomes. The banks will do well, too, and supply the necessary round of speeches supporting the whole process.

Boosting the Bank Rate

Thus we had Gerald Bouey, for fourteen years, trying to impose stability on the nation by hammering the Bank Rate higher and higher and higher until it hit 21.24 per cent on August 7, 1981.[44] All other credit charges hang from the Bank Rate, and when it reached this height, the Prime went to 22.75, consumer loans to 25.00, and mortgages to 21.25.[45] As it happened, this did not bring prosperity to the land, but massive unemployment, and the Trudeau government, to distance itself even further from the carnage, allowed the Bank to set the Bank Rate at 0.25 per cent above the average selling price of ninety-day Treasury bills. When economic collapse led, as it was bound to in the end, to lower interest rates for the very good reason that no one could afford to borrow at the Bouey-induced ones, the governor felt vindicated. His only regret, he told Michael Babad and Catherine Mulroney, was that he hadn't struck harder, faster.[46] He also felt that the Bank should concentrate on the single task of providing price stability to the nation.

Bouey was succeeded by John Crow, who followed the same high-interest-rate policy. This did not mean Bank Rates of 20 per cent, and Prime Rates even higher; interest rates are high or low in comparison with the general run of the economy. If the economy is in deflation, as happens, interest rates of 3 per cent would be high. More normally, an interest rate of 10 per cent in an economy in which prices are advancing at 7 per cent annually is a "real interest rate" of 3 per cent. Real interest rates in Canada were 1 per cent or less for the two decades before monetarism became the creed; during the 1980s, they averaged 3.5 per cent on short-term investments, and 4.6 per cent for longer terms. Canada had higher interest rates than any of our major trade competitors, and among the highest of any developed country.[47] The effect of these high and forced rates was to transfer billions of dollars every year from people who have to spend most of their incomes to those who are rich enough to be able to save.

Crow went further than Bouey, and came out four-square for "zero inflation," which was to be the Bank's policy from now on. He told the

Financial Post on February 2, 1988, that "the only acceptable inflation rate is zero."[48] This despite the fact that we have had inflation in Canada every year but one since the Bank of Canada was created in 1935, and the United States has had inflation every year since the U.S. Federal Reserve was created in 1913, except for years of outright depression or war. This was price stability with a vengeance, and, even if we didn't achieve it, we would give it the old college try.

The "Natural" Rate of Unemployment

To give a rationale to the process by which increasing numbers of Canadians were disemployed, and larger and larger amounts of money were delivered to the well-heeled, and their bankers, the Bank of Canada embraced a theory worthy of George Orwell's satires: "the non-accelerating inflation rate of unemployment," or NAIRU.[49] This concept, first born in the bowels of the Bank for International Settlements (BIS), the bankers' bank, in 1981, suggested that, any time unemployment gets too low, the working classes will get uppity and undermine price stability. The BIS, in its 1981 annual report, even dreamed of the day when restrictive monetary policies would lead to "more satisfactory levels of unemployment," that is, higher ones.[50] Instead of joblessness being bad, it was good, because it promoted price stability, which is the thing most devoutly to be desired. The NAIRU, now about 10 per cent, was the rate above which the unruly masses would get uppity and undo all the fine work that had gone before. It followed that a government need not worry about unemployment until it exceeded the NAIRU—which turned out to be adjustable, so you could raise it when necessary to prove that joblessness was simply the inevitable trade-off for price stability. One economist told the *Globe and Mail*, a trifle bitterly, "The Bank of Canada's estimate of full employment is always one percentage point above the current rate of unemployment."[51]

While the acronym refers to the "non-accelerating inflation rate of unemployment," it is referred to more euphemistically around the Bank of Canada as the "natural rate of unemployment." If you don't have a natural rate of unemployment, whatever you have is unnatural. What this grotesque theory pretends to mean is that, any time fewer than 10 per cent of the labour force are unemployed, we will have inflation.

Thus, it must be the foundation of our policy to keep people from working. Of course, that will cost the economy several billions a year in lost production, to say nothing of the billions more poured out in unemployment and welfare benefits, but there is a way around the latter. Cut them off. Punish them for their shiftlessness by "workfare." Unless they can get one of the jobs we have pounded out of existence, they don't deserve to be supported on the public weal. We can't afford them.

The Bank of Canada has managed to sell this inanity, not merely to Premiers Mike Harris and Ralph Klein, but to the federal government, first under the Conservatives, and now under the Liberals. It is a policy which, by no coincidence, accords exactly with the wishes and philosophies of the private banks. We take a perverse pride in the fact that the Bank of Canada is held to be "non-political." Why should that be? Why should the most crucial areas of economic, and now social, policy be set by people who have no responsibility towards those whose lives their policies destroy?

We are not meant to know; all we can be told is that, if we allow the jobless rate to sink below the NAIRU, those pesky rascals who work for a living will be in a position to ask for a raise, to the detriment of all. To support the principle that raises for the workers are inflationary, while those paid to people who are already rich are merely their just deserts, the Bank put through a set of secret raises to its own deputy governors in 1995, while the rest of the staff continued on a five-year salary freeze. The 10 per cent salary hikes put the deputies at $133,500 annually, higher than the deputy minister of finance.[52] At about the same time, Governor Thiessen got a boost of 6.2 per cent—or approximately three times the rise in annual living costs—from $253,200 to $269,000. Then he told the Bank staff to tighten their belts; in order to keep costs down, 600 of them were going to lose their jobs (which average $38,000 a year). When word of the raises leaked out, Thiessen apologized—not for handing them out, but for concealing the facts.[53]

This inhumane approach could never have become public policy except for the fact that the government had already signed off on its right to control the money supply. The Bank was, and is, making the fundamental decisions that drive the economy, without the advice, acceptance, or even acquaintance of the men and women who are elected, in theory, to run the country.

The banks, needless to say, approved heartily of monetarism, the search for price stability, and the struggle to make the Bank independent of government interference. If there is anything bankers agree on, it is the need to cut government activity, and monetarism pointed the way. There was, as well, the ancient and ineluctable question: What's in it for me? The answer turned out to be, Quite a lot, because the artificially high interest rates meant that they were forced to consume more and more of the nation's output in order to keep inflation in check, and, what is even more scandalous, they managed to make the national debt, whose growing size they so deplored, soar.

Whose Debt Is It?

The bankers, and the Bank of Canada, sold the nation on the notion that excessive government spending had caused a debtload we could not support, and that, to rid ourselves of this burden, the banks were compelled, with deep regret, to take more and more from government revenues in the form of interest payments.

It ought to be a simple matter to test this argument. If government spending on programs has caused our ballooning debtload, we will be able to trace the phenomenon easily enough. Table 8 in the Appendix throws some light on this matter; it shows that, in the three decades from 1965 through 1995, federal government spending on programs—health care, air-traffic control, whatever—was less than government revenues, except for the years 1975–85. The program spending spree during those thirty years added $40 billion to the national debt. However, interest charges added $490 billion to the debtload; 92.3 per cent of the increase was due, not to the wages of hospital workers, or social-security payments, but to the huge interest charges which the banks argue were necessary to curb government spending. If those interest charges had been paid in large part to the Bank of Canada on borrowings from that body, we would have no national debt.

Let us put the case bluntly: the banks kept, and keep, demanding cuts in public spending to bring the national debt under control, but nine out of every ten dollars of the debt that has been created in the past three decades has been due to interest charges, the vast majority of which were paid over to the same banks who call for the cuts. If we can borrow money through the Bank of Canada, paying less than 1 per cent, and instead borrow most of it through the commercial banks at many times that, whose debt is it?

Needless to say, these numbers are never mentioned in banking circles, where a chorus echoes the same old line: government spending will be our ruin, and the only way to attack it is to curb costs, through high unemployment and high interest rates. Bank executives refer to the joy to be gained from curbing government spending and eradicating the debt; none of them mention either the amount or the proportion of that debt which is being handed over to the banks themselves in the form of interest paid by the government. And the Bank of Canada not only goes along with the notion that the chartered banks deserve more and more of the nation's wealth, it has become the cheerleader for monetarism, no matter what damage is done to "the economic and financial welfare of the Dominion."

What would make a nice life perfect would be if the banks could invent a similar bizarre theory that would allow them to get rid of those troublesome reserve requirements, so that they could go out and create endless supplies of money (in the name of monetary control) and flog them all at high prices.

This they proceeded to do.

CHAPTER 7

The Gnomes of Basel
Unleash the Banks

The vital function of cash reserves is to enable the authorities in the Bank of Canada to be able to control the amounts of deposits—or bank money—that the chartered banks can create. By imposing fixed reserve requirements, Ottawa can limit the growth of bank deposits.

—Paul A. Samuelson and Anthony Scott,
Economics, Second Canadian Edition, 1968

Primary reserves have always been like a "tax" on banks and their clients—banks are forced to leave balances with the Bank of Canada for free—the tax is equal to the amount of interest the banks could have earned by lending out the balances.

—*Canadian Banker Magazine,* January 1992

THE BANK FOR INTERNATIONAL SETTLEMENTS (BIS, pronounced "Biss") began life in a converted store between a pastry shop and a jewellery establishment, near the railway station in downtown Basel, Switzerland, in 1930. It was, in large part, the inspiration of Montagu Norman, the legendary head of the Bank of England. Among his other accomplishments, Norman persuaded Winston Churchill to return Britain to the gold standard after the First World War, a move that Churchill later described as "the biggest blunder of his life."[1] Norman believed in the old-fashioned things—gold, good manners, and no interference from government. According to historian Carroll Quigley,

> Norman had no use for governments and feared democracy. Both of these seemed to him threats to private banking. Strong-willed, tireless and ruthless, he viewed his life as kind of a cloak-and-dagger struggle with the forces of unsound money which were in league with anarchism and Communism. When he rebuilt the Bank of England, he constructed it as a fortress prepared to defend itself against any popular revolt, with the sacred gold reserves hidden in deep vaults below the level of underground water which would be released to cover them by pressing a button on the governor's desk.[2]

The Bank of England governor used to rush about the world by steamship, wearing a black slouch hat and a long black cloak, under the assumed name "Professor Skinner." Debarking through the steamship's freight hatch, he would give impromptu press conferences to newsmen who had been tipped off that he was about to land on their shores, laden with wisdom and looking like Zorro.[3]

Norman argued that every nation should have a central bank as its "bank of issue," and that the bank should be autonomous, "free from political pressure." He felt this so strongly that he refused to have anything to do with government officials, except those of his own country, to whom he gave necessary advice, and "if some were in the same room when he met central bankers, he would confine his conversation to the latter."[4] With Benjamin Strong, president of the Federal Reserve Bank of New York, he spread the gospel of autonomous central banks through a series of conferences in Europe during the 1920s; by the end of that decade, there were fourteen central banks in various countries, along with one master bank, the BIS, dedicated to promoting cooperation among the rest. And dedicated as well, it appears, to promoting scorn of governments, democracy, or anything that would interfere with the bankers banking as they damn well pleased.

Central banks come in a variety of shapes, sizes, and duties. The

Bank of England, at that time, was a privately owned corporation, which nevertheless had a number of wide-ranging functions, including those of issuing bank notes, managing the government's accounts, directing monetary policy, advising on financial policy, operating the reserve requirements, and even regulating the other banks in the system. It was nationalized in 1946, and in 1979, its power to license, inspect, and supervise the private banks, which had always been the custom, was given legal status.[5] The chiding, guiding, and regulating roles over deposit-taking institutions which are carried out in Canada by the Bank of Canada, by the Office of the Superintendent of Financial Institutions, and, in some cases, by the provincial authorities, are all left, in England, to the B of E. Essentially, it has become the mentor of the commercial banks, at least as much as their guardian. Margaret Thatcher's "Big Bang" of October 1986, which removed most of the restrictions on British banks, was, as much as anything else, the work of the Bank of England.[6]

The hope was that, if enough rules were shredded, London would become the official international financial centre for the European Community, but that did not happen; Frankfurt won out. Still, London became an international financial market of some consequence, in large measure because of the room to romp given the private sector.

The Federal Reserve—A Strange Mixture

The Federal Reserve, the American central bank, founded in 1913, is a strange amalgam of public and private enterprise. It consists of twelve regional Federal Reserve Banks, which are wholly owned by their member banks, all of them privately owned, and coordinated in Washington by the Federal Reserve Board, the only part of the system that is government-owned. The chairman of this body, appointed for a seven-year term, is by far the most important financial figure in the United States, miles ahead of the secretary of the Treasury.[7] As in every modern financial system, the process of money-creation begins when the Federal Reserve Board decides that there should be more cash in the economy, and causes the government to issue bonds, which the Reserve Banks buy with cheques drawn on themselves. They print new bank notes to cover the cheques, depositing the bank notes in the commercial banks to the credit of the government.

Each American bank note carries a rosette identifying the Reserve Bank that issued it. However, unlike the Canadian system, in which the interest on the bonds that started the process is paid to the Bank of Canada, in the United States this interest is not paid to the owners, the Reserve Banks; instead, about 2 per cent of it is used to run the system, and the rest goes to the government, as a self-imposed tax on the Reserve Banks. When the new cash hits their vaults, the commercial banks create deposits, after setting aside the required reserve, representing a multiple of about fifty times the reserve requirement.[8] The Fed, like the Bank of England and the Bank of Canada, is financially independent of government. Indeed, the Fed is so proud of its independence that, if the president of the United States calls in the Fed chairman for a little chat about interest rates, stock prices plunge, because it is feared that politicians will start to mess about in monetary policies which belong by right to the private sector.

The independence of central banks varies from country to country. Our central bank began as a private bank and migrated into a national bank, but, as we have seen, no one would call it a creature of the government. The Bundesbank, Germany's central institution, refused to support the weaker currencies of western Europe in 1992 and 1993, and caused the European Community's Exchange Rate Mechanism to collapse, despite the specific wish of the Bonn government to keep it going.[9] Japan's central bank seems to be the creature of the nation's giant corporations, while the Banque de France was, until recently, seen as heavily under the thumb of government. Today, it operates under a law passed in December 1993 giving it the power to "formulate and implement monetary policy with the aim of ensuring price stability," although there is a proviso that this should be within the general framework of the government's economic policy.[10]

Central banks which are subject to any sort of government control on monetary policy are described as "weak" by the banking community, while those that can thumb their noses at finance ministers are "strong." Which tells you all you need to know.

The tendency is to create more and more central banks, including a central bank for the European Community itself; even Namibia has a central bank; so does Russia. At last count, there were 110 of these institutions with accounts in Basel, although only 33 of them are full-blown members of the BIS, with share ownership.[11] Despite their many divergences, all these institutions appear to be working towards two common objectives: stability and independence. By "stability," they mean price stability, our old friend.[12] By "independence," they mean dispensing with government interference and imposing their dream of price stability on the nations they represent.

There is no secret why they are alike. "Central bankers like to huddle together" is the way Marjorie Deane and Robert Pringle put it. "Their camaraderie, we dare to suggest, is cemented by resentment." Resentment, that is, against governments who want to horn in on the action. "Central bankers therefore take an almost malicious joy in the exclusiveness of their club."[13] That club is the BIS, an institution which, whatever its faults, is absolutely essential to modern international banking.

Central Banks and Money Clearing

Whatever other functions they serve, central banks are the key to the speedy clearing of large and complex financial transactions among their members and between nations. It was this aspect, in fact, that first persuaded R.B. Bennett to dismiss the complaints of the bank lobby in Canada during the 1930s and establish his own national institution: "I learned to my surprise that there was no direct means of settling international balances between Canada and London, that the only medium was New York and the value of the Canadian dollar would be determined in Wall Street. I made up my mind then and there that this country was going to have a central bank."[14]

The model Bennett had in mind was the Bank of England, a private institution run by and for business. As the number of central banks grew, more and more of them were government-owned, but they continued to operate, in the main, on behalf of private business. The establishment of these central banks made a great difference to the complex process of balancing all the payments between banks of one nation and those of another. Instead of hundreds of banks in the United States, for example, having to clear cheques with each of hundreds of banks in France, the central banks took on this task.

The process would be made even more efficient if there was a central bank of central banks, through which all clearing could be done, instead of multilateral clearing among dozens of nations—one funnel, instead of fifty. The BIS took on this task, although it was not, in fact, originally designed to do it. It was created mainly because Germany's war reparations following the First World War had to be settled with many nations, in many currencies. The BIS was supposed to handle the international transfer of these monies. But the bank's charter says nothing about this; instead, its purposes are "to promote the cooperation of central banks and to provide additional facilities for international financial operations."[15]

Reparation payments, in fact, were suspended before the bank had been in operation for a year, and, when a worldwide financial crisis erupted in 1931, there was very little the BIS could do but assemble a package of short-term loans for nations that were hardest hit by the flight of capital—Germany, Hungary, Poland, Austria, and Yugoslavia—and hope for the best. Short-term loans were not what was needed, but a massive infusion of new money; however, the bankers, as usual, could see no way out of the morass except cutting costs and trimming government expenditures everywhere. The result was the long-drawn-out disaster of the Great Depression. However, as two chroniclers of the BIS put it, "Chivvied by Norman, central bankers continued to assemble in Basel, exchange opinions, blame the politicians, and go home."[16]

During the Second World War, there were suggestions that the BIS had been too chummy with the Nazis, in particular, by instantly turning over to them all the funds that belonged to the government of Czechoslovakia when the Germans marched into that country. When the International Monetary Fund (IMF) was established at the end of the war, Henry Morgenthau, the Treasury secretary of the United States, and a Jew of German descent, proposed the abolition of the BIS, by way of punishment, and a resolution to that effect was adopted by the international meeting at Bretton Woods, New Hampshire, that set up both the IMF and the World Bank. Resolution V called on the partners to the Bretton Woods Monetary Agreement to liquidate the BIS "at the earliest possible moment."[17]

It was never carried out. When the Marshall Plan began to finance the reconstruction effort in Europe, the BIS acted as a clearing agent for multilateral financial deals essential to the operation. The IMF, an agency of the United Nations, was given the job of making financing available to nations in balance-of-payments difficulties, and helping to improve their economic management. The World Bank, officially the

International Bank for Reconstruction and Development, provides loans and assistance to developing nations, and, like the IMF, is an agency of the United Nations. Both are creatures of the governments they represent; neither was especially adapted, as was the BIS, to moving money around among and between banks in various nations. Thus, whether anybody loved it or not, the BIS had a role to play.

Today, it is housed, with a staff of 460, in a black tower that soars more than 200 feet above the provincial town of Basel, 53 miles northwest of Zurich, Switzerland. To get inside, you open one glass door and step in; there is another glass door, still closed, in front of you. When you are suspended in amber, as it were, a voice asks you what you want, and unless you have an appointment with someone willing to vouch for you, that is as far as you get. The door behind you opens, and you slink back out onto Centralbahnplatz, defeated. If you have an appointment, you won't get much out of it. The BIS talkers, even more than other bankers, and bureaucrats, are masters of the lifted shoulder, the raised eyebrow, and the repeated suggestion that these matters must, of course, be put to my superiors, who do not happen to be here, or on earth, for that matter, and why don't you call again?

It is here, ten times a year, that bankers assemble from all over the world, like pigeons coming home to roost. But not to coo; mostly to squawk about governments, and to huddle about new plans to make their members more independent, and government less intrusive, in the brave new global village. The meetings begin with a swank dinner on Sunday evening, at which the real business is done, followed by more formal meetings the next day, with specific topics raised in subgroups. It used to be that whatever happened in these meetings was soon out on the street, but those leaks only led to headlines, attention, even interference, so the boys—they are almost entirely middle-aged males—now keep a silence that would put any Canadian cabinet to shame. We don't know what they do, or why they make the decisions they make; we can only look at the resolutions that become public, occasionally, and the press releases they issue.

There are no government members on the BIS directorate, which is made up of senior members from the central banks of Belgium, France, Germany, Italy, the United Kingdom, and the United States. The member banks, which own 85 per cent of the shares of the corporation (the rest are held by private individuals and companies), can also nominate and elect up to nine directors at large, who are governors of central banks. The Bank of Canada governor is one of these.[18] The 473,125 shares currently outstanding pay dividends annually in Swiss francs, free of tax. The reason there are private shares is that, when the BIS was being set up, the U.S. Federal Reserve would not buy stock, because of the isolationist mood of the country, so the corporate charter was amended to allow the central banks that were members either to buy shares in their own names or to place them with other buyers, and the Americans placed them with a syndicate of U.S. banks.

No elected politician ever gets past the glass doors; this is a place for bankers alone; just because decisions made here have an immediate and heavy impact on the national economies of scores of nations is no reason to have their representatives interfering. The last time a governor of the Bank of Canada met with the provincial treasurers, whose lives and finances he rules, was in 1982, but he attends meetings of the BIS an average of eight times a year, and always comes home with great ideas that he shoves under the door of the minister of finance, who says, Gosh, why didn't I think of that? and puts them into practice.

The Basel Accord Is Born

One of these ideas was the "Capital Accord," or "Basel Accord," offi- cially, "International Convergence of Capital Measurement and Capital Standards," which was pasted together by the Basel Committee on Banking Supervision on July 15, 1988.[19] And just in time, too. The past few years had been a hell of a period for the banks of the Western world. They had plunged into real estate loans, oil loans, Mexican hat- dances, and other dubious ventures, and now they were all going sour. The U.S. savings and loans debacle was beginning to smell, and even the mainline banks were coming under increasing pressure. Banks were div- ing for shelter, or collapsing entirely, in the United States, Italy, and Germany, to say nothing of the Third World. One of the juicier scandals involved Robert Calvi, known as "God's banker," because he acted for the Vatican in many of its financial transactions. The president of Banco Ambrosiano, which was in debt to the tune of $1.3 billion (U.S.), he was found hanging by the neck under Blackfriars Bridge in London.[20]

Then there were the clouds of corruption drifting around from the collapse of the Bank for Credit and Commerce International (BCCI), discussed in Chapter 9, and, what with one thing and another, the outlook was grim indeed for bank shares.

The reserve requirements, which varied from country to country but ran somewhere between twelve to one and thirty to one, were an added burden. (That is, for every dollar a bank created, it had to have somewhere between $3^1/3$ and $8^1/3$ cents in reserve.) In Canada, the figure at this time was about eighteen cents, made up of two reserves: a primary reserve of about eight cents, which was held on deposit at the Bank of Canada (and on which no interest was paid), and a secondary reserve, which the banks could hold in Treasury bills, or other government blue-chip investments, in their own vaults, and on which they did earn interest, paid by the Bank of Canada. The secondary reserve was really a liquidity reserve, and didn't hurt much (the banks were and are bound to keep enough cash or readily negotiable notes on hand to ensure that reasonable demands for legal tender to replace bank money can be met). The effective reserve in Canada was the primary reserve of 8 per cent, and that represented a real problem to the banks.

Think of it this way: Your bank has a capital base of $5 billion, a nice round figure, but you have unbuckled your wallet to the Reichmann brothers of Olympia & York Developments, and now a billion of that has vanished, because O&Y is in receivership and may never pay it all back. You can use various dodges to postpone the evil day of reckoning, because banks are not required to follow ordinary accounting rules. Still, sooner or later, you have to write the money off.

Now, your capital base is reduced by $1 billion, which means that your ability to create money (i.e., make loans) is reduced by the leverage of the reserve requirement. If the requirement is 8 per cent, as it was then in Canada, you have lost $12.5 billion (100 divided by 8) worth of lending room. That is, if you are still solvent, you will either have to come up with a lot more capital or close down the wickets.

The obvious solution is to abolish the reserves. However, the public was becoming alarmed at banks toppling over, and bank presidents hanging from bridges, so somebody had to do something about the security of the banks, or we were going to see a run on some of them that would make the Boston Marathon pale by comparison.

What the BIS did to meet the financial crunch was a product of American political pressure. The U.S. Congress had been asked to advance another $8.4 billion to the International Monetary Fund, and the congressmen insisted, as a quid pro quo, on some tightening in the regulations, which seemed so evanescent at that time. (The IMF, in reality, had very little to do with the stability of individual banks.) To satisfy Congress, without actually bringing governments into the act, Paul Volcker, the Fed chairman, proposed one of the famous "level playing fields" so dear to American hearts. Instead of using the clumsy, interventionist reserve system, all the BIS banks would operate by a common set of rules for "capital adequacy."[21] As long as a bank had enough money to back it, nothing could go wrong, right?

The theory was imperfect, as the world would soon learn. With money whizzing about the globe the way it does, it is virtually impossible to measure the capital adequacy of any large financial institution. When the BCCI crashed in 1991, it appeared to be based on a mountain of capital, except that most of it was fraudulent. When Barings Bank sank in 1995, its capital consisted, in large measure, of fake figures tapped into a computer in Singapore. Who cared? The great thing about the capital-adequacy requirements was that the banks themselves would look after them; you didn't need the heavy hand of government. Moreover, the capital was kept in the bank's own vaults, not shipped off to some central bank.

If you want to see the wording of these requirements, which were adopted after some fiddling around with the details by the BIS, and came into effect in 1989, step into your neighbourhood bank and ask for a copy of the annual report. You will find them, usually, under a heading that says "Regulatory Capital," in dense bankers' prose. The CIBC version starts with this pronouncement:

> According to guidelines issued by the Office of the Superintendent of Financial Institutions (OSFI), pursuant to the Capital Accord (1988) of the Bank for International Settlements (BIS), all balance sheet assets and off balance sheet exposures are assigned weighting factors reflecting credit risk. A financial institution's total regulatory capital (including common and preferred equity and subordinated indebtedness) must be at least 8% of its risk-weighted assets.[22]

It gets even more exciting after that, with references to Tier 1 and Tier 2 capital, and the good news that the bank meets the regulations, and more.

Killing the Reserves

The BIS, in its wisdom, decided that the old, government-run reserves were out of date, and should be replaced by what it called "risk-based capital reserves," which would be held in the bank, not in some central government vault, and which would be based on what banks thought was a fair risk ratio. According to the BIS, a reserve of 8 per cent represented a nice, conservative figure. Thus, any bank should have on tap $8 of liquid reserves—cash, or readily negotiable securities—for every $100 of its loans. This is the current regulatory capital level.

However, the argument continued, not all loans are equally risky, so, if the most dangerous loans need to be backed by an 8 per cent reserve, others could be covered at a lower rate. The lower rate was expressed as a percentage of the regulatory capital level: for a loan that represented no risk, the percentage is zero; a moderate risk, 50 per cent; and a heavy risk, the maximum, 100 per cent of 8 per cent. For example, real estate loans, which are considered quite safe, astonishingly, are deemed to have a risk ratio of 50 per cent. Thus, for every $100 in this sort of financing, the bank must have reserves on tap of $4. Business loans are considered to be much less certain, and have a risk weight of 100 per cent. Thus, for $100 in new business loans, the bank must set aside $8 in capital.

However, loans to governments which are members of the Organization for Economic Co-operation and Development (OECD) carry no risk whatever, according to the BIS rules. The OECD nations range all the way from Austria, Canada, and the United States to Portugal, Turkey, and Mexico. There is no need to set aside any covering capital for these. The actual wording provided is that this waiver of risk applies only to OECD nations that have not had to re-evaluate their currency within the past five years. How safe is this waiver of risk? Let me give you an example. When Mexico did its most recent financial flop in 1995, it was within a few weeks of having all its bonds reckoned as "risk-free."

The BIS rules, which were phased in over the next few years, were intended to replace reserve requirements entirely, but only three of the member nations were stupid enough to go along with this part of the deal: Switzerland, which is ruled by two laws: keep it clean, and do whatever the banks want; the United Kingdom, under Margaret Thatcher; and Canada. The Americans, despite Volcker, cling to a modified, but still real, reserve system based on the deposits on hand in the banks, in addition to the risk-based capital reserves mandated by the BIS. For once, following the American lead would have been a wise decision.

A brief pause here to note that government bonds are anything but risk-free, whether they are owned by banks, corporations, or individuals. If interest rates increase, the value of bonds goes down. Think of it this way: a government issues bonds paying 8 per cent for the next five years, and I buy $1,000 worth. Soon after, it issues more bonds, paying 10 per cent. Now I will make $80 in interest during the year, but anyone who bought a new bond will make $100. If I want to sell my bonds—and very few bonds are actually held to term—I will have to sell at a discount representing the difference between 8 and 10 per cent. This applies whether I am an old-age pensioner, a large corporation, or a bank. But the banks get around the loss of value by carrying the bonds on their books at the purchase value, on the grounds that, sooner or later, they will be sold for the face value, although common sense and experience both tell us that a bond worth $1,000 in face value today will be worth less, in current dollars, when the time comes to cash it, say, five years hence. "Risk-free" is one of those terms that means what you want it to mean.

In Orange County, California, the government issued risk-free bonds to finance a little frolic into derivatives trading, in late 1994. Almost overnight, the county lost $2.5 billion and was plunged into bankruptcy. The value of the bonds had evaporated. When a *Wall Street Journal* reporter asked an executive of Franklin Resources of San Mateo, California, which runs the world's largest municipal bond fund, how his firm planned to calculate the value of its Orange County bonds, "he hung up."[23] Still, the thesis of government infallibility has been accepted, when convenient, by the bond-rating agencies. Months after the California collapse was under way, Standard & Poor's and Moody's, the two most influential bond-rating agencies in North America, both continued to maintain high credit ratings on the county's bonds.

Governments: Safe or Risky?

Can it be, you will be asking yourself, that the same bank presidents who constantly warn us that all the Western governments are headed to hell in a handbasket because of social spending, deficits, and other fripperies also believe that these same governments are so solid that their debt instruments are entirely free of risk?

You bet. The contradictory arguments serve different purposes. The hell-in-a-handbasket argument is aimed at curbing government spending, both for ideological reasons and for the inevitable tax reductions. The governments-cannot-fail argument is aimed at allowing the banks to escape controls. Both arguments are aimed at increasing the profitability of the banks.

The process of replacing the reserve requirements by the Basel Accord was accomplished in this country without raising any undue fuss. If you go searching through *Hansard*, the official report of debate in Ottawa, you won't find a word about it; it was never discussed in the House of Commons or the Senate. When Jordan Grant of the Bank of Canada for Canadians Coalition asked for documentation of this monumental change, the Bank of Canada produced four items in toto.

The first consists of two paragraphs in the government White Paper *New Directions for the Financial Sector*, released on December 18, 1986. This was the paper that removed many of the rules governing the financial sector, so our banks could go out and play in the global markets. The first of these two paragraphs says: "The availability of broad commercial lending powers to non-bank institutions increases the importance of addressing the issue of competitive equity, as between bank and non-bank institutions, which arises from requirements on banks to hold non-interest-bearing deposits at the Bank of Canada."[24] This is the banks' reserves-are-a-tax argument; they have to put up reserves, but the trust companies, their competitors for these same loans, do not. There is no "level playing field." The obvious way to correct this imbalance would be to put reserve requirements on the trusts, credit unions, and *caisses populaires*, as well as the banks. Indeed, that was the solution proposed by the Porter Commission in 1964 in Canada, and the solution the Americans adopted in 1980, with the Depository Institutions Deregulation and Monetary Control Act, which empowered the Fed to "establish required reserves for all depository institutions."[25] But our banks didn't want that.

After all, they own most of the major trusts themselves; what they were really after was a level playing field with no fences. This argument had nothing to do with the solvency of banks; that point was dealt with in the second paragraph: "These required deposits, over and above the amount needed for clearing purposes, have no bearing on the solvency of banks. They are used to assist in the implementation of monetary policy, but they have the side effect of imposing unequal costs on institutions competing for the same business. These deposits are no longer essential for the implementation of monetary policy and will be phased out beginning in 1990."[26]

This was the first, and last, indication that the reserves were scheduled for removal. No argument, theory, or documentation was put forward to support the remarkable statement that reserves "have no bearing on the solvency of banks," though it is true that their main function was, not to meet this problem, but to keep the banks under the control of the monetary authorities. The matter is considered so important in the textbooks that the quote from *Economics: Second Canadian Edition* carried as an epigraph to this chapter appears in red ink in that august university textbook.

The argument of the White Paper, to the extent that there was any argument, was that, while the reserves assist in the implementation of monetary policy, they impose "unequal costs"—the same argument—and that they are no longer necessary.

The other three items obtainable as the official record are three Discussion Papers, prepared under the direction of one of the Bank of Canada's deputy governors, Charles Freedman, and issued between September 30, 1987, and September 1, 1991.[27] They *begin* with the assumption that the reserve requirements will be eliminated, and deal entirely with technical arrangements to control short-term interest rates by varying the amounts the Bank of Canada requires the commercial banks to deposit to cover overnight balances. Any bank that does not have enough cash on hand to clear cheques, and automatic banking machine transfers and other electronic negotiations aimed at it each night, has to take an advance from the Bank, and is charged interest, at the Bank Rate. The Bank can affect these short-term rates both by changing the interest charge and by requiring the banks to hold more or less than is strictly needed. This is, in fact, the system now in place, and it says nothing, does nothing, about controlling the growth of deposits or the multiplication of money, two significant aspects of banking today.

These background papers did not discuss any of the other implications, which, as we will see, were considerable, for the banking system. With no public discussion, debate, or consideration, the change was slipped into the massive amendment of the Bank Act, passed in 1991, and implemented in 1992, in language so convoluted that it is no surprise that it went right over the heads of journalists and MPs alike:

> On the first day of the first month following the month this section comes into force, the primary reserve referred to in subsection (2) shall be reduced by 3 percent, and thereafter on the first day of the first month of each of the next three succeeding six month periods, the primary reserve as modified by this subsection shall be reduced by 3 percent, and on the first day of the twenty-fifth month following the month in which this subsection comes into force, the primary reserve referred to in subsection (2) shall be nil.[28]

In plain English, it said that primary reserves will be taken off gradually over the next two years, until they are all gone in 1994. And that is what happened.

In place of reserves, which provided much-needed stability, we were given day-to-day jacking around with short-term interest rates as the sole instrument for controlling the money supply. This was not as radical a change, perhaps, as I make out, because, in practice, the Bank had been using interest rates as a hammer for some time. The real significance of the change was that it turned the banks loose to increase their monetary multiplier (which doesn't exist, according to them, so that's all right), and enshrined monetarism as a permanent policy in the Bank of Canada.

In Funereal Silence

The entire process was put together with the sort of dignity, and solemn silence, you will notice at any first-class funeral. The only person I know of, outside banking circles, who caught on to what had happened was William Krehm, a lively, grey-haired gent who lives in Toronto, in a Rosedale apartment he carved out of a lovely old house owned by the Gooderhams, of whiskey fame. (There are huge vaults in the basement, once filled with Prohibition booze.) After a career in journalism with the CBC and *Time* magazine, Krehm made a modest fortune in real estate development, the income from which he now spends making things uncomfortable for the banks. He is the chairman of the Committee on Monetary and Economic Reform (COMER), and publisher of that body's monthly bellow of rage, now called *ER*, an abbreviation of its former title, *Economic Reform*. He spotted an article in the *Wall Street Journal*, in which the former head of the U.S. Federal Deposit Insurance Corporation, and the current head of the Securities and Exchange Commission, remarked that "the risk-based capital rules were a mistake, and they should not have been adopted."[29]

Krehm had never heard of the risk-based capital rules, so he put on his journalist's hat and set out to find out what they were. He backtracked the way the change had been made in Basel, and then in Ottawa, and then looked at the results.

He concluded that the banks were putting themselves at enormous risk, because they were sitting on long-term bonds with low rates. If a recovery ever did set in, these bonds would lose value, as interest rates rose, and their holders, the banks, would be in trouble. Furthermore, it was obvious that, if you make it easier for banks to lend to governments by buying their bonds than to lend to business, they will do it. If you have to set aside eight dollars of capital to back a business loan, and no dollars to back the purchase of a Treasury bill, which would you back? In the United States, the banks' portfolios of government bonds jumped by 68 per cent in the two years after the Basel Accord; real estate loans went up 27 per cent, and business financing plummeted.[30]

Canadian banks put their own spin on it. From the point of view of the chartered banks, "Reserve Reform" meant, primarily, that "banks and their customers [are] no longer subject to primary reserve tax,"[31] and that "banks will be on a level playing field with non-bank financial institutions."[32] About time, too; no longer would the Royal Bank have to face unfair competition from the credit union over at the mall.

The article in *Canadian Banker Magazine* written by two senior bankers from which these quotes come noted that the change would allow quite a lot of money, unspecified, to flow back into bank coffers. Between December 31, 1990, and December 31, 1995, deposits at the Bank of Canada owned by the chartered banks dropped by $2.2 billion,[33] so we can put a figure to this; the haul was $2.2 billion, and that money became available to be multiplied into loans. This was the good news, although not spelled out in *Canadian Banker*. The bad news, according to the article, was that the banks would have to be "more accurate" in estimating their overnight clearing needs. You don't want to end up paying interest on money you had to leave on hand to cover your overnight clearances. I would have thought trading $2.2 billion in found money for having to be more accurate in estimating overnight requirements was a pretty good deal for the banks, but the article makes it seem mainly a technical matter, and not worth bothering about.

Moreover, even the need to get the number right or suffer can be fixed, and a new proposal is making the rounds in Ottawa—it is no more than that, as I write—that would have the Bank of Canada paying the banks for any excess money they kept on hand there. That is, a bank could leave more on tap than it thought it needed, and if it proved to be wrong, the Bank of Canada would slip it interest on the excess, as a kind of recompense for having been stupid.

We started with a system in which, in return for the enormous benefits conferred on them by government—especially, money-creation—the banks were required to keep non-interest-bearing reserves with the Bank of Canada, as a method of controlling the creation of deposits and loans, and thus, monetary policy. We wind up with a system in which those reserves disappear, because they aren't fair to the banks, and now we will pay them for having to hold enough money on hand overnight to cover their own cheques and charge cards.

Just as in the United States, the overwhelming effect of the new rules was to persuade Canadian banks to back out of the business lending which had proven so tricky for them, and load up on government securities.

Billions Poured into Government Paper

In the five years after the Basel Accord went into effect, the total assets of Canada's chartered banks increased by $208.7 billion. Of this, $1.3

billion went to new business loans to small and medium-sized businesses, $41.2 billion to large business; $17.6 billion to personal loans; $81.4 billion to residential mortgages; and an amazing $69.2 billion to government securities.*[34] When the process began, the banks held $25.7 billion in government paper; five years later, they held $94.9 billion, a jump of 269 per cent. The banks poured fifty-three times as much new money into government bonds as into small business; they put $151 billion into loans that required between 0 and 4 per cent of capital set-asides, and $60.1 billion into loans that called for 8 per cent.

Who could blame them? The new rules said that business loans are a 100 per cent risk, and government loans bear no risk whatever. Look at it from the point of view of the loans officer at your local bank. Ten business people are clamouring for loans to start new companies, which, if the loans officer approves them, will amount to $500,000. To get this business, he or she has to spend several hours going over loan applications, calling up credit bureaus, and doing all that leg-work. The same $500,000 can be placed with one phone call to buy Treasury bills, and, even if they don't bring in quite as much profit, they don't take up any capital, either.

It is this unintended and unsuspected (at least by the naive among us) impact of the new rules that led to the drying up of funds for business. The new rules, as well, had an immediate impact on the way in which government debt is held in this country. You will remember that the great advantage of the portion of federal debt that is held by the Bank of Canada is that the interest comes back to us, while bonds held by the banks pay them. As the banks gobbled up more and more government securities, the Bank of Canada backed off, to make room. In 1985, the Bank of Canada held 17.8 per cent of the federal debt; ten years later, it held 6.2 per cent.[35]

The late John Hotson, an economist at the University of Waterloo, calculated that the difference between the interest the chartered banks would have earned in 1995, had they kept their holdings of federal securities steady, and the interest they earned by loading up on bonds as the Bank of Canada surrendered them amounted to $3 billion per annum.

---

* These figures add up to $210.7 billion. There was a loss of about $2 billion in "cash and deposits at the Bank of Canada," the drop brought about after the required reserves were abolished.

And, since this was all done with no capital requirement, it was gained without risk, effort, or cash:

> The banks were being paid simply for storing public debt in their strongboxes, without advancing any of their own money. The central bank could have done that at no cost to the taxpayer. It was in fact a $3 billion annual welfare program in aid of the banks—almost three quarters of the banks' total profits for the year.[36]

This, in turn, has a huge impact on the Canadian deficit. If we are transferring to the chartered banks $3 billion and more per year in interest payments that we used to earn for ourselves, the total involved is staggering. Jordan Grant, the head of the Bank of Canada for Canadians Coalition, performed a calculation showing that the "Total Extra Interest Cost" to the taxpayer since the Bank of Canada began cutting its holdings of federal securities amounts to a staggering $67.9 billion.[37] Enough to wipe out the deficit, and, before long, the federal debt itself.

You will notice that this long tale of intrigue, policy change, and international skulduggery had three sets of victims—taxpayers, the business sector, and borrowers at large—but only one set of victors—the banks. They had it made. Or, at least, they appeared to. They had cast off the reserves, done in governments, increased steadily their capacity to manufacture money, and multiplied their profits. They were all set to venture into far-off fields, with results we examine in the next chapter.

CHAPTER 8

The Largest, Established, Permanent Floating Crap Game

It was the opening of the market—anything could happen, anything was possible. It was very dangerous. I could step forward and with just one wave of the hand buy or sell millions of pounds' worth of stuff. And it was just stuff: it wasn't milk or bread or something you could use if the world all came to an end. My products were notionally called Japanese Government Bonds, or futures, or options, but nobody cared what the hell they were. They were just numbers to be bought and sold. It was like trading ether.

—Nick Leeson,
Rogue Trader, 1996

RISK NOT THY WHOLE WAD

—Sign on the wall in the trading room
of the Hongkong Bank of Canada, 1996

WE ARE ON THE TRADING FLOOR of one of Canada's largest banks, in downtown Toronto. The setting is much like the scenes on television, in programs such as "Traders," where money magicians sport in the reflected light of computer monitors, and empires ebb and flow. The room is huge, lit by banks of overhead fluorescents and the computer screens. The traders, who crouch over their keyboards or mutter into telephones in a cryptic language all their own, or jump up to shout at each other, or wave their fingers in symbolic gestures like a regiment of Masons exchanging greetings, are ranged in long ranks of desks that form a giant U based on a huge display that carries the latest news from the front—the London, New York, Hong Kong, and Chicago stock exchanges. Nobody pays the slightest attention to this display, since the same information is available, in greater detail, on the desk computers, but the flashing lights up there look impressive. In this room are assembled nearly 500 trading positions, each with its own phalanx of monitors, and its own stern sentinel, a man or a woman (mostly, a man) in uniform. For the men, a shirt, white or pastel—possibly, on the part of the greatly daring, with stripes—a good silk tie, knotted and in place; pants from Harry Rosen or equivalent. For the women, a smart suit, or dressy blouse and skirt; good shoes; a little, but never too much, makeup.

I feel, looking around this fashionable and foreign throng, a little out of place. They are nearly all of an age, for one thing, late twenty-something or thirty-something. In part this is the case because theirs is a new profession—it did not exist a decade ago—so computer trading has no coterie of white-haired old hands. The old boys here can cast their minds all the way back to those grinding days of the Quebec Referendum, when prices lurched and rumbled, soared and tumbled, with every passing poll. A year and a half ago.

Around the perimeter of this giant U are the offices of the Lords of Money, vice-presidents, and others. There is no shortage of these; banks have vice-presidents the way a dog has fleas; there are always a few of them hopping about. These overlings can actually look out of the windows, and see traffic on the streets and signs of human habitation. They have little to do with what goes on here, at the heart of the machine, except to call in a trader, from time to time, to say, Well done, Harry or Larry or Mary, when one of them has made a million dollars on the day—and it is done—or to ask what the hell he or she is playing at when one of them loses it—that is done, too.

I am sitting at a trading station three-quarters of the way down one of the long aisles, in the middle of the derivatives-trading section of the bank. We call it "Risk Management Trading," and we are part of the bank's

Treasury Group: viz., we are supposed to make the Treasury richer. Eight computer monitors line the back of the twin desks of this two-person position, which trades "currency swaps and cross-currency derivatives" and which is the exclusive fiefdom of a young man we will call Larry, to my left, and, to my right, a man we will call Harry. They work in tandem, like a pair of trained sheepdogs, rounding up deals, driving them forward, settling them into the pen with a bark of triumph. They do it all day, every day, from seven-thirty in the morning until six or seven at night, and they never flag or fail, although sometimes they curse a bit and slap the desk when the market makes one of its inexplicable convulsions and leaps off in a new direction, leaving the traders, as Harry says, "like Bambi in the headlights," waiting to be mowed down by numbers. Between us and the two-foot wall of computer monitors are four little black boxes, tilted slightly towards us, on each desk. Two of these represent our own telephone switchboard, controlled by computer, with 400 numbers ready to dial by punching a button, from here to Hong Kong. The other two are the "hoot and holler boxes," microphones and receivers that let us communicate, if we wish, without picking up the telephone headset that sits at one side of the desk.

Straight in front of us is another rank of computers on the desks of other derivative traders, backing onto our desks, and, beyond that, another rank, and another, and another. Three aisles away, in No Man's Land, the bank's area gives way to the rows of traders who belong to an investment company owned by the bank. They are another tribe, friendly, but other—on the far side, if you like, of the Chinese wall that separates our trades and theirs. Our team is here, around us, and, through our computer links, in other parts of the empire. This is a world, complete unto itself, driven by numbers flickering onto the screens, poured out into the ether by other trading centres all over the globe. Harry says he likes his job, despite the tension, because "there is a feeling of camaraderie." So there is; the frenetic fellowship here is based on its own language, laws, and religion; that religion, of course, is money.

This is, not to put too fine a point on it, an electronic gambling joint, although neither Larry nor Harry would accept that.

"We are providing a service for the customer," Harry says carefully. "If we were not doing that, if we were not bringing real value for money, sure, it would just be a crap shoot." He adds, "What it really is, is a warehouse, for assets."

A Deal Is Done

Suddenly, Ben is on the other side of the desk, trailing his telephone cord, long and lanky, luminous with excitement and the prospect of a deal. Ben is a salesman, not a trader. He spends his time trolling for customers, men and women who have dealt with him before, and whom he calls, constantly, in exactly the same way and for exactly the same reason that a travelling salesman piles into his car and does the rounds.

Ben has been talking to a businessman who operates in the lumber industry, and ships his product to the United States. He is paid in U.S. dollars, but he spends his money, on plant, salaries, lighting, energy, fuel, in Canadian dollars. He knows what he is going to make, roughly, over the next few weeks, but how about next year, and the year after, and the year after that?

Let us suppose, for argument's sake, that the U.S. dollar is 20 per cent lower in three years, when translated into Canadian funds, than it is today, but the price of his wood remains roughly the same. His income, once the proceeds are exchanged, will have dropped by 20 per cent. But not his mortgage, or his fuel bill, or his labour costs. His charges will be the same, his price to his American customers will look the same, but he will be able to buy only four-fifths as much with the income.

He needs some way to protect himself against the variations that will be visited on his cash flow by the vagaries of currency exchange. One way to do this is to buy derivatives based on currency exchanges between Canadian and U.S. funds. Derivatives, as the name implies, derive from something else. They are the offspring of stocks, and bonds, and money-market instruments, rather than the stocks and bonds themselves.*

Our man wants to be sure his income, in Canadian dollars, based on his best guess as to what is going to happen in his industry, is steady. Or, at least, calculable. So he "hedges." That is, he buys derivative products

---

* Derivatives are part of the world of futures, a phrase that covers any contract to buy or sell commodities—anything from pork bellies to soybeans or copper—or financial instruments, any time in the future. Futures have been with us for centuries and, until recently, belonged exclusively to the world of securities trading. However, as the markets grew, and the Four Pillars were dismantled, the deposit-taking institutions moved into derivatives with a vengeance.

over a period of years on both sides of the market; with one bunch of derivatives, he guesses that the value of the Canadian dollar will go down;
with another, he guesses that it will go up. And he keeps moving back
and forth between these positions as the derivatives mature. He may not
make a fortune this way, but he won't lose one, either.

He has bought a series of derivatives covering the next three years,
and hedging on either side of the future value of the Canadian dollar.
This morning, he thinks he can see the way ahead. He thinks the dollar is
going to go up, and he is confident enough in this to want to, as Harry
puts it, "take off his hedges"; he no longer wants to hold the derivatives
that will pay off if the dollar drops or holds steady, because he doesn't
think it will. Look at it this way: if he is buying notional Canadian dollars in a future market, through derivatives, at 70 cents, 72 cents, 74
cents, 78 cents, and 80 cents, he is safe, whether the dollar holds steady,
goes down quite a lot, or goes up quite a lot, because he has covered all
his bets. But, if it goes up, as he thinks it will, and he has bet only that
side of the market, he will gain more. If he is holding the right to buy
Canadian dollars for 70 cents and he can sell that right on a basis of 80
cents, he will do much better than if he was punching in at everywhere
from 70 to 80.* Our man is going to get rid of his higher bets, the ones
that won't earn him much if the dollar rises, and stick with the lower
ones, which will make more if that happens, so he wants to sell these
higher bets. Frank wants us to give him a price on his higher bets.

There is a lot of gabble back and forth. "Show him 98," Harry
shouts across to Ben, who disappears, like a diving duck, back to his
own desk and computer. Then Harry turns around and consults another
trader, who deals in spot-price trading on the Canadian dollar—that is,
money being bought and sold this very minute. When Harry offered his
98, he didn't know the exact spot price on which the future-price guess
will be based, although he had a pretty good idea; he was just giving
Ben an "indicative price," to see how the customer would react.

Ben looms up again. "Acceptable, but can you do better?"

---

* In a game of roulette, you can bet on one number, or a group of numbers. If you
bet, say, 8 and the ball lands on 8, the payoff is 36 to 1. If you bet that any one of,
say, twelve numbers will win, you have a better chance of collecting but the payoff
is proportionately smaller.

Harry looks up. "Give me a minute. Now," he says, "we will sharpen the price." He and Larry poke at their computers.

The deal is not cut, not yet. Harry and Larry know, and so does Ben, that the customer has access to almost as much information as they do. Not quite as up-to-date, but nearly so. He has also been in touch with other banks, to see if they can better our offer. Within two minutes, Harry says, "Give him 100."

Ben bobs, mutters into his phone.

"One hundred. Done." He throws up a thumb. The deal is concluded; the "back office," on another floor, will produce all the paperwork in due course, send out all the cheques, bring in all the bills. They have a tape running all the time, which records the transaction as it is made. The bank has bought all the customer's positions in more than a dozen forward derivatives that would make money if the dollar dropped. Now Larry goes to work selling these positions to other customers who think the dollar *will* drop, or who want to hedge that way.

The bank will make money, if it does, on the difference between what it paid the customer for his positions and what it will get reselling them to other customers.

I splutter, "My God, you're a used-car salesman!"

Harry winces, thinks about it. "Exactly," he says. Better than being called a crap-shooter.

"The more you can chisel the customer on the buy, the more you make," I tell Harry. He doesn't like that much, either, but he agrees. "The thing is, the customer can try other markets, he knows what they are; if you get a reputation for trying to grind the customer, you will soon be out of business."

A used-car salesman, of course, will seldom get blind-sided by the dozens of sudden changes that shape and shake financial markets; a sudden abrupt change in the Bank Rate, for example, or a spectacular failure in a foreign market, or the simple, dizzy whims that strike the exchanges, from time to time, and send prices scuttering for no apparent reason. This is the business of gambling in futures, and you have to wonder, What does it have to do with banking?

Harry's answer is that it provides a service for the customer. The banks' annual reports answer that it helps with risk management: For example, one bank, the CIBC, uses derivatives as an end user, to adjust our asset and liability risk profile. We employ a variety of derivative instruments, primarily swaps, in managing our exposure to fluctuations in market interest rates and foreign exchange rates.[1]

In a word, the bank is hedging, just like our man in the lumber industry. If it does well, it can not only cover its bets, but make a little money on the way through. Larry and Harry are expected to clear $100,000 on a good day. Against these benefits must be set two drawbacks. One is the risk involved in these volatile markets; derivatives are the TNT of financial planning. What if the party on the other side of the risk loses, and then can't pay? What if exchange rates wipe out the gain? What if the whole market collapses? The other drawback is the fact that the entire process is almost impossible to calculate, let alone control. Larry and Harry must do a summary every day to show their trading positions, and guess from that whether they have made or lost money for the bank during the last shift. Some of their transactions, like the one outlined above, are easy enough to gauge, since they are completed quickly. But many transactions involve taking on positions that will not unwind for years, and nobody really knows whether the bank will win or lose until the derivatives mature.

Options and Other Derivatives

Options—which are the right, but not the requirement, to buy or sell a given financial instrument within a certain period of time at a specified price—are the most common form of derivative. Anyone who buys or sells an option makes a guess as to which way the market is likely to go, and acts accordingly. If Silver River Snake Oil stock is trading at $40, and she thinks it will go up, she will buy a "Call"—the right to purchase Silver River stock at $40 within the next three months from someone who thinks she is wrong. She will pay a fee, called "the premium," for this right, a fraction of the price, which varies with the length of time the option is open, and the price at which it may be exercised. If the price hits $45, she will exercise the option, buy at $40 and sell at $45. Although the option cost her less than $1 a share, she will make $5 a share; she will be well pleased. If she is wrong, and the price goes down, she will not exercise the option, and will forfeit the premium— the price she paid for the option—but nothing more. The premium is usually only about 2 per cent of the stock price, so she can take a whirl on the stock without having to risk a lot of money.

Conversely, if she thinks the price of the stock is going to go down, she will buy the "Put" on the same shares, which is the right to sell them for today's current price—$40—within the next three months. If the shares drop to $20, she will exercise the Put, and sell at $40 the shares she bought for $20. She will be even more pleased. And, she has taken this gamble in the knowledge that at least she cannot lose more than she invested.

But there is a way to take care of that, for any stock trader to gamble more for less, and take a greater risk. It is the "naked" option, the most common form of trading, these days. In this case, the "writer" of the option—the person who makes the offer—does not own the underlying stock. Let us stay with the Silver River scenario. We are sure it is about to take a fall, so we write a Put at the current trading price of $40 on 10,000 shares (options are usually sold in bundles of 100). The premium price is $8,000, but, like most people who buy and sell options regularly, we have a "margin" account with the trading house, which allows us to put up only 10 per cent of the price. We have to come up with only $800 in cash. We turn out to be right; the shares go down to $20; we buy our 10,000 at that price, and sell them at once for $40 to the poor yob who thought they were going to go up. We make $20 per share, less the price of the premium, or $192,000, but the only cash we actually parted with was $800 (plus a commission to the broker who handled the deal).

But, suppose we are wrong; instead of going down to $20, Silver River, buoyed by a totally fake rumour that there is a shortage of snake oil in Afghanistan, goes to $60, and we don't have any shares. Now, the holder of our Put wants the 10,000 shares, and we have to go out into the market and buy them at $60 each; they will cost us $600,000, although the premiums cost us only $8,000, and we put down only $800. We have lost a fortune on a gamble that started out with $800. Welcome to the world of leverage.

With options, and "naked" options, there is still some connection between the instrument traded and the underlying stock, but we can make the gamble bigger by buying derivatives based on a whole index of stocks, or on money-market instruments whose value will go up and down, depending on what happens to the stock indices. Or, we can buy interest-rate swaps. Suppose our company, the Lock, Stock, and Barrel Company, wants to protect itself against a possible rise in interest rates, and another firm, Hammer and Nail, Inc., thinks interest rates are going to fall, and would like to make a little money if they do. Lock, Stock will "lend" Hammer $100 million at a fixed rate, say, 10 per cent, and Hammer will "lend" Lock, Stock $100 million at a rate that varies with the Bank Rate. The $100 million appears on the books of both companies, but it does not actually exist; it is "notional." Every month, the two companies balance accounts; if the variable rate is greater than 10 per cent, Hammer pays Lock, Stock the difference; if less, Lock, Stock pays Hammer.

There is a real value to the market in interest-rate swaps, as there is in some of the other derivative products, for serious investors who want to hedge against changes in interest rates. The problem is that today's market consists of about 1 per cent legitimate trading, and the rest straight crap-shooting. The swaps can take on a value, and a life, of their own that has nothing to do with hedging. A derivative can be created by having a computer program look at today's interest rates; figure out how much income a given swap will generate, and for whom; and calculate what the swap is worth. Then the right to buy or sell that swap is turned into an option, and sold. Other derivatives can be created by gambling against changes in currencies. The potential income from, say, a block of U.S. Treasury bills can be set against a stream of income from a portfolio of Japanese stocks. The right to buy or sell either side of this gamble becomes a derivative, whose value will go up, if the yen goes up, for the person holding the Japanese side of the bet, and down, if it goes down. One of the favoured derivatives is created by buying an option based on a guess as to whether the value of a whole range of stocks on a stock exchange will rise or fall. Nick Leeson, who sank Barings Bank, did a lot of his gambling on the Nikkei 225 Index, based on the value of 225 stocks traded on the Tokyo Stock Exchange.

By this time, the actual value of these instruments as financial futures has gone out the window, and we are dealing with them simply as a way to roll the dice. It is as if you set out to buy a bushel of tomatoes down at the market for twenty dollars, and ended up betting the twenty instead on whether the farmer who grew them had a moustache. Then you could buy and sell the right to bet on what kind of moustache he had. There are more than 1,200 financial derivatives currently offered—the list grows daily—including such items as "harmful warrants," "worthless warrants," "death-backed bonds," "limbos," and "heaven and hell bonds."[2] The "junk bonds" that ravaged markets in the 1980s were models of propriety compared with these.

Dangerous Derivatives

It is the more complex, and higher-priced, derivatives that interest the banks, because banks are always moving currencies around the world, and they have the capital to back the kind of gambles that are required. There is no limit to the variety of derivatives or, apparently, to the money that can be risked upon them, as some of the recent spectacular cases show:

- A Chilean government employee, Juan Pablo Davila, lost $207 million (U.S.), about 0.5 per cent of Chile's Gross National Product, playing copper futures.[3]
- The German conglomerate Metallgesellschaft lost $1.3 billion (U.S.) in oil derivatives.[4]
- Showa Sell Sekiyu of Japan, an affiliate of Royal Dutch Shell, lost $1.6 billion (U.S.) gambling in currency derivatives.[5]
- Bankers Trust New York Corporation, a bank acting for a number of customers, led them into derivatives trades that lost them millions. Procter & Gamble, one of these, has lost $157 million (U.S.) so far on trades that are far from finished, and Bankers Trust was fined on charges that its salesmen hid the risks of the contracts they sold.[6]

And then there was Barings Bank, Britain's oldest merchant bank, which was brought down by the derivatives trading of one of its traders in Singapore, Nick Leeson. Leeson was supposed to be trading, like the Bankers Trust operatives, only on behalf of customers, but, when a couple of trades went wrong, he claims, he went into the market directly, to cover up the losses. Soon, he was trading more and more for the bank's account, and losing more and more. Like most derivatives traders, and all bank traders, he spent most of his time and the bank's money on hedges, to cover his bets on both sides, but, as the losses piled up, he realized he could never clear the books that way, so he took off all the hedges and made a series of monumental, and mistaken, bets that the Nikkei 225 Index, and Japanese Government Bonds, would increase in value. When an earthquake hit Kobe, all Japanese stocks took a hit, and Barings was called upon to pay off on a whole lot of lost bets which amounted to £827 million (about $1.8 billion Canadian)—more than the bank's capital base. It was wiped out.

Leeson had concealed what he was doing from the bank, whose incuriosity about daily shipments of up to £30 million to cover his bets was a wonder to behold. The bank thought it was making money when it was losing, because Leeson had fraudulently invented a bank account with lucky Chinese numbers, Account 88888, which was supposed to have as much as £78 million in it, although it did not have a dime. In the book he wrote about his short but lively career from Tanah Merah Prison in Singapore, where he is serving a sentence of six and a half years for deceiving the auditors of Barings and cheating the Singapore Exchange, Leeson makes two points well worth considering.

One is that, although there were supposed to be dozens of checks on the operation he ran, including a daily meeting of the Risk Management Group in the bank's London office, and constant contact with his superior in Singapore, bank management did nothing as long as he appeared to be making profits. An official inquiry in Singapore concluded that "the Baring management could have remained ignorant of account 88888 up to the time of the collapse only if they had persistently shut themselves from the truth."[7]

The other is that the British authorities, especially the Serious Fraud Office, were singularly uninterested in having Leeson, who was arrested in Frankfurt, Germany, tried in England, although his most serious offences, in deceiving Barings, took place in London, not Singapore. Leeson suggests that no one in Britain wanted to have the details of how dangerous derivatives trading really is trotted out before the courts, so he was allowed to plead guilty in Singapore, with very little said.[8] The Bank of England got a slap on the wrist, in a report to the British Parliament, and Barings management were raked over the coals, but there were no recommendations to change either the derivatives gambling or the way in which the central bank supervises the commercial banks.[9]

The major difference in structure between the way in which trading took place in Singapore under Nick Leeson and the way Canadian banks operate in the derivatives market is that Leeson was able to control both the "front" and "back" rooms. That is, he could control the way in which his trades were reported, and the daily balance on the various accounts, which he always showed to be in line. No Canadian bank allows that in any of its trading offices anywhere. In any Canadian bank, the Leeson debacle could not have happened the way it did. However, it must be noted that the series of checks on Canadian derivatives trading are exactly the ones used at Barings—except that Barings didn't use them.

Derivatives trading remains a dangerous business indeed, and all our banks are into it up to their hips. The *Wall Street Journal* estimated the 1995 derivatives market at over $35 trillion worldwide.[10] A year earlier, it was $10 trillion.[11] This is a market that is not only huge, but growing far too fast for anyone to comprehend, let alone control. To put the numbers in perspective, the Gross Domestic Product of the United States in 1995 was about $7 trillion. The derivatives market is about five times that. And, about 90 per cent of derivatives trading, according to one Toronto securities analyst, is accounted for by the banking fraternity, either on their own behalf, or, more often, as commissioned sales people on behalf of customers all over the world.[12] As you will see in Table 9 in the Appendix, the Big Five Canadian banks, at the end of 1995, had more at risk in derivatives trading than their entire Shareholders' Equity.

The banks' annual reports show the "Credit Risk Equivalent"—some of them call it, more guardedly, "Credit Equivalent"—involved as part of their off-balance sheet transactions. This is determined under rules established by the Office of the Superintendent of Financial Institutions, and it represents two risks. The first is the cost of replacing, at current market value, all the bank's derivative contracts, in the event that the parties on the other side fail or withdraw. The second is the potential for future losses on the contracts. In Table 9, I have compared the Credit Equivalent of the Big Five banks to the Shareholders' Equity of each, to give you some idea of the size of this trading. You will see that the risk appears, in every case, larger than the equity. In fact, if one of the other banks it were dealing with collapsed, and could not make a payment, the derivative instruments would have some cash value, and could be sold to reduce the damage. In addition, there is often collateral involved, which could be kept.

No One Knows How Much Is at Risk

So, the complaint of those who object to this trading is not that any Canadian bank is about to disappear because of it, but that no one really knows exactly what the risk is. What Table 9 shows is that, whatever the real number that ought to be attached to the gamble, it is huge. I cannot imagine any of these banks lending money to someone who, when asked for a statement of assets, noted that he owned a house worth half a million dollars, but had a million in chips on the tables at Las Vegas.

The table also shows that the total trades in derivative instruments of the Big Five in 1995 had a notional value of nearly $5 trillion. The notional value, as we saw above, is the amount of a contract in total. If you have an option to purchase $10 million worth of interest-rate swaps, the notional value is $10 million, but you will purchase the option for a fraction of that, and your risk is in the option cost, not the total.

If nobody knows, in fact, how much is actually at risk every day in derivatives, that, surely, should give us pause. It does give Canada's auditor general pause. He has for some time worried about the "capacity of the Office of the Superintendent of Financial Institutions to evaluate credit risks facing the banks from derivatives and securities activities."[13] The retiring superintendent of financial institutions, Michael Mackenzie, repeatedly expressed concern about the involvement of Canadian banks in this volatile field,[14] but no action resulted, or is contemplated.

George Soros, a U.S. derivatives trader, told the U.S. House Banking Committee that "some [derivatives] are so esoteric that the risk involved may not be properly understood even by the most sophisticated investor, and I'm supposed to be one."[15] Soros, incidentally, made more than $1 billion gambling, correctly, that the British pound would have to be revalued, and then lost $600 million in two days by gambling that the dollar would rise against the yen.[16] It didn't.

Even the most staid and stolid members of the business press (in the United States, anyway; in Canada, the subject scarcely comes up) are beginning to sound alarmed. *Business Week* magazine, under a headline that read, "Once again banks are leaving investors in the dark," noted:

> Under today's accounting and disclosure rules it's almost impossible for outsiders to get anything but the sketchiest pictures

of a given bank's derivative activities. Citibank's credit exposure (to derivatives) is now at least 86% of its equity, Morgan's
is 141%, and Bankers Trust's is 213%.[17]

The difficulty is to see how the banks can possibly pull back. In some
cases, bond-rating agencies have been known to lower the ratings on a
corporate bond issue because the company was not using derivatives;
there is even an expression for this—"failure to derivate."[18]

In any event, the official response of most regulators has been, Who,
Me Worry? The reaction of the American authorities to the collapse of
Barings Bank was for the Federal Reserve chairman, Alan Greenspan, to
go before the House Banking Committee to support the repeal of the
Glass–Steagle Act, which attempted to limit the ways in which American
banks could invest, a struggle that is still under way as I write this.
According to the *Wall Street Journal*: "Mr. Greenspan argued that the
Barings debacle, and others like it, shouldn't impede moves to abolish
what he called 'antiquated' barriers. 'Human nature is going to do what
human nature has always done—bad things on occasion.'"[19]

Even the BIS is beginning to get a little leery of the wild gambles now
taking place. In a report issued early in 1996, the central bank noted that
"many banks don't appreciate the size or complexity of settlement risk,
and ... they lack formal mechanisms to measure and cope with their ex-
posures."[20] In some derivatives deals, the report suggested, an entire
bank could be wiped out by the failure or inability of the other side of
the bet to pay off. Despite this, some of the eighty major international
banks which were the subject of the study acknowledged that their senior
management "had never been fully briefed" on the risks involved.[21]

The BIS, if pushed, "might" begin to impose guidelines on commercial banks, although it believes the best solution is "self-regulation."[22]
The Bank of Canada, needless to say, rejects any attempts to control derivatives' trading by the banks.

The banks argue that there are controls in place to safeguard us all.
There is the Office of the Superintendent of Financial Institutions, to keep
an eye on the banks, and the Canada Deposit Insurance Corporation, to
mop up the blood, both government institutions we shall now examine.

CHAPTER 9

Puff the Magic Watchdog

The essential truth about the ordinary bank is that it is no safe deposit box. Ultimate safety—a strong box full of currency—would avail the bank nothing. Every bank under the sun balances a book of loans on a sliver of capital.

—James Grant,
Money of the Mind, 1992

Bank watchdog John Palmer has a novel approach to struggling financial institutions: Let 'em sink.

—Gord McIntosh,
Canadian Press, 1996

WHEN I ASKED DOUG PETERS, the secretary of state for international financial institutions (but who is, in fact, the junior minister of finance), why we don't write a definition of "banking" into the Bank Act, now that it is under review, he replied that he couldn't see how it would make things better.

"Other nations have definitions," he said, "but do they have any better systems?"

He added, later, "It's too bad Canadians can't take pride in some of the things we do well, but I guess that wouldn't be Canadian, would it?"[1] By "the things we do well" he meant banking.

Peters was a banker for thirty-seven years before he became a politician, so I guess his position isn't surprising, but he reflects a view widely held in this country. We have a successful banking system, much better than those rogues south of the border, so we should just leave it alone.*

But what if it's at risk and we don't know it? Or, what if we're busy fixing it, through amendments to the Bank Act, but we are fixing the wrong things, or the right things in the wrong way?

The aspect of our banking system that appears to make us proudest is its stability. While American financial institutions keep falling over the cliff, ours go chugging along, year after year, racking up ever-fatter profits. Well, the Big Five do; no doubt about that. Their end of the year results are extraordinary, as you saw in Table 2.** The main reason for this, I have already argued, is that they operate as an oligopoly. They have such a stranglehold on the financial world that they can survive almost anything, even their own stupidity.

Alix Granger, who wrote an informative book about the banks in 1981, put the point nicely: "The OPEC cartel sets world oil prices, and for most of Canada's history, the bankers have set the price of banking services."[2]

OPEC is in no danger of going broke, as long as the gang clings together, and the same can be said for our big banks. However, we are

---

* Since this subject is not directly germane to the argument of this chapter, but comes up so often, let me go to a footnote to point out one great advantage American bank customers have that most Canadians have never even heard of. In the United States, if you are holding a mortgage, and interest rates go down, you have the right to get a new mortgage at the lower rate, on payment of a small administration fee. In Canada, your mortgage usually contains a penalty clause that effectively wipes out any savings. It requires you to pay the bank the higher of: three months' interest on the mortgage, or the difference between the current rate of interest and the new one over the remaining term of the mortgage. Under the U.S. system, most Canadian mortgage holders could have saved hundreds of dollars a month over the past two years; under the Canadian system, the banks got to keep millions of dollars.

** In the 1995 fiscal year, the Big Five racked up a total profit of $4,933 million, up 21.8 per cent from the year before, while the Gross Domestic Product increased 2.3 per cent. In 1996, they did even better: $6.3 billion in profits.

moving into unchartered waters, with bank deregulation. The end of reserves, the exposure to derivatives, and the yearning to drop in a few hundred millions and see what happens that seems to fill our bankers' bosoms every time they encounter a nation run by a friendly, tinpot dictator (Mexico springs to mind) may undermine our stability.

To protect us, and to rescue us if the worst happens, we have the Office of the Superintendent of Financial Institutions (OSFI), and the Canada Deposit Insurance Corporation (CDIC). The OSFI is charged with "regulating and supervising all federally chartered, licensed or registered banks, insurance, trust, loan and investment companies, cooperative credit associations and fraternal benefit societies."[3] The CDIC is "a federal Crown corporation created in 1967 to protect the money you deposit in member financial institutions in case of their failure."[4] Think of them as the watchdog and the fire brigade. And if you want to know how effective they are, take a look at the record of recent financial disasters in this country.

In Unity, There Is Weakness

If we go back to the Unity Bank, born 1972, buried 1977, we find a financial institution founded on a brilliant idea—a bank to service the sectors of the nation that were ignored by the mainstream banks—but one that got into the hands of a man named Richard Higgins, who was charming, charismatic, and crooked enough to stand unseen behind a spiral staircase. When the bank was being launched, Higgins was vetted by the House of Commons Standing Committee on Finance. One of the questions put to the inspector general of banks (as the watchdog was called in those days) was whether Higgins was "a man of banking experience and integrity."

The inspector general replied, "I have no reason to doubt it."[5] Nor had he. He had interviewed Higgins, once. Had he bothered to contact the Bank of Montreal, where Higgins had worked, and which Higgins had attempted to hornswoggle, he might have come to a different conclusion. Higgins had set up a deal, when he was running the B of M in Grand Cayman, through which he sold the land the bank had assembled to establish a regional office to a pal of his, a private developer, who then undertook to build the building and lease the ground floor back to the bank for enough money to cover construction, rent, and a tidy profit. Whatever the developer made on the rest of the building was gravy. The deal was signed the day before Higgins sent in his letter of resignation to the B of M to take on his new job at Unity, shares in which, incidentally, were bought by the friendly developer. The B of M, when it caught up to the details of the arrangement, killed the deal, bought back the property, and built its own bank.[6]

The inspector general didn't know about any of this, and the Bank of Montreal didn't bring the matter to his attention. When it came to light (it was I, in fact, who uncovered the deal), Higgins was invited to resign as president of Unity Bank, and he found it prudent to do so. By this time, what with a number of his dubious financial arrangements, and a hard economic climate, Unity was sinking fast, and was saved from insolvency only by being swallowed by the Provincial Bank. Then the Provincial was joined in holy matrimony to the Banque Canadienne Nationale, to form the National Bank, about the time Richard Higgins was finishing a short jail sentence for accepting a bribe from a British Columbia businessman in connection with a loan from Unity.[7]

Throughout the whole process, the inspector general had no comment to make. After word leaked out that the bank had loaned $7 million to a Toronto industrialist subsequently charged with defrauding his own firm, and the financial world was getting a tad nervous, the assistant inspector general, William Kennett, was asked whether things were going awry over at Unity, and whether his office was forcing the merger with the Provincial. He replied that there was "some evidence" that Unity was losing the confidence of its depositors, but "no pressure was taken on our part in this amalgamation."[8]

The waters closed over Unity Bank with scarcely a ripple, and the Canadian Bankers Association was able to continue with its proud pronouncement that no Canadian bank had gone bankrupt since the Home Bank, in 1923. Canadian banks don't fold; they are engulfed.

Not long after, Kennett was promoted, and became the inspector general of banks in time to deal with the next two crises, involving two western banks, the Canadian Commercial Bank (CCB), and the Northland Bank.

The Rise and Fall of the CCB

The CCB was launched in Edmonton, in 1976, in the midst of a real estate and energy boom, and quickly made some bad financial moves. One of these was the purchase of a minority interest in a California bank called Westlands, which turned out to be a money-sink, because it had so many bad loans. G. Howard Eaton, who ran the CCB, moved to Los Angeles, which seemed a strange place from which to run a Canadian bank. Kennett, when this was pointed out to him, called Eaton in to explain his actions, instructed him to move back to Canada, and gave him two years to do it.[9]

Then the CCB got itself entangled in what came to be called "The Trust Company Affair." This involved a series of real estate flips by three trust companies in Toronto, at ever-rising prices, with the risk being assumed by the depositors, and the profits by three men who controlled the trusts. The incident ended with the heads of all three companies becoming numbered guests of Her Majesty the Queen for periods of up to five years, with time off for good behaviour.[10] The CCB had advanced $7 million to Leonard Rosenberg, one of the trio, and the chubby charmer who initiated the scheme, and that failed when the firms were taken over by the government of Ontario, their supervisor, which was not so shy about exercising its muscle as was the inspector general. Then it turned out that Rosenberg and his partners owned or controlled nearly a third of the CCB, although the law said, and still says, that no single shareholder or group can hold more than 10 per cent of a chartered bank. Eaton was forced to resign, and the CCB was sent reeling.

Mr. Justice Willard Z. Estey, who wrote the inevitable government report on this one, noted that the impact of the vanished $7 million on the CCB, already in financial difficulty, was "a loss of confidence and a run on deposits, driving the bank to the Bank of Canada for liquidity support."[11]

To keep going, the CCB indulged in some interesting accounting practices, such as accruing interest on loans when the payments had not been met. That is, the borrower owes $1 million in interest on a debt on January 1, but, when January 1 comes along, no interest is paid. The lender then says, Never mind, I know you're good for the money, and rolls the loan over, with interest chargeable on the whole new amount.

The interest had not been paid; whether it would ever be paid was a matter of conjecture, but it showed up on the CCB balance sheet as income. The bank's auditors approved the books without a murmur, and the inspector general said, in effect, that if it was good enough for the auditors, it was good enough for him. At the time, the inspector general had a total of eight inspectors to scrutinize the activities of fourteen Canadian and more than fifty foreign banks,[12] but instead of clamouring for more staff, he tended to rely on the banks' auditors.

The CCB now moved into a twilight zone, a period where everyone, especially the government spokesmen, pretended it was not moribund, while, on the side, putting in an order for flowers, shovels, and a hearse. When Eaton was forced out of the bank, anxiety descended on the stock market, which is driven by equal amounts of greed and paranoia, and it seemed likely that there would be a stampede for the exits. Gerald Bouey, who was at that time the governor of the Bank of Canada, stepped in to calm things down. He telephoned the *Globe and Mail* to insist that the CCB was a "solvent and profitable bank,"[13] information that came to him, presumably, via tea leaves or a Ouija board.

The *Globe* duly ran this bit of good news, though with raised eyebrows. Every few days, an opposition member would rise up in the House of Commons with a rude question and be reassured that all was fine. Still, a general sense of unease led to the withdrawal, over the next few months, of $1.3 billion in deposits from the CCB,[14] which made the bank's position that much worse.

On March 25, 1985, a government press release set out to prove that everything was under control now, because the six largest chartered banks, the governments of Canada and Alberta, and the CDIC, collectively referred to as "the Support Group," had weighed in with a rescue plan. The banks, collectively, and the governments, separately, put up $60 million each, a total of $180 million. For its part, the CDIC put up $75 million. This infusion of $255 million would look after all the soft loans out there, and William Kennett, the inspector general, gave the banks a letter to assure them that, with their help, the CCB "will ... be solvent."[15] He had tea leaves, too. He had never done an inspection to determine whether the assets against which the CCB had issued loans were still worth the figures shown on the books.

Not that the banks doubted him, of course, but they wanted their own look at the loan portfolio. Accordingly, George Hitchman, the retired deputy chairman of the Bank of Nova Scotia, began a study of the CCB's loans on July 2, 1985, and, by August 1, had concluded, "It is clear that the CCB is insolvent."[16]

Bit of a shock to Bouey, Kennett, and those who had contemplated whipping their deposits out of the bank, but had left them in on the basis of the official reassurances. Bit of a shock, as well, to anyone holding CCB stock who clung to it on the basis of the same soothing syrup. In a six-month period in 1985, the Bank of Canada advanced $1,272.2 million to the CCB,[17] pumping in cash at one end while it leaked out at the other. Finally, it became obvious to all that the bank could not survive, that no other bank would marry it and pay off the mortgage, and that there was not going to be another rescue package. The CCB was put out of its misery on September 1, 1985.[18]

Some Very Dodgy Numbers-Crunching at Northland

At the same time that the CCB was spiralling into the ground, so was another Western bank, Northland, which was centred in Calgary.* Like the CCB, it was born in the energy and real estate boom in Western Canada, put out hundreds of millions of dollars in real estate loans backed by shaky assets, and then, when these loans became non-performing, indulged in some very dodgy numbers-crunching. Mr. Justice Estey described the accounting methods used in the CCB and Northland cases as "imaginative," "energetic," "bizarre," and "risky" at various places in his report. The weak loans were placed in a "workout" category, and the figures were made to look better by calculating "the projected success of the workouts and anticipated improved economic conditions generally." That is the description of Mr. Justice Estey; I would call it financial faith-healing. The auditors believed, and the inspector general believed them, and Northland staggered on. In fact, it extended more loans, in hopes of getting some good ones to cover the bad ones.

---

* We need regional banks, particularly in Western Canada, and it is a pity that two recent bankruptcies involved regional banks, but these failures had nothing to do with regionalism, everything to do with skulduggery.

Mr. Justice Estey, in his only flight of fanciful writing in 641 pages of prose, noted, "The financial statements became gold fillings covering cavities in the assets and in the earnings of the bank."[19] By 1983, Northland was insolvent, but whistling past the graveyard, while the inspector general was otherwise occupied.

The collapse of the CCB in March 1985 led to a rapid withdrawal of deposits from Northland, which was seen, correctly, to be in the same danger, because it was operating in the same markets, and in the same way. Again, the Bank of Canada stepped in, with a total of $517.5 million in advances.[20] Despite this, the inspector general's office approved a new issue of debentures by the bank amounting to a new loan from the general public of $16 million. In connection with this, the investment firm which had undertaken to float the debentures onto the market was told that "the OIGB [the Office of the Inspector General of Banks] was aware of nothing which would make it imprudent to proceed with the issue."[21] What is more, the governor of the Bank of Canada, Gerald Bouey, rejected a proposal from the bank to reflect in its financial statements the write-off of a large segment of its loans portfolio, on the grounds that they would never be paid, and might as well be laid to rest. This would certainly have spooked the market by more accurately reflecting what had happened, but the calamity was averted.

Finally, the OIGB bestirred itself enough to look into Northland's bizarre banking practices and, reeling, tried to get the National Bank to merge with Northland, to save it. National Bank inspectors took one look at Northland's smelly loan portfolio, and backed away hastily. A curator was appointed in September 1985, and the bank was liquidated in early 1986.[22]

The eventual price-tag picked up by the federal government for the two banks was more than $1 billion.[23] The six chartered banks which had put in $60 million lost it. However, uninsured depositors in the banks were reimbursed, at a price of $875 million. These were mostly people who had more than the $60,000 maximum for CDIC insurance. Normally, they could collect that amount only in the case of a bank failure, but in the case of the CCB and Northland, some depositors collected several times the $60,000 "maximum." In Ottawa, opposition MPs made quite a fuss about this bailing out of the fat-cats, but Governor Bouey argued that "the causes of the present situation already existed at the time the official assurances were given,"[24] which was the crucial point. Without these assurances, from himself and others, the depositors would certainly have hauled out their money long since. It would not have been right to punish them for being stupid enough to take the word of the official regulators.

In March 1986, William Kennett, the inspector general of banks, retired at the age of fifty-three, saying that he was "in need of a rest."[25]

The liquidators for the CCB and Northland brought lawsuits against the former directors and officers, and the auditors of both banks, Ernst & Young International and Peat Marwick Thorne. In 1990, the defendants settled for $82.5 million in the CCB case, and $43.2 million in the Northland case.[26]

The lesson was pretty clear; the official regulators of these two banks had only the sketchiest notion of what was going on within them; and, when the danger became manifest, the instinctive official response was to pretend there was a light at the end of the tunnel right up until the moment that light turned out to be the headlight of a freight train that ran over the taxpayer.

What could be more natural, when the nation discovered that its regulatory system was not up to the job, than to deregulate? So, that was done. The lines between banks, trust companies, investment firms, and insurance corporations were blurred, as we saw in Chapter 4, and the Office of the Inspector General of Banks was rolled into the new Office of the Superintendent of Financial Institutions, in 1987.[27] The OSFI has to "regulate and supervise":

- 9 domestic banks;
- 53 subsidiaries of foreign banks;
- 19 loan companies;
- 31 federally chartered trust companies;
- 7 cooperative credit associations;
- 21 provincially chartered trust and loan companies, which the OSFI looks after as an agent of the CDIC;
- 19 investment companies;
- 33 fraternal benefit societies; and
- 135 federally registered life insurance companies.[28]

These 327 firms, many of them huge, nearly all of them involved in incredibly complex financial deals, are overseen by the OSFI. Oh, yes, and the office hires itself out to the Canada Pension Plan, on the side, to help oversee its finances.

This is about as efficient as you would expect, as we will see in the cases of the Bank of Credit and Commerce International (BCCI), Standard Trust, and Royal Trust.

Crooks and Creeps International

The BCCI, also known as the Bank of Crooks and Creeps International, is particularly interesting because it represented the kind of international financial giant that our own banks would like to become, although, I hope and trust, they do not aspire to its crookedness. What they do aspire to is the absence of regulation that allowed it to flourish before it foundered.

The BCCI was founded in 1972 by a Pakistani with a gentle smile named Agha Hasan Adebi, who turned it into a personal piggy bank for a number of people whom the police of various nations were anxious to have assist them with their inquiries. Adebi nonetheless managed to connect his bank with a number of respected international financial houses, including the Bank of America, which bought a small quantity of the shares.

Although the bank began in the oil-rich sheikdom of Abu Dhabi—which was why the Bank of America invested, for the entrée to the oil lands—Adebi decided to incorporate it in Luxembourg, as BCCI Holdings, SA.[29] The secrecy laws are strict in the duchy, while other regulations are evanescent and taxes are negligible. Later, another corporate headquarters was established in Georgetown, Grand Cayman, and a third in Gibraltar, giving the shareholders three places to play where the constituted authorities are singularly incurious about what goes on in the vaults.

By the mid-1970s, the BCCI, financed by Arab money, started in Abu Dhabi, incorporated in three other nations, with a solid connection to the United States, was off and running. Pakistan was the second major centre of expansion, after Abu Dhabi, but soon the bank was popping up all over the Middle East, the Far East, then Africa, then Europe, and, before it was done, there were 400 branches in seventy-three countries,[30] all lending vast sums of money. It became involved in a lot of noisesome, not to say crooked, operations, floated out loans based on dubious collateral, and indulged in some unusual giveaways to the customers—fun sessions with prostitutes in place of pop-up toasters as an incentive to do business, for example. A bank which is willing to shove money over the counter with only a cursory glance at the collateral does not have any trouble finding customers, and BCCI business mushroomed.

As the years passed, a rather noxious stink was beginning to emanate from the BCCI, due to various of its shady operations. It had laundered quite a lot of drug money for various unsavoury characters, among them Manuel Noriega, the Panama dictator well known for his American ties and his key role in the cocaine business that fed the U.S. drug market. Quite a number of banks have laundered drug money over the years, some of them have known about it, and some of them have not. The BCCI's sin was that it was caught knowing about it, and had to plead guilty to charges in that connection.

Drug dealers brought cocaine into the United States, sold it, deposited the take in BCCI accounts in low-denomination money orders and certificates of deposit, to make tracing more difficult, and then wired the cash offshore. The bank collected handling fees. In addition, satchels of cash were shipped to Saudi Arabia, turned into gold, and plugged back into the system. When the BCCI was caught by officers of U.S. Customs, you might have thought that that would have blown the lid off the entire racket, but it did not. Customs referred its evidence of the drug rackets and their financing to the Justice Department, which did nothing about them; the BCCI was allowed to plead guilty to money-laundering charges, and paid a $15-million fine. Among the many items concealed from the public during this process was the fact that the BCCI owned six U.S. banks, through sham nominees, although it was illegal for it to do so.[31]

The BCCI also got into gun-running, financing the sale of arms into South America out of an office in Boca Raton, Florida; bankrolling the sale of helicopters to Guatemala; and putting up the cash for an abortive attempt to ship prohibited materials from the United States to Pakistan, to help with its nuclear weapons program.[32]

The CIA, which actually used the BCCI to pay off operatives, had submitted a report on the bank in 1986, pointing to money-laundering and other illegal activities,[33] but no action resulted, and the BCCI, by

1987, had managed to turn itself into a truly global bank, with 16,000 employees, branches all over the world, and assets listed at more than $20 billion (U.S.). Four of these branches were in Canada.

The money was poured in through the Middle East, the bank's main operation centre was in England, but its corporate headquarters were split among Luxembourg, Grand Cayman, and Gibraltar. No national regulator was willing, or able, to take responsibility for what it got up to.

But, alas, it was now failing, as more and more of its large loans began to go sour, some because the assets against which they were borrowed, such as real estate, had lost much of their value, and some because the loans were fraudulent from beginning to end, or, at the very least, high-risk. The Gokal shipping family of Pakistan owed the BCCI over $700 million in a series of transactions that slipped through the bank's offices in Grand Cayman for which a subsequent audit could discover only $65 million in security.[34] The bank was kept afloat by sucking in new money at high interest rates to cover the bills as they came due, thus piling up more debts.

Adebi had a heart attack, and not a moment too soon; he was given a heart transplant at Cromwell Hospital in London in February 1988, and, while he recovered, he was removed from virtually all banking operations, which became even more frantic with the absence of this key figure. The BCCI's problems were about to be visited on the regulators, like it or not.

In March 1990, Robin Leigh-Pemberton, governor of the Bank of England, was handed an audit report prepared by Price Waterhouse that showed that the BCCI was in such severe financial trouble, because of fraudulent and imprudent loans, that it would require $1.78 billion in new funding to stay afloat.[35] The American authorities demanded, and received, a copy of this audit, and began digging into their old files on the BCCI.

When the ailing Adebi resigned from the bank, Zafar Iqbal, the BCCI country manager in Abu Dhabi, took over, and cooperated with the British and American investigators who had now evinced some interest in what was going on. With Adebi out of the way, the bank's senior staff began to provide some of the hard information on soft loans that had been concealed for so long.

The bank was kept going, and the extent of the damage was concealed, for fear of causing a run on deposits. Leigh-Pemberton would later justify this course of action in a quote that should be stitched in needlepoint on the pillow-sham of every institutional investor: "If we closed down a bank every time we had a fraud, we would have rather fewer banks than we have."[36]

This rationale did not provide much comfort for anyone who bought shares between the time the Bank of England knew the BCCI was up to its ham hocks in disaster and the time of its demise.

You will be glad to know the governor got his comeuppance. The severe criticism of the Bank of England's performance in connection with the BCCI scandal was followed by a pay-raise of 17 per cent for the governor in May 1991.[37]

Two new audits into the bank's operations, one by the bank itself, another by and for the Bank of England, turned up enough evidence to spur criminal investigations in both Britain and the United States. They showed that the bank was in debt to the tune of at least $5 billion (U.S.), and perhaps two or three times that, and revealed that, while the bank's annual reports showed robust earnings until the late 1980s, it had possibly never earned a profit in its entire history.[38]

On July 5, 1991, bank regulators in eighteen countries seized the assets of the BCCI in a coordinated shutdown, and bank branches were restricted in forty-four other lands. The accounts of 1.25 million depositors were frozen, businesses were paralysed all over the globe, ships were stranded in ports, factories shut their doors, and thousands and thousands of paycheques turned into useless little slips of paper in the hands of people who had never had anything to do with the BCCI except to work for a company that kept its accounts there. In a score of cities, customers massed in front of the closed bank branches, demanding their money, in vain. Deposit insurance applied in only a handful of the nations where the BCCI operated; most of its depositors were left to the mercy of bankruptcy proceedings, still going on; most of them will probably never collect a penny.

In Canada, rumours that the BCCI was running amok had been circulating for years. The government had been receiving tips, some of them anonymously, from BCCI employees, and from the Canadian Bankers Association, warning that the bank was operating in a wicked way, since the early 1980s.[39] The complaints were passed along to the minister of finance, Donald Mazankowski, but nothing happened. It was all put down to sour grapes, one of the crops in plentiful supply in the financial community. However, after the cracks in the BCCI's structure began to appear abroad, and the Canadian subsidiary began to leak losses, it was put on a short leash, with a charter limited to three months of operation at a time. That was the situation when the Bank of England and the U.S. Federal Reserve System hauled out the handcuffs in mid-1991. Then, the OSFI stepped in and closed the doors of the four Canadian branches. The long process of trying to realize on the remaining assets scattered around the world began, and will probably continue for many years.

What the BCCI case shows is that the Bank of Montreal comment quoted in Chapter 1 to the effect that no single nation can control its banks is quite correct, and applies with particular vengeance in any case where a bank is allowed to operate from the base of one of the many nations that pride themselves in having no rules. This is a powerful argument against the globalization of the banks, although they see it as the opposite.

Not Up to Standard

At the time the Office of the Superintendent of Financial Institutions was reluctantly investigating the BCCI, it was also beginning to suspect that all was not well with some of the Canadian trust companies it was now overseeing. This brings us to the case of Standard Trust, a firm founded in 1963 by Steven Roman, the mining magnate, and owned by a holding company, Standard Trustco Ltd. It was allied to an insurance company. A little less than half the stock was sold to the public, while Roman retained control. It grew to be the nation's ninth-largest trust company, and, like a number of other firms, got into trouble by issuing imprudent loans on real estate in the 1980s. The most troublesome of these involved Owl Developments Ltd., of Edmonton, to which it lent more than $100 million. Owl, in turn, was involved with a Winnipeg company, Berland Estates Ltd., a condominium development. Owl's president, John Barath, introduced Eric Stewart, the vice-president of mortgage production for Standard, to Victor Schultz, one of the principals in Berland, and, before the dust had settled, Standard Trust was lending Berland $2 million, and Barath was pocketing a $35,000 fee for this clever work.[40]

When Berland Estates went into bankruptcy in 1988, Owl could not keep up its mortgage payments, so Standard wound up with a lot of real estate that it really did not want. There were other, similar deals. In Newfoundland, Standard took over a strip mall which it had financed, when the owners went bankrupt. To get rid of that one, Standard auctioned it off to the highest bidder—who turned out to be one of the mortgagors who had gone bankrupt. Standard, unbelievably, turned around and lent this same man the money to buy back the strip mall at a knock-down rate. And then, of course, couldn't collect from him.[41]

By the spring of 1989, Standard was in serious trouble. The record now available shows that, by April, 8 per cent of its entire mortgage portfolio was in arrears. You wouldn't know that from the information made public at that time. In July, Standard Trustco Ltd., claimed a record six-month profit of $7.8 million, up 24 per cent from the previous year. The unpaid mortgages were taken care of by having the trust company simply accrue the missing interest, just the way the Canadian Commercial Bank had done. Instead of looking like money lost, or potentially lost, it was carried forward. People who bought the company stock without the slightest hint that it might be in trouble, and people who had money on deposit in the thirty-seven branches of the company, were in a perilous position.

However, this time the OSFI did catch up to the fancy accounting. On September 12, 1989, Donald Macpherson, the deputy superintendent of financial institutions, wrote to Brian O'Malley, the chief executive of Standard, and told him to stop accruing interest on delinquent loans. No other action was taken.

In April 1990, as part of its rescue of Owl Developments, Standard breached the regulatory rule that prohibits lending more than 1 per cent of its assets to a single borrower, and, when that didn't work, wound up taking over the real estate. The company president, Juli Koor, would later admit that at least ten of the firm's loans were in breach of the regulations.[42]

On June 25, nearly a year after it had originally found reason to suspect there was something going wrong, the OSFI began an examination of Standard's books. It quickly discovered that the company's assets were overstated and that there was no adequate provision for loan losses. Again, the public was not given a sniff of this. Instead, the company reported a profit of $5 million, and declared a quarterly dividend of twenty-five cents a share.

It was not until July 27 that Standard announced that a special audit was being conducted. The stock, which had been selling for $17.75 in June, dropped to $16.00. The quarterly dividend was called off, on instructions from Michael Mackenzie, then the superintendent of financial institutions.

The results of the special audit were not released until November 9. They showed that Standard's non-performing loans totalled $215 million, and the "profit" of $5 million shown in June was instead a loss of $50 million. The stock went into free fall.

Standard was required to present a "Business Plan" to the OSFI, showing how it intended to keep in business. This plan showed that it was losing money at a rate of $2.5 million a month; the only way to keep its liquidity requirements in line with the law would be to sell securities and its good mortgage loans. Standard's leverage was 25; what this meant was that, under trust company rules, the firm had to have $1 in capital for every $25 in deposits. Standard had $1.5 billion of the public's money, so it needed $60 million in capital. In short, it would have to sell its sound assets, making its continuation even more improbable. Again, the public was told nothing of this, although the company did issue a press release saying that shareholders' equity had dwindled by $10 million, to $27 million. The stock plummeted to $3.

Frantic attempts to sell the trust to anybody with the necessary money took up the next few months, and then, on April 5, 1991, Standard delivered its 1990 audited books to the OSFI for its annual inspection. These showed that the insurance firm allied with Standard Trust had lost $102 million on the year. Again, the public was not informed, although, on April 9, the company announced that its loan-loss provision for 1990 would come to $117 million.

On April 16, the Ontario Securities Commission got into the act, accusing Standard directors of releasing misleading financial statements. The next day, the OSFI seized the trust, padlocking its branches and head office. Five days later, on April 23, creditors of Standard Trustco, Ltd., the holding company, forced it into bankruptcy, and the usual swarm of lawyers and accountants descended.

The depositors were covered—at least those with less than $60,000, the limit of the Canada Deposit Insurance Corporation—but the stock-holders were out of luck.

The OSFI defends the imposition of a cloak of silence over the failing trust company with two arguments. The first is that its job is to protect the public, especially the depositing public. "We did everything we were required to do on that account," a spokesman from the OSFI told me, from behind the cover of a promise of anonymity. The second is that, if the regulator went public with every breach of regulations that came to light, its job would become impossible. "No one would trust us with any information" is the way it was put to me. "There has to be a certain amount of trust in this business."

A Royal Mess

Royal Trust was gathered into the bosom of the Royal Bank on September 1, 1993, in the culmination of a series of events that amounted to a disaster. Royal Trust was one of our oldest, and most respected, financial firms for nearly a century. Founded by the Bank of Montreal in 1899 to "coddle the estates of its valued clientele,"[43] it was the epitome of the Old Guard in Montreal's financial world, so conservative in approach that it was known as "The Rusty Trust."[44] Control of Royal Trustco Ltd., the holding company for the firm, passed to Canadian Pacific, then to Montreal financier Paul Desmarais, and finally, in a series of background purchases during the 1980s, to the Hees–Edper holding group, owned by the Bronfman family. The core business of the company had been residential mortgage loans, trust management, and, to a lesser degree, managing assets abroad for Canadian investors, but all that changed. Royal's managers, under the Hees–Edper umbrella, were required to buy shares in the company, and the higher the shares went, the more they earned. Not surprisingly, they shook off the stodgy, and safe, approaches of the past and plunged into a series of investments that included real estate ventures in England and California, and financial services companies in Britain, Hong Kong, Switzerland, and the United States.

Royal ventured into mutual funds, credit cards, an estate agency, control of Pacific First Financial Corporation in Seattle, and substantial loans to Olympia & York's collapsing empire, in both London and Toronto. For a time, share prices soared, and the business press echoed the praises of the shrewd and hard-headed management style that was leading the somnolent old trust company into snappier investments. The complexities of the transactions managed to keep shareholders—and, apparently, the OSFI—from discovering that anything was going amiss until late 1992. So far as the general public knew, Royal was the nation's second-largest trust company, with $27.1 billion in assets, and a solid reputation. The OSFI issued a guarded statement complaining that the managers of trust companies were showing more loyalty to their controlling shareholders than to the institutions for which they were responsible, but neither Royal, nor any other company, was named.[45]

Then, abruptly, the sour real estate loans and other foreign gambles, which had begun to go awry in 1989, had to be written off, and Royal Trustco admitted losses of $943 million between July 1992 and March 1993.[46] In December 1992, Michael Cornelissen, who had been running the trust company for Hees–Edper, departed abruptly—with full salary and pension until 1998, along with consulting fees and "certain additional annual payments thereafter."[47] Pacific First Financial was unloaded, a number of other bad debts were written off, and in March 1993, the Royal Bank stepped in with an offer of $1.6 billion for Royal Trustco, taking out the Hees–Edper group and all other shareholders.[48]

Between that time and the closing of the deal on September 3, there were a spate of newspaper articles wondering about the wisdom of the process, but there was no public criticism from the OSFI, no attempt to find out what had gone so disastrously wrong, and no reference whatever to the Mulroney government's pledge to keep one large financial institution from swallowing another. The general tenor of press coverage was to reflect profound relief that the Royal Bank had stepped in to rescue the trust, even if it was bound to lead to the dismissal of more than 2,000 employees.

This affair did not result in a bankruptcy, and did not, like so many other trust company collapses, lead to a raid on the coffers of the CDIC. However, it did suggest, once again, that the regulatory system is incapable of doing much but stand around wringing its hands when financial firms gamble with depositors' and investors' funds.

Deposit Insurance

Failures such as the CCB, Northland, and Standard have cost the CDIC hundreds of millions in payouts. Can it continue to support such massive bailouts and still offer the consumer protection? The solution proposed by the Canadian Bankers Association and the C.D. Howe Institute was to adjust the cost of deposit insurance, now paid for by a small charge against each deposit, by "co-insurance,"[49] a euphemism for making the insurance deductible. Only 80 per cent of the money would be insured; the depositor would bite the bullet for the first 20 per cent (just as the car-owner pays the first $500, or whatever, on deductible collision insurance). That is enough of an incentive, the banks argued, to ensure that prudent investors would look out for their interests more sharply than they do under a system where it literally doesn't matter if the lending institution to which they have entrusted their funds spends it foolishly.

The difficulty is that, the day after such a change was made, money would begin to flow out of the trust companies, credit unions, and small banks into the vaults of the Big Five. They aren't going to founder, because the government can't afford to let that happen. So, why would people gamble with 20 per cent of their savings when all they have to do is deposit it all with a big bank?

This is not so much a scheme to save deposit insurance as one to wipe out the last shreds of competition. And it is based on a false premise. In case after case, we have seen that the public hasn't the foggiest notion what goes on inside our financial institutions. As a *Toronto Star* editorial put it: "How can the C.D. Howe Institute tell ordinary depositors that they should be able to smell trouble brewing when it says that the expert regulators who get paid to monitor financial institutions 'have consistently failed'?"[50]

The regulators don't know, until it is too late, and, even when they do know, they can't tell the rest of us. And why not? Because it would cause a run on the institution involved. There's a Catch-22 for you.

It would be irresponsible to change the deposit insurance and allow hundreds of thousands of old-age pensioners, and other depositors, to be wiped out because they weren't shrewd enough to realize what only a handful of people can possibly know about the operations of any given institution. Cooking the books has become an honoured profession; a reasonable person cannot possibly keep up with the wily numbers-crunchers. Remove the deposit insurance, or even co-insure it, and you will only ensure that the smallest rumour will start a run on any bank or trust company, no matter how well run.

A step in that direction was, in fact, taken by the CDIC in 1993, without any formal decision. Prenor Trust, yet another company that got blind-sided by an ambitious loans policy in a declining real estate market, failed in January 1994, and was taken over by the CDIC. In June 1993, the board of directors of the CDIC had issued an order that, in such cases, no interest would be paid on deposits after the takeover. This meant that 80,000 depositors, with $879.5 million on deposit with Prenor, lost their interest for at least the two months it took to return them their capital. People with Registered Retirement Savings Plans in Prenor (or any other failed trust company) also lose. That is because the CDIC liquidates the RRSP certificates by selling them to a bank, which transfers them into a daily interest account. My wife had about $7,000 in a Prenor RRSP which went from earning 11.25 per cent to earning 0.25 per cent. She could not have cashed it, because it was in a five-year Guaranteed Investment Certificate and had another two years to run. She eventually reinvested it at 5 per cent; her contribution to Prenor's demise was several hundred dollars, despite the ads that tell us we are "fully insured" by the CDIC.

In short, we had already adopted a form of co-insurance, without ever having formally decided to do so. Tom Delaney, the nation's top expert on RRSPs, argues that "the bankers' lobby appeared to wield such power that the CDIC board effectively changed the law without Parliament's consent."[51]

A New Mandate for the OSFI

In the late 1980s, the public was increasingly angry at the Ottawa authorities as case after case of insolvency, defalcation, deceit, or default came to light. From 1989 to the end of 1994, we lost fifteen banks, seventeen trust and loan companies, thirty-three life insurance firms, and seventy-four property and casualty insurance firms.[52] In most cases, the failing firm was merged with a former competitor; in every one of the bank cases, there was a cost to the public, and Jean Chrétien's Liberal government, when it took office in November 1993, promised reform.

What the administration delivered is a change; whether it is real reform remains to be seen. In June 1996, a new law, Bill C-15, "An Act to Amend, Enact and Repeal Certain Laws Relating to Financial Institutions," was proclaimed.

It contained two key provisions that touch our discussion here. The first was a series of regulations allowing the OSFI to step into a wayward institution earlier in the proceedings.[53] The OSFI had always taken the position that it could act only once one of its charges was actually insolvent. It was required to "regulate and supervise" them; it was also responsible for the "maintenance of public confidence in the Canadian financial system."[54] Surely that implies the duty both to bring institutions to heel as soon as they begin to stray and to tell the public what it is doing and why. That was not the view the bureaucrats took, so the new law made it clear that the superintendent of financial institutions has the right to step in as soon as he has reason to believe something is going wrong. The exact terms of this new oversight role have not been spelled out as I write this; they will be contained in the regulations accompanying the bill. One thing is clear, and that is that the OSFI will not have the right to remove the chief executive officer of a wayward firm, or any of the directors, although it will be able to veto the appointment of a new director or senior executive to a troubled financial institution.[55]

The Mind Boggles

The other provision was to change the system of deposit insurance. To give the Liberals credit, the idea of co-insurance was dropped, despite the fact that it was supported by both the banks and the CDIC. The Liberal caucus, and in particular the Ontario caucus of the Liberal caucus, rebelled, I am told, at this self-serving proposal. In its place we are to have a system of "risk-based" premiums charged to all deposit-taking institutions to finance the CDIC. That is, if one financial institution seems to be getting into trouble, the OSFI will put the directors on notice that the company is now getting wobbly, and will therefore have to pay higher premiums for CDIC coverage.* Under the new system, there are to be five levels of premium, a base rate, plus four step-up rates, depending on how serious the problem seems to be (the exact rates are as yet undisclosed).

Now, here is the surprise. The public is not to be told when a bank gets into trouble. It may be headed for disaster; the bank shares you hold may be increasingly worthless. (And, most of us do hold some, indirectly, since almost every pension plan in the nation has bank shares as part of its portfolio.) But you will have no advance warning, although those on the inside do.

The argument was put, in a rather rambling way, by the newly appointed superintendent of financial institutions, John Palmer, before the Standing Committee on Finance, when the bill was working its way through Parliament in August 1995:

> If we lifted the veil of secrecy and we announced publicly, for example, that we had marked institution X down to a category 2 institution, and we've got four categories of troubled institutions. So this is a category where there are some serious concerns, but the institution has a good chance of working itself back to financial health ... If we were to announce that publicly, then what's likely to happen? The public knows the OSFI is concerned. The most sophisticated depositors will rush for the exits ... the less sophisticated depositors won't understand the significance.
>
> In any case, the amount of institution money pouring out of the institution, given its relatively low level of capital, will be enough to sink it.
>
> Who's left holding the bag? It is the least sophisticated and the longer-term depositors, and their losses may well be a lot larger than would be the case if we were allowed to work with the institution quietly to encourage it and its management to work it back to health.[56]

---

* Up until 1992, the premium was 0.1 per cent of deposits, but the corporation lost $861 million that year, so, in 1993, it was raised to 0.125 per cent.

This is the Leigh-Pemberton argument, the co-insurance argument. Don't let the yokels know what is going on, or they will panic the first time a bank gets into trouble. In fact, it is an argument for dismissing the whole idea of risk-based premiums out of hand, because what is obviously going to happen is that depositors and shareholders alike will flock to the Big Five the instant there is any rumour of trouble anywhere, and competition for the oligopoly will become fainter than ever.

There is another problem. Banks issue shares, and float debentures, and are required to file a prospectus every time they go to the market. The fact that a bank has been put on notice by the OSFI, and charged higher premiums by the CDIC, would seem to be vital information for any prospective purchaser of that institution's instruments. Will these people be told that the bank they are putting their money into has been downgraded?

Doug Peters told me he didn't know. "In the United States, where they have a similar system now, the banks are expressly forbidden from revealing this information," he said. "It's part of the regulations."[57] However, he didn't know what position the CDIC, which will actually administer the scheme, will take when it draws up its regulations for Canada.

The essential problem in every one of the cases cited in this chapter is that the regulator did not have enough staff, or enough knowledge, to move in on the wavering institution before it was too late. This problem has simply been ignored in the new legislation. The OSFI is given some new powers to intervene, but no new personnel to do thorough inspections. Apparently, we cannot afford the staff it would require to keep on top of things; we can afford only a billion dollars or so for the bailouts, when they come.

Given an impossible mandate, John Palmer, the new superintendent, has come up with a new approach to regulating the financial institutions of this country, which I guess you could call tough love. He told Gord McIntosh of Canadian Press:

> The fate of the financial institution is the responsibility of the management and the board of directors ...
>
> Our primary objective is to minimize losses. If we can do it by encouraging the institution to steer itself out of trouble, terrific. But if we have to put it down to minimize losses, we'll do that.[58]

The difficulty is that it is the Canadian taxpayer who will take the knock. While no one can blame Palmer for not wanting to tackle a job for which he has neither the resources nor the inclination, the end result is bound to be a smaller band of larger companies, and when one of them gets into trouble, there will be no question of letting it sink. It will be absorbed into the maws of rivals, and the cost transferred to the public purse.

Let us suppose that one of the Big Five stubs its toe in derivatives. Do you suppose the OSFI, the CDIC, or the federal cabinet will stand aside? Not a chance.

What we have achieved is a state of mind that says that real regulation is not possible. If our financial institutions want to run amok, too bad; we don't have the will to control them, and we don't believe they should be controlled, anyway. As Palmer put it to a combined meeting of the Canadian and Empire Clubs in Toronto, the "death of companies and the birth of new ones is normal and fundamental to the economic system."[59]

The death of a corner store, maybe. The death of a multibillion-dollar bank, no. It is not fundamental to a sound economic system to let financial institutions play with depositors' money, and then pay another institution hundreds of millions of dollars out of the public purse to take them over when they collapse. Nor is it fundamental to a sound economic system to nurture financial institutions whose policies seem curiously indifferent to the damage being inflicted on the range of businesses which they are supposed to serve.

In Part Four, we will see that indifference as it affects ordinary Canadians.

PART FOUR

A Consumer's Perspective

As long as Canadian financial institutions hinder the progress of Canadian businesses rather than lend them what they need to survive, we will continue to face hard times.

—Susan Bellan,
Small Business and the Big Banks, 1995

CHAPTER 10

Giving the Business to Small Business

Providing services that make our customers' lives easier is how we do business with millions of Canadians. One customer at a time.

—Royal Bank advertisement, October 1995

While Canada's branch banking system is efficient in aggregate terms, representatives of all the major banks admitted to failings in their relationship with their small business clientele, blaming their own large size, failure to communicate appetite for risk and, perhaps most important, their high level of account manager turnover.

—*Report of the Standing Committee on Industry*, October 1994

DUNCAN PHYPER IS MADDER than hell. Once the owner of a booming car-leasing operation in Calgary, he now lives in very modest retirement in Vancouver, working on a book he hopes to write about the Canadian banking system, based on his own financial dealings with the Bank of Nova Scotia. It is a tangled tale, highlights of which I have reconstructed, in the main, from the findings of the trial judge who heard the original case.[1]

In 1981, Phyper was persuaded to move the business of his automotive company, Dunphy Leasing Enterprises Ltd., from the Toronto-Dominion to Scotiabank by an offer of better terms on his financing for a line of credit and other benefits.

That was just in time to catch the fallout from a recession that made the bank nervous about its deal with Phyper, among others.

In March 1982, head office decided to quash the loan agreement, against the advice of the branch manager in Calgary, who wrote that "we consider the value of the leases and automotive security to hold loans safe."

Phyper had no written notice that the rug was about to be pulled out from under him; nor that the bank, in the words of the judge who later heard the case, "ignored the conditions in the loan agreement ... and unilaterally ... amended the loan agreement." The background to this decision was that there had been some problems with this loan from the bank's point of view, which included a claim that Phyper was not giving the bank required financial details, and that the loan did not conform with the bank's Automotive Finance Manual requirements, the contents of which were unknown to him. The line of credit was originally for $5 million, but the loan eventually ballooned to $6.2 million. Then head office ordered the branch to begin transferring money from the account of Dunphy Leasing, Phyper's company, to pay interest on, and reduce the principal on the loan. Between March and June, the bank took $1.048 million this way and applied it to principal alone, although "no written communication was provided to Dunphy Leasing by the Bank advising that there was to be yet another departure from the provisions of the loan agreement."

The effect was to put Phyper into an untenable financial position; he became delinquent in his payments. The bank then gave him twenty hours to repay the entire amount, and, when he couldn't, declared the loan in default. Receivers were sent in and they immediately began to liquidate the assets of Dunphy Leasing and one of its subsidiary companies. He was out of business.

As usual in receiverships so hastily imposed, the money raised from the sale of assets did not cover the entire amount owing, so the bank sued for the shortage between the money it had advanced and what it felt it was owed.

Phyper sued the bank back for damages, including damages for trespass and the conversion of the assets of his business.

On March 26, 1990, after eight years of legal process, and a trial that lasted sixty-three days, Mr. Justice Power of the Court of Queen's Bench in

Calgary delivered a judgement harshly critical of the bank personnel, for "mismanagement and incompetence," as well as their failure to communicate with Phyper, or give him any reasonable notice of the actions the bank was about to take. The court awarded Phyper $1,095,456 for compensatory damages, and $100,000 for "the trespass to and conversion of [the company's] principal assets." The judge also concluded that the bank had improperly calculated the interest involved.

The bank then appealed, and, on November 25, 1991, the Alberta Court of Appeal ordered the whole business to be tried again, from scratch. The reasons given were mainly that the trial judge had not made it clear in his judgement whether Dunphy was put out of business by the bank, or whether he was already in such trouble that he would have gone under anyway, and that the trial judge had made contradictory findings of fact. Even though the appeal court found that some of the bank's arguments were flawed, this issue of exactly how much blame lay on each side deserved another trial. Suppose Phyper was headed for the high jump anyway? The trial judge didn't say he was, but he didn't say he wasn't, either. Didn't that make the bank's actions less damaging? These are interesting legal matters, if you happen to be wrapped in ermine and sitting on an appeal court bench, rather than out on the sidewalk wondering where all your money went, so the appeal court thought it worthwhile to crank up the machine once more, and hold the whole trial again, although Madame Justice Fraser, who wrote the decision, recognized "the great cost and difficulties that this may pose for all parties."

The interest-calculation argument led to a new legal action, which the bank eventually won in a separate proceeding that went to the Supreme Court of Canada. Its method of calculating interest was accepted by the court.

That was in 1994. So, after twelve years, Phyper was back at the beginning, still out of business, but now out hundreds of thousands of dollars in legal fees as well. And another trial was looming ahead. By 1995, he had run out of money to pursue his action against Scotiabank.

When Phyper came to me and asked me to write a book about his problems, I said no, and he accused me of being "afraid of banks." I said I wasn't afraid, just prudent. And poor.

The other difficulty, alas, is that his situation is not unusual enough to make a book. I won't say that it is commonplace, but it is hardly rare for a bank to inflict damage on the small and medium-sized business community it is supposed to succour. When I raised this point with Doug Peters, who was a banker for thirty-seven years, he told me:

> You know, I suppose out of every hundred cases (where a business borrower complains about the banks) there is probably, I don't know, 25 to 30 per cent of them where the business man is really wrong; maybe 10 to 20 per cent of them where the bank's wrong, and the rest of them fall somewhere in between.[2]

So the banks blunder in one out of five, or, let us be generous, one out of ten of these troublesome cases, of which there are, by conservative estimate, about 10,000 per year in Canada.[3] If our financial institutions screwed up this often in their dealings with General Motors, Canada Packers, or Hollinger, Inc., they would be in serious difficulty, and they would get their act together in a hell of a hurry. And yet, it is the small and medium-sized businesses that provide more than 90 per cent of new jobs in this country.[4] While the small concerns tend to hire people as fast as they can, the large ones often fire them as fast as they can. The fact that the financial houses prefer to lend to the latter does not reflect a prejudice against earning workers; it's merely easier and more profitable to make a few huge loans than hundreds of little ones, even if the results are catastrophic for the economy as a whole. As Susan Bellan, the entrepreneur quoted in the epigraph to Part Four, notes:

> We end up with a situation where profitable banks are bursting with funds that they withhold from small business because these businesses are supposedly uncreditworthy. Yet we see society straining under the weight of persistent unemployment, spiralling welfare costs, rising taxes, declining public services, and growing public debt, much of it owed to domestic and foreign banks.[5]

166

The Bank That Couldn't Be Bothered

Andrew Bekes, an undergraduate at the University of Victoria, founded a computer company called Abaco Systems in 1986.[6] He secured a number of contracts from the government of British Columbia, and he and his wife operated the business out of their home. In 1989, he won a contract to supply computers to the government, and went to the manager of his local CIBC to get what was originally a $5,000 line of credit increased so he could finance the deal, which would require $70,000. The manager explained that Bekes would have to go to the downtown branch. The downtown branch refused the loan, even after Bekes's father, Albert, a retired developer, offered to guarantee the amount. Albert then lent the money to Bekes himself. Abaco won more contracts, so many that, in 1993, he needed $100,000 to expand to fulfil the business he had secured. Andrew Bekes went to CIBC and asked for a loan under the Small Business Loans Act, federal legislation which guarantees chartered banks up to 85 per cent of the amount of a loan to finance equipment, fixtures, and renovations. The CIBC manager said there was no need to go through all that; if Andrew could convince Albert to put up $200,000 in Guaranteed Investment Certificates, which he owned, this time the bank would expand Abaco's credit. Shortly after Albert did that, the CIBC abruptly cut the line of credit, and began to bounce cheques, even though it was still holding $200,000 in security. The explanation given was that the financial institution didn't want to have to sue the family for its funds, in case it turned out that Abaco wasn't doing as well as it appeared to be. The company was saved, but only by more cash injections from the family.

The Royal Treatment

Amy Brooks and her husband, Bob, ran a successful catering business, Millbrooks Gourmet Foods Ltd., in Calgary, sold it, and wanted to start a new business, a neighbourhood pub and restaurant called Buffalo Bob. Amy asked a branch manager of the Royal Bank, with which she had dealt for twenty-five years, for help with the financing. She was told to prepare a business plan, and to pay $1,200 in a commitment fee, of which she understood $1,000 would be repaid if the deal did not go through. She did that.

The Royal then prepared an Offer to Finance, under which the bank would advance $133,000, on conditions that were, to say the least, un-usual. The interest rate was prime plus 2.5 per cent; there was a $600 an-nual charge, even if the money was not used; the bank would advance funds in increments of $5,000, so Amy would be paying interest on money she didn't need; there was to be no banking with other institutions (this was apparently to prevent cheque-kiting, which is illegal, a provision that made Amy furious, with its implication that she would cheat); and—the biggie—security for the $133,000 loan was to be provided by personal guarantees of $180,000 from Amy's parents, David and Betty Milner (solid citizens, and long-time Royal Bank customers), $150,000 from Amy and her husband, a caveat on the title to the parents' home, a second mortgage on Amy and Bob's home, and a general security agreement against all the assets of the Milbrooks.[7] Or, to put it another way, about $1 million in guarantees to back $133,000 in credit. When Amy turned this down, the bank hung onto all but $400 of the commitment fee—Amy's understand-ing was not what appeared in the offer. She screamed bloody murder for three years, but got nowhere. A bank vice president wrote her, at one point, to say the matter had been "thoroughly investigated" and that "Our findings conclude your request for financing and subsequent concerns were dealt with reasonably and in a fair and equitable manner." Buffalo Bob turned out to be a great success, despite all.

The Loans That Wouldn't Float

Ellen Cullen, who owned a successful bookstore called Canterbury Tales in Moncton, New Brunswick, complained to a parliamentary committee that she had to deal with three different bank managers in three years, and start all over again with each. Then, when she re-invested some of her profits in computer equipment, rather than buying books, the bank pulled her loans, giving her thirty days to wrap up her business, and charging her a "monitoring fee" of $50 per week, during the shutdown, which she refused to pay. (The bank eventually relented.) She found al-ternative financing, and told the bank, "I don't want to deal with a bank that is going to treat me like this."[8]

The Case of the Vanishing Credit Line

Susan Bellan, who has been running the successful, and profitable, Frida Craft Stores on Front Street in Toronto since 1979, encountered the same problem of rotating loans officers. She began the business when she returned to Canada after a number of years abroad. On graduating from university, she went to work for two years with Canadian University Services Overseas (CUSO), in Botswana, for the national handicraft industry, and was offered a job as a consultant in London for Freedom, Rights and Independence of Developing Africa—Frida— founded by a rich and eccentric Spaniard. "I said fine, but before I took it, I spent six months travelling all across Asia on my own, to try and learn about handicrafts in different countries. It was my sabbatical."[9]

After two years in London, living in hotels and eating in restaurants, she decided that she wanted to return to Canada—"I wanted a personal life." Frida offered her a job as a consultant in Canada, but "it was a sort of nutty organization, and they forgot to pay me for six months, so there I was, living on my savings."

So, she proposed a joint venture, a new store in Canada. "I had managed to put aside $10,000 in two years, because I have to say, as a young woman, people were always insisting on paying for my dinner." The result was a Toronto store, opened in 1979, which Bellan took over, paying off the Spanish share—$100,000—out of the profits over the next six years.

As the business expanded, she went to the Toronto-Dominion Bank, just around the corner, to establish a line of credit.

"We had to mortgage our house to buy inventory, because you couldn't go to the bank to get that kind of money. And the store expanded from a cash flow of half a million dollars to almost $1.6 million. Even so, it was very difficult to get any expansion in credit. The head of small-business lending for the branch came in here and said, 'Who would buy this stuff?'"

The store was held to a credit line of $65,000, the same amount as when it was generating less than a third of the income, and Susan and Willie put up real estate as collateral to keep afloat.

"I felt I was building up the business, and they wouldn't lend me any more money. God, it's as hard to build up a business as it is to be in a period of decline, and the bank would not lend us any more."

Then, in 1991, dealing with her fourth bank bureaucrat at the Toronto-Dominion in seven years, she was horrified to discover that the bank was reluctant to provide a $25,000 "bulge" in credit the store used each year to bring in Christmas stock. The banks were retracting their commercial loans, and Frida was made one of the victims of the new policy, even though it had never missed a payment. The new manager demanded that the company bring its credit line, which had been wrestled up to $100,000, back down to $65,000, before he would even consider the request for another $25,000, without which the store would be bereft of stock during its most profitable sale period of the year. To get the necessary money, Susan and her husband sold a rural property, collected some money owed to the company through the GST program, and used an income tax rebate. When all this was done, they had met the bank's conditions. Still, the bulge loan was refused. When Susan confronted the local bank manager, he conceded that the process was a trifle heavy-handed, and authorized the $25,000. At the same time, he warned Bellan that the company's balance would have to be brought down to zero by January, when the credit line might be cut in half, or eliminated entirely—not because anything had gone amiss—a former loan of $80,000 had been paid off in full—but because "the retail sector was very risky right now."[10]

The bank also indicated that it was about to call another loan, guaranteed under the Small Business Loans Act, which had been paid down to $20,000, used to help establish a second store. In dismay and despair, Bellan called the Office of the Superintendent of Financial Institutions, the bank watchdog, in Ottawa. Surely, that office could keep the banks from running companies out of business, or what was it for? She was told that, "while we could make a formal complaint, he said his office would just turn it over to a vice-president of the bank, and then we would be in even more hot water for having contacted the authorities."

Talking about this in her basement office in Frida Craft Stores, Susan Bellan waves her arms, rolls her eyes, shrugs her shoulders, recalling the weeks and months of turmoil and tension her family went through at the hands of her friendly neighbourhood bank. The dynamic business woman is ingenious, assertive, and tough; the bank had picked on the wrong person. At one point, when she besieged the loans officer in the bank, and he went off on a break, she followed him, every step of the way. "Poor guy; I wasn't going to let him out of my sight."

"I couldn't eat, I couldn't sleep; I was going to lose my house, my business, everything." Finally, figuring that she had no alternative, she went public, and phoned a newspaper. A story appeared in the *Toronto Star* headlined, "Rich banks accused of squeezing too hard." An avalanche of telephone calls, letters, and faxes descended on the heads of the bankers and their watchdog, and first thing you knew, the TD decided it could fork out the money, after all. Frida Craft Stores is alive and well, and still making a profit, but the TD's role in this process is somewhat murky, to say the least.

However, Bellan is one of those sore winners, and she wasn't willing to leave it at that. She soon found herself wrapped up in a campaign to help other businesses battle the banks, as chair of banking issues for the Canadian Organization of Small Business. Now, she devotes the time she has left over from running a successful business and raising three children to firing off complaints to the banks, appearing on panels, and wrestling with proposals to bring some element of common sense and fairness into these issues. She has even written a book, *Small Business and the Big Banks*, full of bright ideas (we will come to some of them in Chapter 12) and cautionary tales about the banks' dealings with our native entrepreneurs. Choosing her words carefully, she notes: "The damage that was done to the Canadian economy in 1990–1993, when thousands of companies were destroyed unnecessarily, can never be put right."

The Bank Broke the Broker

Ben Skovsgaard ran a small real estate brokerage, Remax Twin City Realty Inc., in Kitchener–Waterloo, Ontario, which was struggling, in tough times for real estate, with a loan from the Toronto-Dominion Bank. On July 27, 1990, the TD sent him a letter warning that he would have to come up with $50,000 or lose his line of credit. The letter said: "In the event a cash injection is not possible, we request the company arrange alternate banking facilities before Aug. 31, 1990."[11]

So Skovsgaard scrambled around to do what was required. On July 30, he wiped out a $29,913 overdraft in the company account, and made arrangements to raise the $50,000 demanded by the bank. He had good reason not to want any trouble in the company accounts at this time; he had a group of agents lined up to buy out the brokerage. However, on August 9, three weeks before its own deadline, TD began bouncing cheques from Remax Twin City. This drove off the potential purchasers of the company, and effectively killed the looming deal. Five years later, an Ontario court ordered the bank to pay $494,000 for the damage it had inflicted on the client. The bank appealed, but lost, and paid up in November 1995.[12]

Blind-Sided by the Bank

Joe Murano, who ran a series of video stores in Kitchener, Ontario, wanted to expand by buying out another chain, and went to see the account manager—the third to handle his account—at the Bank of Montreal. He explained that he was going to close one of his stores, to free money for the proposed purchase, and move the inventory to another store. Was that all right? The manager did not refuse. The store was closed, the inventory transferred, and then, one night, a B of M employee, driving past the empty place, concluded that Murano was pulling a "midnight run." He called the bank's regional office in London, Ontario, and they sent in a team of specialists, who closed all Murano's video outlets. Claire Bernstein, the Montreal lawyer and columnist who wrote about the case, called it "a bank execution."[13] She points out, "No one on the specialist team bothered to call Murano to check out their information. That wasn't in their manual." The result was the total collapse of Murano's business. A series of comments by the bank to the effect that he was dishonest finished him. He sued, and after several years of litigation, Justice George Adams ordered the bank to pay him approximately $5.5 million.

Even so, there was no money for punitive damages to pay for the years Murano spent working in his father's pizzeria while the case worked its way through the courts, and, as Bernstein points out, "nothing to change a bank system that puts *all* its emphasis on protecting itself."

You mustn't think that all bank business customers are treated this way. As we have already seen, Olympia & York Developments was able to get into the ribs of the Canadian banks for more than $2 billion on security that turned out to be lighter than air. Similarly, Rogers Cable Systems, in need of $2 billion to take over Maclean Hunter in 1994, had no difficulty finding the funding. Of course, Rogers paid $50 million in commissions to the lending banks to help the thing along. It is remarkable how far a $50 million sweetener can go in persuading a bank to unlimber the wallet. As Bellan points out in her book, "This $2 billion the banks lent to Rogers was half of the $4 billion that they had cut in small business lending during the early 1990s."[15] No jobs were created by the Maclean Hunter takeover; the $4-billion slash-and-burn campaign the banks went through, on the other hand, resulted in the loss of hundreds of thousands of jobs.

Well, why not? The banks, as they keep telling us, are duty bound to protect the interests of the shareholders, not the poor yo-yos who try to get ahead by building small businesses from scratch and sweat. The banks can find far better things to do with their money than lending it to people like Susan Bellan, Andrew Bekes, and Amy Brooks. The difficulty they are in, though, is that, while they would rather dine with Robert Campeau than chew a sandwich in the basement of Frida Craft Stores while discussing loan terms, they don't want anyone else horning in on their territory. They hate it when MPs suggest, as Jim Peterson, chair of the House of Commons Finance Committee, did to me, that, "if the banks don't want to lend to a small business, I don't think we can make them. Perhaps we ought to have some other way of looking after these people."[16]

A Four-Pronged Defence

Under almost constant attack over the past five years for the poor job they do financing small and medium-sized business, the banks have responded with a four-pronged defence that owes far more to public-relations bafflegab than to fact, but it has worked brilliantly.

First, they flatly denied that they do a bad job; the complaints, they aver, are those of a disgruntled few, and based solely on "anecdotal evidence." That is, stories of people who have actually been clobbered, rather than reassuring statistics, or "hard facts." When case after case was unrolled against them, they retreated to a previously prepared position, which is that nobody's perfect, but we have the best banking system in the world, so don't mess with it.

Second, when a suggestion was made to monitor the banks' treatment of their business customers, they outwitted consumers. In 1994, Democracy Watch, a small, but active, Ottawa lobby, came up with a bright idea. There ought to be an ombudsman to represent ordinary Canadians who come up against the banks, said Duff Connacher, the feisty young Ottawa coordinator of Democracy Watch. Connacher, a long, blond, young man who looks as if he might play the sheriff in a western, served an internship with Ralph Nader, the American consumer advocate whose very name strikes chill in corporate boardrooms across the United States, and he has borrowed a few ideas from Nader. One was to have a neutral referee, financed by government, or by the corporations themselves, to help consumers—thus, a federal bank ombudsman, such as exists in other countries. This made such eminent sense that the House of Commons Standing Committee on Industry embraced the notion in its October 1994 report in straightforward language:

> The Committee recommends that the government establish an independent office of the Bank Ombudsman to investigate complaints of breach of duty or maladministration by the banks. As in the United Kingdom, the ombudsman should have the power to require banks to pay compensation to complainants for financial loss, inconvenience and stress.[17]

The banks recoiled in horror, and sent their army of lobbyists into action. In due course, what resulted is a system which would be comic, if it weren't so serious. First, the major banks established internal ombudsmen to deal with complaints from small business. One of those who tried to use this system told me that he called up the relevant number at his bank to complain about the way his credit line was handled, and was told, "If you don't like it, sue us." So, that didn't seem to be the answer. After more pushing and shoving, the major banks themselves established a federal ombudsman for small business in June 1996. His name is Michael Lauber, and he is an accountant. The way it works is this; if you are a small-business person and you think you have been wronged by your bank, you phone the bank and ask for the ombudsman. When you are told to get lost, you telephone Lauber's office in North York, and you get an automatic telephone machine, answering in the name of "The Canadian Banking Ombudsman, Incorporated."

It gives you a good deal of information about the ombudsman's office, and, if you push enough numbers, reminds you sternly that "the ombudsman's office requires that all complaints be first referred to the bank," adding that "most of the major banks have an ombudsman to deal with small business."* If you are still not satisfied, and want more information, the voice tells you, in the language of your choice, to press more numbers, and you get switched to another machine, which tells you that there is no one available to take your call, but offers to take a message, which can be up to three minutes long. With sufficient perseverance, however, you can reach a person, who will have nothing to do with you until you can prove that you tried the bank's ombudsman, and are not satisfied with "either the procedures or the result."[18]

So, only when you have been brushed off by the individual bank's ombudsman will Lauber's office agree to look into the case. And, here is the catch: while this office has the power to review complaints and make recommendations to the banks, none of its findings is binding on them.[19]

It is impossible to overpraise the slick way the banks have gone about this process. The roar of business dissatisfaction has been turned into the murmur of a series of reports to Parliament, which will list the number of complaints made, the banks involved, how many complaints were resolved to the customer's satisfaction, and how long it took to achieve a resolution. It is better than nothing, but it is a country mile from the original proposal. The ombudsman was to have been established by the government; instead, he was established by the banks, and is a private corporation. He was to have been independent; instead, he is, in Duff Connacher's words, "funded by the banks."[20] He was to have the power to enforce his findings; he has no such power. What he can do is to issue reports full of numbers, and hope for the best.

The ombudsman does not, of course, accept this characterization, and his office put out a press release on May 6, 1996, to say that "the Canadian Banking Ombudsman is not an employee of the banking industry. He will report to an eight-person, independent, board of directors." What the press release does not say is that five of these directors are bankers. He is not paid by the banks, but his office is funded by

---

* There are eight banks now in the system, including the Big Five, the National, Hongkong Bank of Canada, and Citibank.

them. Obviously, there is some disagreement about what constitutes independence.

Third, the banks, when they were ordered to collect the statistics that would reveal what they are doing for, or to, Canadian small and medium-sized business, fought a rearguard action worthy of the Russians' fallback on Moscow during the Second World War. They argued that releasing figures on how much they lent, and to whom, and whom they refused, and on what grounds, would amount to giving away trade secrets. The Standing Committee on Industry, attempting to penetrate the fog, collected the numbers provided by the Bank of Canada, which came from the chartered banks, and showed that, in the period from 1989 to 1993, there was "no evidence of a significant decline in lending on a year over year basis."[21] However, when they went over the figures of the Office of the Superintendent of Financial Institutions (OSFI), which included a great many statistics not reported to the Bank of Canada, including commercial mortgages, they found "a substantial decline in loans outstanding over the past two or three years," in a number of business sectors.[22] If we spread the net a little, the decline in business lending becomes clear, even in the Bank of Canada numbers. In the decade between 1983 and 1992, total commercial loans, as defined by the Bank of Canada, increased by 50 per cent. At the same time, business loans under $200,000, measured in constant dollars, dropped 30 per cent.[23] The banks, having wiped out most of their competition, now account for nine out of every ten dollars lent to the small-business sector,[24] and the effects of their withdrawal have been devastating. They are knee-capping the one area of the economy that creates jobs, and replying to any criticism that it is off the mark.

The committee concluded that the banks were being less than frank:

> While the Committee understands that we have been in a recession, during which the call on credit would naturally go down, we believe that the actions of the banks have exacerbated the situation. Evidence gathered informally, as well as in the letters and testimony received, strongly suggests that banks called in credit in order to get their houses in order. The banks allege that the evidence of small and medium-sized business borrowers is "anecdotal", by which they suggest it may be unreliable or inaccurate because confidentiality restricts their

ability to respond. We do not agree. It is not credible that so many small and medium-sized business borrowers would imagine a false situation.[25]

The obvious answer was for the banks to come clean on the numbers, but they hemmed and hawed and said that they didn't have them, and, if they did, it would cost them too much to produce them.[26] The committee, politely but firmly, dismissed this excuse. Every bank branch, as you would expect, is required to keep regular track of its loans; to whom they are made, how many, how much, and the kind and size of business served. Perhaps, the committee suggested, the way out would be to set up quotas, as suggested by a number of witnesses, and require the banks to meet them.

The banks then agreed to release some statistics, but only when they could release them together. The solidarity was short-lived; some of the banks began to feed out their own numbers, in self-protection. In the end, they agreed to provide a set of numbers which can be monitored by the committee.

However, what the banks have grudgingly condescended to provide is a long way from what is required. They are to produce what is called "Performance Benchmarks for Small Business Financing by Banks,"[27] which will be based, mainly, on surveys. That is, the banks will sample their customers, using professional polling systems, to produce annual estimates on such matters as "Approval Rates" (sorted by the gender of the owner, sales level, number of employees, the age of business, and industry sector).[28] What they will not provide is a full breakdown of their lending practices.

As Democracy Watch's Duff Connacher points out, "What is needed is the hard numbers, not samples. We need to know who is being turned down, and why. We need to know how many new entrepreneurs are being refused financing, and there is nothing here on that. They will only survey established firms."

In the United States, Connacher notes,

> there are more than 8,000 banks, and they are required to produce hard numbers on their loans broken down by race, economic level and postal code. If you have the postal code,

you know whether one sector of the population is being discriminated against. There is nothing of that here. If the
Americans can do it effectively with 8,000 banks, why can't
we do it with six?

Moreover, the numbers the banks will provide are not broken down
over $1 million. That is, the banks will provide breakdowns of loans up
to $25,000; between $25,000 and $49,999, $50,000 and $99,999,
$100,000 and $499,999, $500,000 and $1,000,000; and "over $1 mil-
lion."[29] The huge middle ground, where the action is, is entirely missing. A $2-billion loan to a giant multinational and a $1.5-million loan
to an emerging Canadian firm will be lumped together.

"The committee meant well," Connacher says with a sigh. "They
just were not very smart."

The fourth and final defence the banks threw up was to go on the
offensive with a series of articles and interviews deploring the "bank
bashing" indulged in by unenlightened folks who either have just been
dumped into bankruptcy by their friendly neighbourhood institution or
know somebody who has. Bank bashing, as *Canadian Banker Magazine*
makes clear in an endless chorus, is based on a misunderstanding of the
wonderful job the banks are doing.

At the same time, most of the chartered banks began to pour out
those wonderful ads featuring Canadian business persons smiling and
carolling the glories of the banking system which has done so much for
them. Some of the cases are real, but most of the ads feature models describing events that have about as much connection with reality as
Tinkerbell. Clap like mad, and your bankbook will balance. They are
all, by the way, anecdotal, which is apparently a sound and solid approach when the stories are used to boost the banks, and only suspect
when they are being knocked.

Going the other way, as it often does, the Bank of Montreal
brought out a series of ads that had the other bankers somewhat irri-
tated, to put it mildly, and which was designed to show the real face of
banking. It used grainy pictures, taken with hand-held cameras, featuring ordinary Canadians holding hand-lettered placards that read, "Are
we going to be O.K.?" "Will I ever own my own home?" "Can I ever
retire?" There is even one showing a bike courier riding around with a

sign that says, "Banks only help the rich." You may pause to wonder why a bike courier would ride around carrying such a sign, a danger to traffic. He's only doing that because the bank asked him to, for the ad. The idea is to answer the ad campaign's underlying question, "Can a bank change?" with the warm and fuzzy feeling that, by golly, at least the Bank of Montreal can change. Here is a bank that understands what life is like when you don't know how you are going to meet your payroll, or your mortgage. (*Frank* magazine, lacking a respectful approach, brought out its own version, a young woman standing under a Bank of Montreal logo and holding a hand-lettered sign that read, "Hell, We Don't Even MAKE Change.")

The campaign, aimed at twenty-five- to forty-nine-year-old Canadians, those most likely to accumulate big debt, was considered to be a brilliant success. According to *Report on Business* magazine, "Change at the bank has been largely positive. In fiscal 1995, it reported record profits of $986 million, up nearly 20% from 1994. There was some unhappiness in one unit, where bonuses were 20% lower than expected. Overall ranks were shaved by more than 1,400 people. [Bank chairman Matthew] Barrett took home $2.5 million."[30]

Or, to put it another way, the bank didn't change anything except its image, the boss got a raise, and a few hundred bank employees got thinned out onto the unemployment rolls. Some observers seemed to think there was something a bit dodgy about the new ads. Geoff D'Eon, the producer of the television comedy "This Hour Has 22 Minutes" told *Report on Business* that his crew decided to do a spoof of the campaign because "we looked at it and went, 'My God!' Stylistically, it's catchy. But its content is Orwellian. It's saying something that is manifestly untrue, but it's saying it with such a puffed-up sense of truth, it's scary."

Clearly, the man lacks an understanding of the bank business, let alone the ad business. The idea is not to change the bank so that it will end up on the side of bike couriers who roll around with rude signs; the idea is to give the *impression* that the bank is concerned. Quite a different matter. In the meantime, perhaps you will shift your account, or your company, over to the good old B of M.

The Banks Can Be Reformed

At the end of the day, a swelling chorus of outrage against the banks, which might well have led to direct and serious action against them, resulted instead, by virtue of the banks' four-step campaign, in little consumer protection. Still, the fact remained that, under sufficient pressure, the financial houses could be induced to disgorge more information, could be put on the defensive, could even be persuaded to admit that not all was well in their relationships with small and medium-sized businesses in this country. The banks adopted a code of ethics, which is vague, but a start. Several of them earmarked special funds for lending to small business, although a number of business people I have spoken to tell me it is still just as hard as it ever was, or harder, to get money on the basis of knowledge or technical expertise.

Clawing and screaming, the banks have been chivvied into the beginnings of reform, and there is some leverage, in the changes already made, to press for more. The good news is that banks can be bullied into providing better service; the bad news is that they have to be.

I cannot leave this subject without relating one of those unreliable personal anecdotes of my own that the banks find so regrettable. My wife and I own a small company, and the company shares—both of them—are going for a dollar each, which is what they went for in 1977, so we figure we are ahead of Robert Campeau, if slightly behind Conrad Black. We think of ourselves as small-business persons, the backbone of the nation, and the pal of the banks, according to their ads.

Not long ago, my wife put $500 into the company bank account, in cash. And not long after that, we got our monthly statement from the bank, with a little notation informing us that we had been nicked $1.10 by that mighty institution to count the cash, which my wife had already done, several times. We were also nailed 75 cents for making the deposit. The rate to count cash by the Bank of Nova Scotia, for a small business, is $2.20 per $1,000, or $1.10 per $500. And no, they wouldn't pay *me* to count it when I took it back out again, a week later.

If I had deposited the money in coin, it would have cost us $2.00 per $100, assuming that we had already sorted, bundled, and, yes, counted, the coins beforehand. I suppose if we had put in a million dollars or so, we might have worked out a volume discount.

I bring this to your attention just to let you know that the banking sector is still actively seeking out small business.

And if they catch us, they're going to kill us.

CHAPTER 11

Service with a Snarl

When I go into a bank, I get rattled.

—Stephen Leacock,
My Financial Career, 1910

We are being nickeled and dimed to death, only it's not nickels
and dimes any more, but fifty cents and a dollar or two dollars.

—Wendy Armstrong,
Consumers' Association of Canada, 1995

IN MARCH 1993, Arlene Murrell of Pickering, Ontario, opened a bank account for her daughter Allison at the Canadian Imperial Bank of
Commerce. She put $53 dollars into the account, the sum of a number of
presents given in cash to celebrate the child's first birthday. Murrell
thought it would be nice for her to have this little nest-egg coddling in
the bank; it would show her daughter that a penny saved is a penny
earned. In February 1995, nearly two years later, someone from the bank
branch telephoned to say that the account was dormant, and if something was not done right away, the CIBC would be forced to extract $20
from it. When Murrell went charging down to the branch, bankbook in
hand, she discovered that the account had already dwindled to $30.65,
because, in April 1994, the bank had begun to levy a 95-cent-a-month
service charge against it because it wasn't being used.[1] Actually, she was
getting a bargain; most banks hit you $1 a month. If you use an account,

they charge you for whatever you did; if you don't, they charge you for not laying yourself open to any of the other charges. Allison was earning 0.25 per cent on the daily interest savings account, which works out to 13.25 cents a year on her birthday savings, or just over a penny a month, against 95 cents a month in charges for not doing anything. Arlene Murrell protested to the bank, and "they justified it by saying that they sent mail to all their customers stating that there would be a change in service charges on certain accounts."[2] She recalled vaguely having received such a notice, but who can make sense of these things? When Murrell went to the *Toronto Star* with her story, the bank said it was all one of those gosh-darned mistakes. The bank has accounts for those under nineteen, on which there are no service charges; Arlene should have had her money in one of these. Or, the girl could have come up with $1,000, because the bank doesn't charge on accounts above that level (and why should it? It is getting the money for a risible amount of interest, and then lending it out, multiplied many-fold, for anywhere from twelve to sixty-four times what it is paying in interest).

Murrell said, "Well, one day she will have $1,000, but the CIBC won't see it. Not in a hundred years."[3]

Some of our ancestors, a suspicious lot, used to keep their spare cash in a sock, and we mocked them, but at least no one can extract 95 cents a month from a sock. What we used to call "saving," that is, putting money away and letting it accumulate, should now be called "dwindling." If you deposited $300 into a bank at today's interest rate of 0.25 per cent, at the end of twenty-eight years, it would have been gobbled entirely, even if the bank didn't get sore at you in the meantime and snatch it from you.[4]

I found myself nobbled by exactly the same arrangement when the CIBC began extracting the same 95 cents from what I thought was a savings account. The teller told me, when I caught up to it, that I had been sent a notice to inform me of the coming change, but when I said I bloody well had not been sent any notice, she put the money back. Then I closed the account.*

---

* Just about a year later, to show you how efficient the CIBC is, I got a letter from the bank's president, Holger Kluge, offering me a cut-rate deal on insurance, as "our way of saying thank you for banking with us."

You have to assume, whether you are a four-year-old girl of no experience, or a rather older and ruder man, that the bank is going to have you, unless you are on your toes every minute of the time. If you don't read, or cannot understand, the gibberish they send you by way of notification, too bad. If you chose the wrong type of account among the myriad options now offered, and which the tellers themselves often do not understand, too bad. I had my money in what is called a Menu Account, but in fact I should have had it in a "CIBC Advantage Account, available upon request for customers 60 & over," but I turned this one down because the CIBC booklet *Personal Banking: Service fees and how to reduce them: Straight Answers* said, "CIBC Advantage Plan 60 benefits not available on Chequing Savings, Personal Chequing, CIBC Investor Rate Account, U.S. Dollar Daily Interest or CIBC Key Accounts." Though the booklet offered few straight answers, it looked to me, and to the woman who helped me make my choice, that I would do better in a Menu Account, which, when I began the process, did not have the 95-cent-a-month levy on it. The smart thing for me to do, when I got the notice which the bank thought it had sent to me, but which I never received, would have been to switch accounts, instantly.

If you assume that banks are going to gouge you at every possible opportunity, you will be better equipped to deal with them than if you think they are on your side.

More Horror Stories

These "I was robbed" stories blossom from time to time, and embarrass the banks, but not enough to make them really change their ways. *Economic Reform*, the newsletter of the Committee on Monetary and Economic Reform (and which was renamed *ER* in 1996), received a draft worth $35 (U.S.), drawn on an Italian bank, and took it to their own financial institution, which said, Forget it; the conversion charge would be just about the same as the face value of the bank draft, even though the sender had already paid a fee. The free flow of money you keep hearing about in the new global economy belongs to the affluent. The rest of us are paying more and more for "one-stop financial services for the convenience of the bank's customers."[5]

184

In 1988, there was a spate of complaints after the House of Commons Standing Committee on Finance brought forward tales of a bank's charging a customer $2 to change a $20 bill into quarters. A United Church minister complained that the church's account had been eroded from $35 down to $26 by service charges.[6] The finance committee at the time was headed by a Tory maverick, Don Blenkarn, who hauled a number of bank presidents down to Ottawa and gave them hell. The committee even proposed to regulate bank fees, although they weren't serious. The executives were suitably, and temporarily, abashed (Matthew Barrett of the Bank of Montreal told the committee, "There is the impression that prices are changed too frequently and without sufficient prior notice")[7] but their explanations were, to put it mildly, curious. The argument of the Canadian Bankers Association was that the banks had invented a whole flotilla of new charges to bring about a "user pay" system, in which customers would actually pay for the services they used, in place of a collective system, which, they argued, meant that large depositors were subsidizing the rest. They called the new system of charging a specific fee for a specific task "unbundling." Then a parade of bankers told the finance committee that they had no idea what it cost to provide any single service. Robert MacIntosh, the CBA spokesman, testified, "I would say there is no such thing as a cost for anything you have sold."[8] What he meant was that any bank could work out only the global costs of operating its services; it could not single out any one task, such as cashing a cheque, and say what that cost. There went the argument that "unbundling" made sense.

Under pressure, the banks promised to reform, and, indeed, began to provide more and more timely information about their charges. They even froze the level of service charges for three years. They also produced a bewildering number of new accounts, such as the Royal's "Leo's Young Savers Account," and "Sixty-Plus," which allow the age-deprived, and age-challenged, to escape service fees entirely, if they can figure the damn things out (see below), although how that squares with a "user pay" concept, God only knows.

As soon as the issue faded from public memory, they were back at it, hiking fees, inventing new ones, and creaming the customer, still in the name of the user-pay thesis which their own executives had demolished in 1988. User pay is with us with a vengeance, with specific charges levied against every form of transaction in accounts that are almost impossible for the individual consumer to compare.

For example, Scotiabank has no fewer than ten different deposit accounts* for individuals. I tried to compare two of them: Scotia Powerchequing and Scotia Chequing. Powerchequing has no service fees, so long as you keep $1,000 on deposit; as soon as you drop below that, you start paying a maintenance fee of $1.00 a month, and service fees of from 45 cents for each Interac payment to 60 cents for each cheque or withdrawal. Scotia Chequing, on the other hand, has no maintenance fee, whether you have $1,000 in it, or $2, or $50,000. What it has instead is an "activity fee," of—guess what?—$1.00 a month. You have to pay $2.50 a month to get a statement on Powerchequing, but it is free on Scotia Chequing. On the other hand, no interest is paid on Scotia Chequing, while it is paid, at a rate that varies from time to time and can be changed without notice, on Powerchequing.

Which is the better deal? If you have to keep $1,000 in a bank to avoid interest charges, you are paying a cost. If you put the same $1,000 into a certificate of deposit, it would bring you, at this writing, $58.50 a year. You will get, in interest on your $1,000 in the account, $5.00 per annum, instead of $58.50. The difference is $53.50 per year, or the cost of 89 transactions at 60 cents each. Ah, but you save $12.00 in maintenance fees, or activity fees, with the $1,000 you leave in the account at low interest, so the real difference is $53.50 minus $12.00, or $41.50. If you write more than 89 cheques a year, you are better off with Powerchequing; if you write fewer, with Scotia Chequing. Well, maybe not. If you want a statement with your returned cheques, you have to pay another $2.50 a month, or $30.00 a year, on Powerchequing. Make a guess.

If you wonder why we didn't go through all these complex calculations in earlier times, the answer is that most of the services were free in earlier times.

Well, then, we can more or less compare these two of the ten Scotiabank accounts with each other, but now we want to know if we should go over to the Toronto-Dominion Bank, where there are two

---

* Scotia Value Account, Scotia Plus, Student Banking Advantage, Getting There Savings Program, Scotia Powerchequing, Scotia Chequing, Scotia Basic Banking, Scotia Gain Plan, Scotia Daily Interest, and Scotia U.S. Dollar Daily Interest.

parallel accounts, Investment Builder and Moneybuilder. The bank's pamphlet explains, under a section called "Withdrawal Fees," that the Investment Builder charges go like this:

- Self-Service Banking* 85 cents
  No-Charge Level $25,000
- Cheques, In-Branch Withdrawals $1.00
  No-Charge Level $25,000
- 2 Free Withdrawals/Cheques per statement period**
  Monthly Maintenance Fee $1.00
  No-Charge Level $250.

So, you pay a $1.00 Maintenance Fee, which is waived if you keep $250 or more in the account at all times, and you can escape all other withdrawal fees only if you have $25,000 in the account.

Both accounts pay 1.5 per cent interest, but the Moneybuilder only charges 40 cents for self-service banking transactions, instead of 85 cents, and 60 cents for in-branch transactions, instead of $1.00 and you can escape these by keeping a minimum balance of $1,000 in the account at all times instead of $25,000.

The $1.00 monthly maintenance fee is forgiven in either account if you keep $250 on deposit. Neither account returns your cheques to you, but either will provide a passbook or monthly statement for free.

On paper, it looks to me as if the Moneybuilder is a better deal because the service charge for writing a cheque is 60 cents instead of $1.00, but you get two free cheques per month on the Investment Builder, so that might be better for someone who doesn't write many cheques. On the other hand, Scotiabank charges 40 per cent less per cheque.

The Investment Builder also appears to be better than Scotiabank's

---

* This means any activity through the bank's ABM or Interac systems, or pre-authorized payments that come automatically out of your account.

** There is an explanatory note for this one that says, "You receive one free Self-Service Banking transaction/cheque/in-branch withdrawal fee per automated payroll deposit per statement period." This does not appear to be correct; when I telephoned for an explanation, I was told that the account earns two free transactions per month, and it doesn't matter if there is an automated payroll deposit.

Powerchequing, because it pays higher interest—at the moment, 1.5 per cent as opposed to 0.5 per cent. But this can be changed at any time, without notice, so I wouldn't count on that.

In short, it is almost impossible to work out which account makes the most sense for the individual consumer, unless he or she is willing to devote a huge amount of time and effort to the project. Then the problem is that the banks keep changing the rules and the accounts, with little or no notice, so you may pick out an account that seems perfect to you—as I did the CIBC Menu Account—only to discover that the bank has added new charges, which they may or may not tell you about. To make life still more complicated, accounts come and go. The Bank of Montreal's *Better Banking Guide* lists five accounts which still exist but are no longer offered. That is, if you have one, you can keep it, but no one else can get one. All of these look better, to me, than the new ones. (For example, the old Daily Interest Savings Account did not charge for cashing cheques, but the new Firstbank Savings charges 75 cents.)

About the only constant in this whole morass is that the banks will charge you whatever they think they can get away with.

Dave Smith, a businessman in Mississauga, Ontario, paid the CIBC $627.35 in service charges during 1995, then got a letter from his branch telling him that he was going to be nailed an extra $5 a month because the bank needed "to be adequately compensated for the administration and service your company is receiving."[9] Mind you, the bank wasn't going to do any more for Smith, it was just going to charge him more.

CIBC chairman Al Flood defended his institution's deposit service charges, which totalled $437 million for 1995,[10] on the grounds that the average Canadian paid only $54 a year this way, less than cable TV, telephones, or newspapers.[11] It was a bizarre comparison. Unless Flood was counting in the entertainment value of standing in line, the actual time spent delivering banking services to a customer comes to a few minutes per month, against fifty or sixty hours of service in the other media. Better to compare service charges with what it actually costs the banks to deliver the services, which they said could not be determined, or to see how the rate of increase in the charges relates to the cost of living.

The Big Five earned $1.8 billion in service charges during 1995, up 19 per cent from 1990, while the Consumer Price Index rose 11 per cent.[12] The banks are slicing off nearly double the general rise in

prices, which means either that they are gouging or that they are inefficient. And when they hike their charges, they are going to call it a price
reduction. In August 1996, Canadian Press announced that the CIBC
was bringing in a "basic 60-cent transaction fee," which, reporter
Sandra Rubin opined, "could revolutionize the way Canadian banks
charge for their services."[13]

Instead of charging you different prices for different items—so
much to make a withdrawal, so much to cash a cheque, etc.—the bank
will nail you 60 cents per dib, thus making life simpler, and, of course,
saving you money. "This benefits the customer, not the bank," a CIBC
spokesperson told Rubin.

The reverse is true. The 60-cent fee replaces fees that ranged between 45 cents and 60 cents, so the customer who saved money this
way would be doing rather well.

But then there is this incentive: "Each transaction involving a bank
machine, debit card or telephone banking will bring a 15 cent credit to
the customer's account, bringing the transaction charge down to 45
cents." These drops are called "Reward$."

Confused, I went into my local branch, and picked up the pamphlet
called *Service Fees Clear and Simple*, which says:

> Here's how it works: you receive CIBC Reward$ of 25% off your
> 60-cent fee every time you make a basic transaction using ...
>
> An Automated Banking Machine (ABM)
> Telephone Banking
> CIBC Interac Direct Payment
> Pre-authorized Debit

Or, to make a long story short, every time you do all the work yourself,
you get Reward$. Instead of paying 60 cents, you pay 45 cents for these
services. Thus, the system of Reward$ appears to be designed to get us
outside the bank, pushing buttons and hoping for the best.

The Crap Shift

The banks don't want us cluttering up the branches, and mean to charge us extra if we insist on doing it. What could be cleverer, then, than to dream up a system under which they don't actually have to see any of us, with rare exceptions (unless we are filthy rich, in which case we get a banker of our very own to wait on us), and charge us more for not serving us than they were ever able to charge us for serving us? This process, now well advanced, is developing along two fronts at once: through the charges levied against us whenever we do business with a bank, or when we just leave our account alone; and through the charges we pay to use credit cards, debit cards, smart cards, and other versions of Electronic Funds Transfer, or EFT.

The economic jargon for this is "productivity enhancement through customer participation." I prefer to call it the "Crap Shift."

Roughly, what the Crap Shift (CS) means is that the modern, lean and mean corporation depends increasingly on transferring as much work as possible onto the customer. The theory came to me when I was calling a hotel in South Dakota, long distance, which did not have an 800 number. After I was switched over to Reservations, they played "Home on the Range" in my ear twenty-seven times in a row. On my long-distance bill. To avoid this, the hotel would have had to employ enough clerical staff to answer the phones, but why should they do that when they can dump the inconvenience, and cost, back to me? That's the Crap Shift.

Other examples of CS abound. As when you get into a lineup in a department store where there are only four people in front of you, and the officer in charge of CS—every store has one—comes along and orders that cash register closed, so you can move to one with fifteen people in front of you. The oil companies did the same when they took away the person who pumped the gas and wiped the windshield, and then hiked their prices to make up for the fact that we now had dirty windshields and gas all over our pants. And the universities did it when they set students to trying to register for classes through telephone answering machines, while raising their fees.

But the process has reached its zenith, or nadir, depending on how you look at these things, within the banks, where we get less for more and then have to read the promotional copy telling us that these changes have come about because of "customer demand." Customers demanded the right to line up in front of an automatic banking machine, or ABM, instead of a warm human person? We have become so benumbed that we never dream of complaining about the things. I stood in line in a supermarket in beautiful downtown Vernon, British Columbia, one day not long ago, while a customer tried, for seven minutes, to get a bank computer to accept payment for her groceries on Interac, the EFT device that takes money straight out of your account. The cashier, who was busy inspecting her nails all this time, finally looked up and, "Gee, that's funny, another customer had the same problem." Then she called her supervisor, who put in a call to the bank, which reported that its computer was down right now, darn it, and would she care to try later? So, the customer went over to an ABM, conveniently located near the register, and took out cash. She did this standing under a sign the supermarket had erected, under the gold and black Interac logo, that said, "For your convenience! Fast! Safe! Efficient!"

The ABM, which is where the banks want us to do our banking, costs up to $80,000, when you include the Pentium computer chips required to handle all the tasks it is now called upon to perform. But it works twenty-four hours a day, unlike a teller; never takes a coffee break, bitches about the boss, threatens to go on strike, or asks for a raise. If a teller grabbed your credit card and swallowed it, you would be surprised and chagrined, but when the ABM does so, you obey its instruction to contact the listed telephone number to find out that it's just a stupid mistake, and you feel you ought not to get mad about it. After all, it's only a machine.

It costs much less to run an ABM than a teller. If the machines have become focal points for con artists, thugs, and fraudsters, well, at least they're open twenty-four hours a day. One banker I spoke to off the record told me that the real motive in pushing us out of the premises and onto the machines is higher productivity. Canadian banks believe they will be able to do with 35,000 fewer employees, once we are properly trained to forgo human contact and do our banking almost exclusively on the ABMs or at home, on computers hooked to the bank by phone. The number was reported elsewhere, in a study produced by the accounting firm Deloitte & Touche, based on interviews with bankers.[14] When I responded that the loss of 35,000 jobs would probably each cost the taxpayer about $10,000 in unemployment insurance, retraining, and social assistance, or $350 million annually, he looked puzzled. What had that to do with the banks?

The ABMs are taking on a whole roster of new duties to add to the old ones of doling out cash, and allowing customers to work with their accounts. You can get a coupon worth 25 cents off a two-litre bottle of Coke if you use one of Scotiabank's machines. They will soon be used to distribute discount coupons for restaurants, sell theatre and airline tickets, and imprint money on the "Smart money" cards we will meet later in this chapter. Some of the banks hope to use the machines as billboards, which will deliver a spiel along with the cash, when you access them.

Even better, you can now access your bank account over the telephone, and pay even more. On the TD Bankline, it costs you 50 cents to find out what your balance is, $1.30 to pay a bill, or $1.50 to have the bank fax you a print-out of the current state of your insolvency. The banks love it; they collect lots of money, and they don't have to have you within miles of the premises.

Among the banks' most recent inventions are two services available at Scotiabank and the Royal, which will give customers a print-out of their ten most recent transactions, in the case of Scotiabank, or their transactions over the previous seven days, through an ABM, at 50 cents a whack. This new service, replacing the free one where you passed your bankbook over and looked at the result, was installed "in response to customer requests,"[15] as usual.

The way around large service charges for items that used to come free, the banks tell us, is to buy one of their package deals for anywhere from $3 to $25 a month.[16] This would be a more persuasive argument if, as already noted, the banks didn't boast in their annual reports about how much they make by switching customers onto these grab-bag arrangements. What seems to me to be happening is that the banks keep raising their charges to the point where a monthly fee seems less onerous, and then they will load more onto the monthly fee, just to make sure no one escapes alive.

Plastic Makes Perfect

The ABMs, along with the phone links and monthly packages, have helped the banks to decrease staff and increase their take from service charges, but they do just as well on credit cards and debit cards. In part, this is the case because they collect at both ends; the customer pays an annual fee for the card (usually), pays stupendous interest rates on any amount not paid off by the due date, and then the retailer forks over a fee, anywhere from 1.75 per cent to 5 per cent of every purchase, for the privilege of being hooked up to Visa, or MasterCard. Canadians currently hold 58.5 million credit cards,[17] 3.3 of them for every adult in the country. The number of transactions on them has risen to a staggering 840 million per annum. In 1995, Canadians spent $61 billion through their credit cards[18] (not all from banks; the trust companies, owned mostly by the banks, and other deposit-taking institutions, have part of the action). On average, Canadians have unpaid balances on their credit cards of $17.4 billion. The rate of interest charged on these cards ranges from 11.75 to 16.75 per cent per annum. The banks refuse to break down their costs and revenues on these cards, but the interest on $17.4 billion at 11.75 per cent would come to $2 billion annually, give or take a doubloon; and at 16.75 per cent, the take is $2.9 billion.

Now you know why you are always getting another credit-card application in the mail, even if you are a few months behind in your payments. On one notable occasion, I was in a war with American Express which had reached the stage when they were sicking a collection company onto me, and I was threatening to sue them, and, right smack dab in the middle of the exchange of hostilities came a warm letter thanking me for being such a wonderful customer, and offering to boost me from mere-mortaldom to a gold card. I told them what they could do with the gold card, adding a caution that, if they took my suggestion, they should watch out for the jagged edges, but I was impressed by their zeal to press new credit on one who, on their books at least, was a deadbeat. (It took about six months for my wife to prove that we didn't owe a dime; in fact, they said they owed us eighteen dollars. Joan told them to put it in the coffee fund. She is nicer than I.) It was not a matter for celebration when Amex announced in 1996 that it was bringing out a credit card to compete directly with Visa and MasterCard.

Almost every week, there is a new card, with a new gimmick—air miles, shopping discounts, reward points, or travel insurance—to persuade us to accumulate more of the things and use them oftener. Two car companies, Ford and General Motors, have deals with credit-card companies under which 5 per cent of every purchase becomes a bonus which can be accumulated, at a maximum rate of up to $500, for seven years, to give you a $3,500 head-start on the lease or purchase of a new car—which has undoubtedly gone up in price by at least that much during the time you saved. The telephone companies will also kick back a percentage of long distance fees into this pool. Then, there are the "affinity" cards, which will kick a small percentage of your purchases into a charitable organization, or a university, as a reward for your continuing loyalty, and spending. All of these gimmicks are based on the simple principle that customers will spend more when they think they are getting something for nothing. Works, too.

The banks are the prime instigators of such gimmicks for the very good reason that the cards represent billions of dollars created in their hands, and they can collect fees, at one end, and interest at the other, on this made-up money. At the minimum transaction fee of 1.75 per cent on $61 billion in purchases during 1995, credit cards created a pool of $1.067 billion for the operators, before they started collecting interest.

With the profits, they can generate nice little pamphlets to tell us that we must be more prudent and financially responsible, because money doesn't grow on trees, you know. Only on plastic.

Visa and MasterCard both started as American cards—respectively BankAmericard, which became Chargex when it came to Canada in 1968, and Master Charge. The parent institutions are now called Visa International and MasterCard International, and the individual companies, such as Royal Bank Visa, the largest issuer of Visa cards, and Bank of Montreal MasterCard, the largest issuer of MasterCards, are franchised from the parents, which are non-profit, private corporations whose operations are not open to public scrutiny. The key point for the consumer to remember is that it is the individual bank, trust, or other card-issuing institution that sets the rates and terms for its cards, and rakes in the profits.

This became a matter of some moment when the Bank Rate began to dip in 1994 and 1995; the institutions carrying both Visa and MasterCard were mighty slow in following the downward trend, and managed to widen the spread between the Bank Rate and their interest rates. The result, according to a study released by Industry Canada in April 1996, was a nice little windfall. Between 1990 and 1996, the report stated, the average difference between the Bank Rate and the Visa rate was 10.5 per cent; after the Bank Rate dropped, the difference widened to 12 per cent.[19] That difference, of 1.5 per cent, works out to $22.50 per year on an average annual balance of $1,500 per Visa customer. It's a little bonus the lenders pay themselves for doing nothing.

The banks explained that they were forced to take more money this way because, as Mark Weseluck, director of operations for the Canadian Bankers Association, told the *Toronto Star*, "We have got to cover off a higher loss," that is, from bankruptcies.[20] Bank policies, of course, contributed to a record number of bankruptcies, 78,690 in 1995.[21] Banks cannot be bothered to do serious credit checks when they flood the market with cards. To cover such losses, they are forced to pull more out of the straitened economy to add to their huge profits.

Credit Card Theft Beats Bank Robbery

Besides bankruptcies, there are frauds, thefts, and counterfeiting to add to the cost of the credit cards. In 1994, according to statistics gathered by the Royal Canadian Mounted Police, the major issuers of credit cards lost $1.75 billion to fraud worldwide.[22] In Canada, the total was $70 million. In one case, the RCMP discovered a credit-card "plant," where the crooks were using the latest in computers and laser printers to emboss, code, and "tip" fake cards.* Corporal Michael Duncan, the RCMP expert who described the operation, noted that "the resulting losses to the Canadian consumer were conservatively estimated to be in the tens of millions of dollars."[23] To beat the fraud artists, the credit-card issuers are developing ever more complicated means of producing their cards, but they cannot stay ahead of the villains.

By and large, the banks meet this problem by a singular incuriosity.

---

* "Tipping" is the process of applying colour to the surface of the account number on the card. It is hard, and expensive, to do, but apparently worthwhile.

My wife and I received a call from MasterCard soon after a trip to England, asking us if we had spent $10,000 or so in the last few days. After I recovered from the fainting fit, I said, No. Well, the funny thing is, the voice from MasterCard said, someone did. Credit-card slips totalling just over $11,000 had been signed in London, and on a trip to Ireland, over a period of five days. They had a hell of a fine time, too—one luncheon cost more than $300; then there were a couple of watches worth more than $2,000, shoes, gloves, and all the fixings, to say nothing of a rental car, ferry tickets, and lots of grog.

We thought we had a pretty good idea of where our card had been held back and copied, and offered to do all we could to help. If MasterCard would just tell us which signature was on the slips—mine or my wife's—we could probably pinpoint it. MasterCard withdrew, with a stern word to the effect that it was none of our damn business, and they would look after the matter. When pressed, MasterCard admitted that what they would do would be to try to hit the merchants involved for some of the money—what were they doing allowing charges long after we had passed our credit limit?—but that it was "very unlikely" that any attempt would ever be made to bring the culprits to heel. It cost too much. Though we did not have to pay any of the pirate charges, we were stunned at the notion that money amounting to about three average bank robberies would be written off this way.

However, in retrospect, MasterCard was no doubt correct. There was very little chance that the fraud could be traced. Someone makes a note of the numbers on a card presented to a store or restaurant. The numbers are embossed onto a new card created in one of the plants that exist all over the world. The new card is sold for a few hundred dollars, used to rack up a few thousand, and then dumped. In the bad old days, the crooks would send the card to Hong Kong, or some other exotic spot, before the spending started, but nowadays they don't bother. The system is too broad for anything as complicated as that.

If the merchant had to go through any serious form of checking the customer, or the clerk who okays the transaction had to do anything more than check the credit balance in the account on a computer, it would slow the process down, and irritate everyone.

The cost of crookedness is just built in to the cost of the card—the parallel is to the cost of shop-lifting—and that's that.

In another case, we were charged twice for the same item by the same store, but it was invoiced under a different merchant name. When we caught it, and complained, the credit-card company told us the same merchant had done this several times in recent weeks, and they were thinking of looking into it. We go over our credit-card statements with a magnifying glass, but thousands of Canadians, probably hundreds of thousands, just look at the bill, groan, and pay it.

Besides the cost to the user, and the inducements to crime, there are other problems with credit cards, including the fact that they often make credit junkies of people who are simply unable to handle them. As our bankruptcies rose in 1994 and 1995, so did the number and use of credit cards, as Canadians tried to employ plastic to keep afloat. In addition, the cards lead to a lot of headaches when, inevitably, things go wrong.

You sign a chit for $56.81, and it gets translated into $568.10 on the account. You scream. The credit-card company tells you to pay up, and you will be credited later with a refund. If you scream loudly enough, and if you have a receipt, you can fax the receipt to the company, and it will withhold payment from the merchant. But you have very little bargaining room. The agreement that governs the card leaves you with little option: "You agree to accept our records of a transaction as being accurate unless you can provide contrary evidence that is satisfactory to us."[24] And, "if a dispute arises about a transaction for which you used your card or charge-cheques, you must settle it directly with the merchant or business concerned."[25]

The money in dispute becomes a debt the moment you use the card. The agreement's statement that "you agree to repay the Debt to the Bank" means that the bank can go into any account you have on the premises to extract payment to square a debt that may not even be legitimate. Furthermore, "you will pay all reasonable expenses incurred by us to enforce this agreement."[26]

As if we didn't have enough trouble with credit cards, now we are gobbling up debit cards, probably the greatest propaganda triumph of the banks in recent history. A Niagara of advertising poured over us, to tell us how we wanted them, loved them, needed them, and when we were taken in, and signed up, more ads told us that we had demanded them. The cards were first introduced in 1991, and by the end of that year, a total of 2.6 million transactions had taken place. By the end of

1995, there were 390 million transactions on 8.2 million cards at 140,000 terminals.[27] With the debit card, the banks again collect twice, once from the customer, and once from the merchant. Moreover, they eliminate NSF cheques—if the money isn't in the account, it will not be transferred, unless the account is covered by an automatic, and expensive, overdraft protection plan. But, best of all, as the CIBC points out in a brochure prepared for retailers, "people who pay with their banking card tend to purchase more than when they pay cash."[28]

The major advantage to debit cards, from the point of view of the banks, is that, while they create the same staggering fees, the institutions do not have to keep money on hand to pay the merchants over the period while they are waiting to be repaid by the customer. In the case of the credit card, you spend $500 at a store, and the store sends the chit to Visa or MasterCard, which bills you and pays the store. If you do not pay the monthly tab on time, you will be charged exorbitant interest; but more and more of us are paying within the required period from the day the bill was mailed to us. This led to a morose complaint from the banks: "Credit-card issuers note that one reason for the large spread between credit-card rates and the bank rate is that many customers pay off the entire balance each month and, therefore, incur no interest."[29]

To bridge the gap between when the bank has to pay out the cash and when we pay it in, the issuers have to keep money on hand. I know of no reliable figure on how much this is, but it must amount to millions of dollars every month which the banks keep to cover payments while waiting for the cardholders to shell out. With the debit card, there is no weary wait. The money comes floating out of the account the moment we sign the chit, and if it isn't in the account, the bank will gladly lend us the cash, at consumer-loan rates, to cover.

Why Canadians regard this as a convenience is beyond me, but there is no doubt that we do, probably because we don't want to carry cash, and debit cards cost less per transaction than a cheque, at most institutions; the Bank of Nova Scotia, for example, charges 60 cents for a cheque and 30 cents for a debit-card transaction; but if you are going shopping, you can cash one cheque and use the proceeds for a dozen transactions, yet many of us prefer to swipe a card and pay a dozen fees. The debit cards are processed through the Interac Association, which also processes ABM transactions. In 1995, the seventeen members of

Interac—banks, trust companies, credit unions, and *caisses populaires*—collected about $140 million in fees; the traffic is not yet close to credit cards, but it is growing even faster.

If we are such bumpkins, why shouldn't the banks vacuum our accounts?

The next step after the credit card and debit card is the "smart card," or "cash card," on which the bank or trust company puts a credit of, say, $500, which is taken off by the machines at the retail level until it is used up, at which point you stagger back to the bank, or an ABM, and request a refill. The Royal Bank of Canada and CIBC were scheduled in late 1996, in Guelph, Ontario, to try out a "Mondex" cash-card system, modelled on a British version that was launched in Swindon, England, in 1994.[30] This card is to cover smaller purchases than the debit card, which retailers will not usually accept on purchases of less than $10.

All of this is part of the move to the "cashless" society. The watchword is "convenience" and we are told that Canadians find money inconvenient. It is the banks and other deposit-taking institutions, in fact, that find the computer-driven world convenient, and profitable. As we move into electronic merchandising, where we will be able not only to bank on the computer, but to go shopping there, we appear oblivious to the dangers, including the invasion of privacy, which is an integral part of modern banking.

Nothing Is Private

Douglas Goold, in *How to Get What You Want from Your Bank*, recounts the story of the friend of a colleague who wrote a large cheque on an account at Canada Trust to cover the purchase of Treasury bills at RBC Dominion Securities, which is owned by the Royal. She got a letter from Canada Trust noting that they were "sorry to see" that she had gone to "other institutions for your financial needs."

Goold asks: "What right has a financial institution to single out a customer's private cheque for attention and then put the make on the customer?"[31] A better question might be: What is to prevent any financial institution from doing this? And the answer is, nothing.

The Canadian Bankers Association adopted a privacy code in 1990 which gives the customer the right to see and challenge the information held by the bank on him or her. But the small print on the bottom of a credit-card application, or almost any loan application, already covers this; it gives the institution the right to "see and exchange" information with "other parties." The Visa application used by Scotiabank goes further, and tells the applicant that

> Scotiabank collects information about its customers. We use this information to offer you products and services, make credit decisions, comply with the law, protect your interests and for other purposes.[32]

To answer Goold's question, you give Visa the right to put the make on you the moment you apply for the card.

This invasion business may work both ways. The real danger, to my mind, in our love affair with digital dealing is that some really intelligent crooks will manage to invade the banks' computer systems. Canadian banks that run computer networks are not on the Internet; you have to dial them on purpose and directly, and gain access with an assigned code. How long will it be before someone breaks a security code and dumps the whole file onto the World Wide Web?

The constant reassurances that this cannot happen, that no bank system can be breached, are so much wind and water. In Pineville, Kentucky, the Security First Network Bank has been operating since October 1995 entirely on the Internet, accessible to anyone with a computer, a modem, and the necessary software. A company official visited Toronto to explain the system to interested Canadian bankers.[33] If they are lured onto the Net, the next thing you know, as anyone who has read the chronicles of our age understands, some fourteen-year-old whiz in Farflung, Saskatchewan, will crack the code and either loot a Canadian bank's customers or bring the whole bank crashing down around our ears.

What we have to remember in all our dealings with these institutions is that they are out to get as much money from us as possible while delivering as little service to us as possible. The exorbitant service fees, credit cards, debit cards, and smart cards are all part of the same sales pitch, which is not designed to make our lives more convenient, but more expensive, with the excess going to the banks. In Part Five we look at some of the ways we can protect ourselves.

Remedies

The view is that the banks are just getting too powerful.

—Paul Zed, MP, April 1996

CHAPTER 12

Last One Out of the Vault, Turn Out the Lights

> Look, I get enough God damned complaints ... about the banks
> and their treatment of customers now. Imagine how many I'd get
> if we had one big bank.

—Doug Peters,
Secretary of State for International Financial Institutions, 1995

> I don't think that anybody can devise a system to replace it. It's
> not that bad. Hardly any of them are going broke.

—Justice Willard Estey,
Toronto Star, 1996

EVERY NOW AND THEN, a bank spokesperson gives the game away. The
banks spend God knows how much money on all those folksy ads with
two jean-clad chaps strolling through the woods and saying how the
friendly bunch down at Grabbit and Run Bank helped them get the
business going. Then the music swells and a deep voice tells us that
Grabbit and Run is on our side. There are people who believe this, just
as there are people who believe that a plastic pyramid, shrewdly placed

beneath the bedsprings, will improve our sex lives. But they are a minority. So when a banker comes right out and says that the banks are taking as much of your money as possible, the spin-doctors can only heave a weary sigh and trot out another ad campaign to undo the damage.

Not long ago, the Bank of Montreal, which alone among our Big Five banks seems to have heard of competition, took out newspaper ads poking fun at the others for paying interest on savings accounts that ranges from 0.25 to 0.75 per cent.

"Quit hanging around with a bunch of zeros," the ad advised, pointing to its own savings accounts, then at 4.25 per cent (but since diminished).

When customers began to flock across the street in response to this lure, the TD raised the rate on its Investment Builder Account from zero to 4.25 per cent, overnight. Not because of what they were doing at the B of M, of course; they had been thinking about it for a while and decided that now would be a good time. The reason they hadn't done this before, said Christine Thompson of the TD, was this: "Some customers prefer to earn less interest because they prefer to pay less taxes."[1] Thus, the bank's idea of being on your side is to skin you at every possible opportunity because they want to spare you the burden of paying taxes on any money they might carelessly leave in your possession.

I do not mean to imply that the banks are worse in this way than any other corporations, all of which exist to make the maximum profit for the shareholder. The real distinction between our financial corporations and any other Canadian companies is that banks are placed in a privileged position by the law; they can create money by government indulgence, and they are protected by government-backed insurance. Responsibilities come with these advantages.

There will never be a better time for ordinary Canadians to contribute to the debate than over the next two or three years, while the task force, and then Parliament, wrestles with amendments to the Bank Act. If we are going to get any real reforms, the banks must be kept with their feet firmly to the fire of public displeasure, the process which they call "bank bashing" and the rest of us call "restoring the balance." A spate of ugly headlines, a couple of days of uncomfortable testimony before the House of Commons finance committee, and the banks discover that the changes they said they could not possibly make are feasible, after all;

whereas, left to their own devices, they are far too busy protecting us from the high incomes that lead to higher taxes to make any of the required changes. Those of us who want earlier action from the task force now assembled for just that purpose should get our ideas down on paper.

The starting point for government is the White Paper produced in June 1996, which suggests that we have a wonderful system in place now, but that it needs updating and improvement to prepare for the next century. The two crucial points are these:

> Canadians enjoy one of the strongest financial systems in the world—one that is efficient, effective and stable. For the most part, it offers a good balance between competition and the stability of financial institutions ...
>
> ... At the same time, the government recognizes that the financial sector is evolving rapidly and that the fundamental questions which have been raised by stakeholders in consultations—mainly on the structure and the role played by financial institutions—must all be addressed to ensure that we have the most efficient, secure and competitive financial sector for the next century.[2]

We probably do have one of the strongest financial systems in the world, but that is not the same thing as saying that it is a good system from the point of view of the consumer, whether we have in mind the average depositor or the business client. The emphasis is on stability; you will note that Mr. Justice Estey, the man who conducted the post mortem on the Canadian Commercial and Northland banks, has argued that the system is working well because "hardly any of them are going broke," a somewhat strange criterion. Hardly any of the giant oil companies are going broke, either. Like the oil companies, our major banks operate as an oligopoly, and any oligopoly is stable; that doesn't mean that it serves us well, only that it serves itself well. Oligopolies are, by their nature, inefficient and non-competitive.

The White Paper's reassurances to the contrary, our banks are not as stable or responsive to consumer needs as they claim. If government were to admit that things are not going well, someone would be bound to ask why they haven't done something about it; better to assume that the need for change is dictated by that useful cliché, the challenge of the future. To the government mind, the challenge of the future is that the financial world is evolving so rapidly that reform is necessary to avoid disaster. To my mind, the challenge is that the banks are running out of control and into danger. Whichever way you look at it, considerable change is coming.

I have eleven proposals for banking reform based on the evidence and arguments of this book:

1. Define Banks and Banking in the Bank Act

As we have seen, the way the law reads today, banking is what banks do, and a bank is a corporation that does it. This spacious view would allow banks into just about any business, in theory; in fact, it already allows them into the casino we call the derivatives market. The banks tell us that they serve as "financial intermediaries," borrowing from their depositors to lend to individuals and businesses, and living on the difference between what they pay the former and charge the latter. The CBA's *Bank Facts* calls it "their vital traditional role: that of society's financial go-between."[3] A clever lawyer could write that into legislation in ten minutes. Let the banks be financial intermediaries, and let them stay out of the trust, insurance, leasing, and securities games, which have nothing to do with financial intermediation. That would by itself greatly curb their adventures in the derivatives market.

2. Restore the Four Pillars

To make the point clearer, the Bank Act should restore the former, and useful, divisions between the four main financial sectors—banks, securities dealers, trust companies, and insurance—by prohibiting any corporation in any one of the sectors from owning more than 10 per cent of any corporation in any of the other sectors. Again, the legislative language ought not to be a problem; all that is required is a recognition that there is a need for such a division. The bank takeover of the trust business has had a smothering impact; the trusts were the innovators who gave us flexible hours, better rates, and a measure of competition in the marketplace. With only two large trust companies left independent of the banks, all that is gone. Who benefits? Certainly not the customers; we do not gain by the fact that there is no longer any difference in the rates offered by every institution of any size in the nation; the only beneficiaries are the banks.

In the same way, the banks' invasion of the securities industry has led to their dominance of that sector, to which the banks brought, not competition, but a deliberate attempt to end competition. They tried to cut off the availability of funds to their few remaining rivals, as we saw in Chapter 4, and they meet the argument that they are placed in an impossible conflict of interest with their customers by a claim, believable nowhere beyond the bounds of the CBA, that they maintain "Chinese walls" between the various sectors of their business. If they did, what would be the purpose in swarming into securities?

The insurance industry thinks it has won the battle to keep banks from selling insurance in their branches, but that is not my reading of what is going on in Ottawa. What seems to have happened is that the insurers simply did a better lobbying job than the banks, by putting pressure directly on MPs to preserve their market, and the jobs that go with it. One Ontario MP told me:

> In the caucus, it was absolutely clear that Doug Peters thought the banks should get the business. He told us we were sticking up for the insurance companies, and the biggest of them were all owned by Americans. I got up and said that in my riding, there were very few banks, and getting fewer, but there were a hell of a lot of insurance agents who didn't sit behind a desk, but were out in the community, active members of the community, and those were the people I was defending.

The government, then, backed off the proposal to give the banks what they wanted because of the uproar in the Liberal caucus, not as a matter of policy, and branch-sold insurance will undoubtedly be one of the matters considered by the task force. In the meantime, Quebec has passed legislation which would allow deposit-taking institutions, including banks, in that province, to sell insurance in the branches by making some tellers into agents for that purpose, thus getting around the law.[4] As well, the banks have set up insurance subsidiaries to sell policies outside the branches while preparing for the glad day when they can sell them inside. The day after the government announcement that banks would remain barred from branch-selling, I got a flyer from the CIBC offering to sell me a policy by mail. So much for the ban; the banks have already nipped around the barrier. A friend of mine was offered one year of personal accident protection, free, for being a Royal Bank customer, along with the opportunity to buy more insurance, of course— from American Bankers Life Assurance Company of Florida!

The arguments against the deposit-takers owning the insurance business have not changed; the business person who applies for a loan, or the householder who applies for a mortgage, is going to be pressured, directly or indirectly, to buy insurance at the issuing bank, whether it is the best deal or not. Indeed, the average consumer will never consider any other deal, will be afraid to consider any other deal, for fear of losing required credit. The White Paper says that the government will explore whether or not new measures are required to protect consumers "against abusive tied selling."[5] (Tied selling occurs if, for example, an individual goes to a bank for a mortgage and is told that there will be no problem if he or she switches insurers to a firm connected with the bank.) A simple prohibition against any deposit-taking institution owning more than 10 per cent of any insurance firm would end this difficulty.

In the same way, the car-leasing companies—again, the largest ones are American—thought they had won the day when Finance Minister Paul Martin said the banks would not be allowed directly into their business, but it is obvious that the subject will come up in any thorough review of the financial sector. The banks say they can deliver leases at a saving to the consumer, and it may be true. They might be able to deliver pizzas at a saving to the consumer, too; but if they take over the pizza racket, prices won't stay down for long. The history of banking shows us that, once the oligopoly gets complete control of another sector, prices go up, not down.

The CBA position comes down to the fact that its major members have such a stranglehold on the financial sector that they are making too much money to reinvest it all in their core business, so they ought to be allowed to expand and expand until either they run the entire corporate sector, or they hit an outer limit, and collapse. What the Task Force ought to tell them is to stick to the work they began, and reinvest more in the business sector, and less in other realms.

3. Say No to Merger Mania

What our banks want, almost more than life itself, is to merge. Curious, really. Just after the part of the speech where the bank president talks about the fierce rivalry and healthy competition that makes his job such a challenge comes the line about the need to leap into bed with the bank next door, as soon as possible. Thus, Holger Kluge, president of the CIBC: "If we want to remain internationally competitive, there may have to be consolidation in the industry ... Whether it's going to be three or four banks, I don't know, but it's definitely going to happen."[6]

Frankly, I don't care if our banks remain internationally competitive; I would be happy if they were to be nationally competitive. What they mean by "internationally competitive" is that only the largest banks get to play lead roles in global finance—things like lending a few billions to Robert Campeau to buy up Federated Stores, which then went bust. Banks make a lot in fees on these massive takeover deals, and, if the takeover survives, in interest. But the takeovers themselves are economic disasters, except for the players. The end result is the looting of the target firm, which is stripped of assets and cleansed of employees to create a quick share profit for the predators. Why should we want to encourage that? Why is it in the interest of Canadians to spur the capture of one multinational by another so that competition may be reduced?

Besides their desire to find fat fees in these deals, our bankers contend that they need more money to buy the expensive technology they want to install so they can make more money. John E. Cleghorn, chairman of the Royal, put it this way in an interview with Art Chamberlain of the *Toronto Star*: "Today, if you look at the high cost of technology going forward, to be low-cost producers, there is an argument that says scale matters."[7] It is the same argument that applies to any corporation anywhere in the world. If we only had one grocery chain, it could cut costs, because it would increase the scale of its operations. It would not pass the benefits on to its customers, because it would have no need to; there would be no competition. The banks have not passed along whatever savings they may have made through new technology; instead, they have increased their charges and kept the profits, as you would expect them to do. Up until now, the law has kept them from merging for the very good reason that common sense and experience, to say nothing of the formal findings of economists and royal commissions, tell us that, if we let them combine, they will benefit, not us.* If they believe new technology makes a good investment, let them invest in it; that is what capitalism is supposed to be about. But if they want us to believe that curbing competition benefits consumers, they ask us to ignore the entire history of economics.

The lads are already making bedroom eyes at each other, and have come together to form data-processing firms. The Bank of Montreal, the Royal, and the Toronto-Dominion announced, in July 1996, that they were setting up a separate company to handle this business, and, three weeks later, the CIBC and Scotiabank announced a similar joint venture.[8] The reasons given are the usual ones, to save money (translation: "slash jobs"), but nothing was said about passing on the savings to the customers.

What is the level of competition in an industry which comes together to handle one of the most crucial components of its operations? As the *Toronto Star*'s Art Chamberlain noted: "The recent alliances joining back-office operations may be a way for the banks to take advantage of the benefits of merging, without drawing political heat."[9]

I suspect that what really troubles the Big Five, however, is that they are no longer in the top ranks in the lists of the world's largest banks. In 1980, they were all on the roster of the sixty-five largest banks on the planet.[10] Today, the Royal's rank is 55, CIBC 63, the Bank of Montreal 66, Scotiabank 72, and TD 94.[11] You might not think this is much of a fall, but apparently, it is almost too much to bear. Cleghorn, the Royal's chairman, warns that: "Since the size of a bank has a major bearing on its ability to do business, we can foresee a gradual erosion of the ability of Canadian banks to compete internationally."[12]

There is no evidence for this claim. Our banks continue to grow much faster than the economy, much faster than international trade; their complaint is that other banks from other lands are growing even faster. Tables 10 and 11 show that the banks have grown, in both size and profit, much faster than the national Gross Domestic Product. Between 1990 and 1996, the capitalization of the largest Canadian banks (that is,

---

* Adam Smith put the point with crystal clarity in *The Wealth of Nations*, more than two centuries ago: "People of the same trade seldom meet together, even for merriment and diversion, but the conversation ends in a conspiracy against the public, or in some contrivance to raise prices."

their share prices multiplied by the number of shares) grew by 214 per cent.[13] That is monumental, but apparently not enough for our banks, because the American banks, on average, grew even faster—by 584 per cent.[14] So what? The U.S. banking system, we keep being told, is entirely different from our own. For one thing, they have more than 8,000 banks, and we have, for all practical purposes, 5. It is entirely possible that the mushrooming growth of the U.S. banks represents massive stock swindles as much as real growth—American banking history is full of watered stock. But no, our banks fear that foreigners, noting that the Royal only has $183 billion, will turn away in disgust, to Japan, home of the world's largest banks. Of course, Japan has its own problems. As Raisuke Miyawaki, an expert on the subject, told Reuters: "Bankers look like gentlemen on the surface. But they are doing bad things and have ties to the underworld."[15] Seven Japanese *jusen*, which are mortgage holding companies in the banking sector, managed to run up $86 billion in loans now judged to be irrecoverable, and, in all, the Japanese banks are looking at more than $500 billion in bad debts.[16] Their bad debts alone amount to 60 per cent of the total assets of our chartered banks. Is this what we should be aiming for?

When I asked Doug Peters about allowing the Canadian banks to merge, he made two points. The first was the obvious one: "The biggest banks are all Japanese and look at the trouble they're in."

The second was: "I try to imagine the Canadian banks coming together, and you have all the chairmen sitting around, and one says, "No, John, you be chairman," and John says, 'No, Harry, you're the best one for the job' ..."[17] And he laughed. I find the first argument stronger than the second. Corporate leaders have massive egos; sometimes, it is all they have. But corporate mergers take place nonetheless, and, if necessary, over the bodies of the egotists who do not want to yield place.

While people like Doug Peters don't think the mergers are necessary, it's clear that our bankers do, and Jim Peterson, chairman of the House finance committee, told me: "I'd have to hear the arguments on both sides, but I have no objection in principle."[18]

Merging is simply done; just remove the section of the Bank Act that prohibits any single person or corporation from owning more than 10 per cent of a large bank (the prohibition applies only to Schedule I banks).

The White Paper does not address this subject directly, although it drops a number of hints, such as this one: "While the level of concentration may have increased over the past 10 years, there is no concrete evidence suggesting that this increase has had a negative impact on the state of competition."[19] This seems to suggest that increased concentration has no bearing on market rivalry, an entirely new approach to market theory. I think we are being set up to swallow the notion that "international competitiveness," that nostrum of our time, will force us to allow the banks to wed, just so our lads can hold their heads up at meetings of the BIS.

When the banks appear before the task force begging to be wed, they should be told to take a cold shower, and forget about it.

4. A Tax on Financial Transactions

Jack Biddell, an accountant, bankruptcy specialist, and author, has developed, with the help of Jordan Grant, chair of the Bank of Canada for Canadians Coalition, a proposal for a financial transactions tax, or FTT (pronounced "fit," which is what the bankers have every time you mention it). It would replace the GST, and would, at a rate ranging from, at most, 0.25 per cent, and, at least, 0.1 per cent, be applied to every financial transaction from cashing a cheque or using a credit card to derivatives trading. Biddell argues that this tax would raise more than the GST—at 0.25 per cent, it would bring in $37.5 billion, enough to replace both the GST and provincial sales taxes—and would be much simpler to operate. You turn the job over to a few financial-service organizations, and monitor them closely. An added advantage to this is that it would, as Biddell put it to me, "tax the big casino."[20] That is, all those millions of transactions flowing through the derivatives market would take a tiny hit; not enough of a hit to wreck the market, by any means, but enough to begin to separate real investment for a financial purpose from mere gambling. The margins on most of the casino deals are too narrow to permit much leeway; the money is made by sloshing millions of dollars around at a time, and taking a tiny cut from each. This is particularly true of arbitrage trading, where the dealer buys in one market and sells the same item in another market at the same time, to take advantage of a tiny and temporary difference in rates. Even a small tax would make this unprofitable, and force the traders to look for deals that represent significant economic activity, rather than mere dice-rolling.

The objection to the FTT is that it would interfere with the free ride the financial sector has been having. There are no taxes on these transactions at all, on the grounds that the players, being rich, will not tolerate any. The traders will simply move the business offshore, or evade the tax. Well, it's an argument. It seems to be based on the supposition that, in order to avoid having to collect a tax on transactions that is so small as to be almost invisible, our banks and other financial traders would become a bunch of crooks. I don't believe it. Biddell, who has had a good deal of experience with banks, doesn't believe it, either. And Jordan Grant, the clever young entrepreneur and bank critic whom we met in Chapter 10, says flatly that "if the tax is low, no one is going to risk going to jail just to avoid it; that's nonsense."[21]

I think the real objection to the FTT was put, unwittingly, by Michael Walker of the Fraser Institute, in an interview with the *Toronto Star*. After arguing that "people will simply set up offshore," and that transactions will simply go "underground," he comes to the nub:

> There is no magic way to avoid the pain of retrenchment. The view that financial transactions represent some great untapped potential for tax is wrong. It avoids the main problem, which is too much government spending. The solution is to get spending in line with the taxes people are willing to pay.[22]

Taxes are not a voluntary effort; they are a matter of gathering the largest amount of feathers from the goose with the least amount of hissing. Walker, and his fellows of the righteous right, start with the notion that there is too much government, and an effective, simple, clean tax that raises a hell of a lot of money is anathema because it does not require a cut in government spending. But if we start instead from the premise that it takes money to support the public purpose, and that a fair way to get some of this money is to levy a small tax on a sector of the economy that now escapes entirely, we are on the way not only to improving the national economy, but to reforming the banking system as well.

5. Recapture the Bank of Canada

The notion that our central bank is under sufficient political control because the government has the right to force the resignation of the governor is a delusion. If we want a central bank responsive to Canada, and not merely to the nostrums of the monetarist school, it must be placed under clear political direction. The minister of finance must be accountable in the House of Commons for the activities of the Bank, including the setting of interest rates. This was the case until 1980.[23] Why do we find it so difficult to accept the notion of political responsibility for the economy? Surely it is the heart of politics. The Bank's original mandate, to concern itself with the general economic welfare of the nation, was a sound one, but it could not exist in a vacuum; the Bank was required to carry out the policy of the government, not vice versa.

Scott Gordon, an economist and bank watcher, set forth an argument in 1972 which has never been bettered:

> Nothing could be plainer than the fact that the functions of a modern central bank are functions of high economic policy ... The Bank of Canada enjoys greater freedom from ministerial control than any branch of government, with the possible exception of the judiciary; yet it is endowed with responsibilities and powers for forming and implementing public policy that exceed those of any other public body, save the Department of Finance.[24]

A strong argument that the Bank needed to be brought to heel was made in *The Monetarist Counter-Revolution*, one of the authors of which, Doug Peters, is now ideally positioned to induce reform, but seems to have lost the taste for it. In his book, Peters called for greater accountability, greater disclosure, more political control, and a clear recognition of the failure of monetarism. Obviously he has not been able to sell his reforms to his own government, and so, in the interests of cabinet solidarity, he gets along by going along. The task force need have no such constraint.

6. Put the Banks Back on the Reserves

The removal of the requirement to keep primary reserves with the Bank of Canada was accomplished in secrecy and stealth. I have argued, along with others far more knowledgeable in these matters, that it was a blunder. At the very least, the Task Force must consider this issue, which is nowhere addressed in the White Paper, but which is central to its mandate to consider all questions relating to "the structure of the

Canadian financial services sector." This is a debate that has not even taken place, yet, but if we don't act soon, the banks will simply say that it is too late to change.

7. Lure the Banks into Stronger Support for Business

Connected to the reserves issue is the issue of business finance. If we set up a system that makes it easier for the banks to buy Treasury bills than to bother their heads about business investments, they will do just that. And who can blame them? Under pressure, they have made a number of improvements, including the establishment of equity funds aimed specifically at small and medium-sized businesses, but these modest reforms do not come close to meeting the need.

The 1996 Ontario Budget laid a temporary capital surtax on any bank equal to 10 per cent of the institution's taxable capital over $400 million within the province.[25] Then the Budget stuck in a "Small Business Investment Tax Credit," through which any institution could wipe out the new tax by advancing "patient capital investments" in small business within the province. There are a number of problems with this provision, including the fact that it is only temporary—it expires on October 31, 1997. As well, none of the experts I talked to within the Ontario government knows exactly what it means. I asked one source, "What is a patient capital investment?" He replied, "We're working on that." I hope they get it straight before the surtax expires.

A much more straightforward proposal is contained in Susan Bellan's *Small Business and the Big Banks*, and borrowed from the United States. There, the Community Reinvestment Act, passed as long ago as 1979, requires any deposit-taking institution to put back into the community from which it draws its deposit base a minimum amount of the money available, and to post a notice in each branch outlining the purpose of the Act and how the institution is meeting that purpose. In many states, similar legislation sets out the proportion of community investment that must be directed to small business—as opposed to mortgages, agriculture, and other loans.

The legislation requires much more disclosure from the banks, including a breakdown, by race, gender, economic stratum, and postal code, of every loan, so that anyone can determine whether the laws against discriminatory practices are being flouted.

In addition, Bellan wants more control for business loans moved back to the branches by "requiring that any deposit-taking branch make business loans up to $250,000, as was done in the past."[26] Head-office interference has done more harm to business lending than almost any other factor, since it inevitably follows the red tape of rulebooks rather than the assessments of the lending officers in the region.

Finally, she calls for incentives based on tax lures. These would include allowing a bank which suffered losses from loans to small and medium-sized businesses to deduct up to three times the loss from its books.[27] The purpose here is to persuade the banks to advance these risky loans, which they are now almost pathologically reluctant to do. The rationale for Bellan's proposal is that it is worth the taxpayer's money to invest in business loans, even if some of them are risky, because the losses are more than offset by the gains realized from job-creation and the numbers removed from unemployment and social-assistance rolls.*

After her book was published, Bellan came up with some more intelligent ideas, which she submitted to the finance committee in March 1995.[28] She argued that the banks ought to be required to produce more and more reliable figures, to begin with, so that their performance could be accurately measured. Then, they should be given targets to meet to increase their loans. Loans under $200,000, which have fallen by 30 per cent in real dollars since 1983, should be increased by 60 per cent to make up for past deficiencies and to recognize this sector as "the source of virtually all new job creation in the 1990s."[29] Loans between $200,000 and $1 million would be increased by 20 per cent, in Bellan's proposal, to make a sector which has just kept up with inflation produce more jobs by increasing faster than the general growth in the economy.

---

* Bellan calculates that tax breaks for creating jobs through risky loans would have to earn the government money. She bases this on a default rate of 30 per cent on $11.5 billion in new loans, a ratio similar to new-ventures loans made available by most provinces. The cost to the public purse is $3.5 billion annually. There would also be the tax cost of loan forgiveness. But what she calls the "net double win," a combination of social assistance avoided, at $10,000 per person annually, and new taxes produced by the new jobs, would return money to the Treasury at the ratio of five to two. The $8 billion worth of successful loans would produce $20 billion in new funds, "which pays many times over for the bad loans."

She would use a combination carrot and stick to jolly the banks along; an annual "charter fee" on bank deposits of 0.25 per cent, which would be increased to double that amount for institutions that failed to meet their targets and reduced or eliminated for those that succeeded.[30]

These ideas are all so straightforward, feasible, and sensible that I can only conclude there is no chance on earth that they will be implemented unless the task force is persuaded that the remorseless opposition of the banks to each and all of them is based on self-interest and not the national interest.

With her experience, savvy, and empathy, the government could do no wiser thing than to make sure that Bellan is attached to any new supervisory body it creates.

8. Give Us a New Regulatory Regime

The White Paper seems ready to relax regulations, with several references to "easing the regulatory burden," but without any sensible reasons for doing so beyond the standard mantra, international competitiveness. The problem with our regulators has not been too much strictness, but too much laxity, as we learned in the cases of the CCB, Northland, BCCI, Standard Trust, and as we are about to learn in the derivatives market. The notion that, because the number of crooks at work, and the sophistication of their methods, are increasing exponentially, the government should give up regulation as an impossible task, is quaint, but hardly useful.

The OSFI, which Bellan argues "has not shown enough independence from the banks,"[31] should be replaced by a body with representation from consumers, all sectors of the financial industry, and business both large and small. The model that suggests itself is the Canadian Radio-television and Telecommunications Commission (CRTC), which, whatever its faults, is public, available, and accountable as it goes about the business of regulating our broadcasters. Call it the Canadian Banking Regulatory Commission, or CBRC. Like the CRTC, it would have full-time and part-time representatives from all of the regions of Canada backed by a staff of bureaucrats and accountants.

It would have jurisdiction only over the deposit-taking institutions, because we have already very sensibly sent the insurance, trust, and securities businesses back to their provincial homes.

9. Reform the Bank Boards

This is another of the subjects allotted to the task force, with entirely the wrong emphasis. Under "Corporate Governance," the White Paper notes: "A 'best practices' paper will be developed by the Office of the Superintendent of Financial Institutions (OSFI) in consultation with industry."[32] What we need is not another meeting of that old gang of mine to make sure nothing changes, but positive legislation along the lines proposed as far back as the Royal Commission on Banking in 1964 to prevent the cosy conflicts of interest that are currently so common. To put it plainly, there should be no cross-over between major borrowers of the banks and bank boards, a complete reversal of present practice.

The Senate Banking Committee held a series of public hearings that underlined the impotence of outside directors, that is, directors who are not directly connected with the company. They get the limo ride, the expense-account lunch, and a wad of money for attending meetings, but no key to the executive washroom. A number of these directors indicated that there was no way they could oppose management. Accordingly, the committee recommended that the executive and directorial functions should be separated on corporations, so the board would hire the president, but he would not name the board. The common rule of Canadian banks, where the chairman is the chief executive officer, would be changed; the positions of chief operating officer and the chairman would always be held by different people.[33]

The committee also urged adoption of a guideline established by the Toronto Stock Exchange, which says that the board of any public company should be run by a majority of directors who are unrelated to its operations. This is to ensure that key decisions are not influenced by management at the expense of the shareholders.

The trouble with the guideline is that it is just that—a guideline, not a rule; there is no enforcement, or attempt at enforcement. The trouble with the recommendation to separate the executive and directorate functions is the same; the committee doesn't think companies should be required to follow the rule; they should just bear it in mind.[34] The only way to impose reform in this matter is by setting down clear rules that every bank has to follow, and sticking to them.

10. Deposit Insurance

The changes recently made in the Canada Deposit Insurance Corporation rules, which set up categories of naughtiness for the deposit-taking institutions, and insurance rates to match, which are to be laid on behind a veil of secrecy, represent the opposite of responsible regulation. If the regulators think a deposit-taking institution is running out of control, they ought to say so, out loud, identifying the bank and the problem, so the consumer can make an intelligent decision, and the authorities can take appropriate action. With an open and vigilant regulator, we should go back to the old rules, with common insurance commonly paid for—in the end, by the customers—so that we are all covered in the same way.

11. Five-Year Bank Charters

Every now and then you run across an idea so simple, clear, and obvious that you wonder why no one ever thought of it before. Such a one is contained in Susan Bellan's book, in four words: "Five-Year Bank Charters." Under the current legislation, the bank charters expire with the Bank Act; that is, they are, in law, ten-year charters already, so this is not a radical change.[35] What makes Bellan's proposal different is that the banks would have to appear publicly, one by one, to justify their continued existence. Just as broadcasters, who also trade on government largesse, are required to submit themselves to periodic public examinations, so should the chartered banks. The Canadian Banking Regulatory Commision, mentioned above, suggests itself as the appropriate venue. The reviews would be staggered, with one of the Big Five under examination each year, to ensure thoroughness. At the review, a series of corrective measures could be levied against any erring institution, beginning with fines and ending with cancellation of the charter. The banks would hate it. The rest of us would love it.

How to Deal with Your Bank

To go with these eleven items of public policy, I suggest ten steps the ordinary consumer can take to protect himself or herself against the practices of our banks.

1. Haggle

Despite the lists that appear regularly in our newspapers showing what banks are supposed to charge for loans and mortgages, it is possible to get better terms. The loans officer, or manager, of the bank branch can make a deal; on a five-year mortgage, for example, you can get a rate as much as 0.75 per cent below the listed rate, simply by asking for it.

2. Complain

Banks are sensitive to the criticism that they are gougers, and if you find yourself faced with any charge that seems exorbitant or unreasonable, your local branch has the option to forgive, or lower, the charge. Naturally, the banks are reluctant to mention this fact, and will reply, when you first complain, that the charge is "bank policy," but, if you persist, you will usually win. In one case, a bank bounced a cheque of mine by error, and charged me for bouncing the cheque, and then added an overdraft charge for covering it—which it had not done. A "customer representative" explained that, although the error was the bank's, there was, after all, a charge against the account, and somebody had to pay it, because that was bank policy. I voiced my view of the policy and got the charges reversed, then was hit with a small interest charge on the overdraft I had never received; this, too, was bank policy. It took three months to get everything straightened out, and I finally received a letter of apology. There never was a policy to charge the customer for the bank's mistake; it is simply the formula dragged out on these occasions. You can complain to the branch, to the bank's customer service centre, to the Canadian Bankers Association, or, in theory, to the Office of the Superintendent of Financial Institutions, although I wouldn't count on much help or sympathy from the OSFI. On page 227 I suggest that the best place to air your grievance is at the feet of the institution's chief operating officer, who, if he gets tired enough of these complaints, actually has the power to do something about them.

3. Keep Your Slips

No human being goes over the transactions that appear on your monthly statements for credit-card, debit-card, or Interac transactions. Random checks are made from time to time, but in the main, we are all at the mercy of the computers, and the people who tap the numbers into the computers. Unless you keep all your slips and check each one against the monthly statement, you are asking to be cheated. My wife, who does the books for our company, has saved thousands of dollars by cross-checking every statement against the slips. Keeping track of them all is, frankly, a royal pain, but not nearly as great a pain as being swizzled. Oddly enough, she has only once found a mistake, a small one, in our favour, and it took her weeks to convince the bank that we owed more than they said we owed. Your statements always carry a telephone number which you can call to inquire about your account, for free. Use it, even though it is a test of patience when you sit on the line listening to a tape recording that asks you to hold on because "your call is important to us."

4. Look for Age-Related Accounts

All the major banks now have accounts on which many regular service charges, such as those for cashing cheques, paying bills, or making a withdrawal, are waived for customers who are under nineteen or over sixty years of age (Scotiabank's "Scotia Plus" account begins at age fifty-nine). In principle, I think these are quite wrong; I can see no reason why a sixty-one-year-old millionaire should escape the cost for having to cash his dividend cheques while his fifty-year-old neighbour is charged to cash his paycheque. Still, the accounts are there, and it would be foolish not to take advantage of them, if you qualify. In most cases, your bank will tell you about these accounts, and provide a brochure explaining how they work (which is dead simple, you just apply). However, as we saw in Chapter 11, some branches of some banks have employees who will not give you this information unless you ask for it directly. You can be shy, or you can be treated fairly by your bank, not both.

5. "Flat-Rate" Service Charges

The decision as to whether to buy one of the packages offered by your bank is a personal one, and, unfortunately, takes a lot of figuring. I have never found one that would benefit someone with my pattern of banking, when compared with the individual fees for cheques and withdrawals, but I do not use debit cards or ABMs, where charges can mount up quickly. Moreover, I have very little interest in all the other gimmicks offered as part of the flat-rate packages, such as a small discount on a safety deposit box, or a discount on the management fee for a self-directed RRSP. As I write this, the Bank of Montreal appears to have the lowest range of flat-rate packages, beginning with the Instabanking Plan, at $3.50 a month. This allows you up to five free cheques and ten electronic transactions per month free, or fifteen transactions through Interac. After that, you pay 60 cents per cheque, or 50 cents per electronic transaction. The regular charges are 75 cents per cheque, and 30 cents for each Interac transaction. The B of M's top flat-rate package, Gold FirstBank Plan, at $13 a month, allows you unlimited transactions, and a number of other gimmicks. The most expensive plans, such as TD Preferred Service, cost $25 a month, and give you, besides unlimited transactions, a free gold credit card, and a number of other freebies, such as free rent on the "smallest" safety de-posit box or "equivalent fee credited towards larger box." Of course, as soon as you get on top of all the details, the banks will change the plans, and you will be back at square one, trying to figure out which, if any, plan works in your favour.

6. Use Your Bank for Banking, Period

If you succumb to the banks' repeated offers to sell you mutual funds, insurance, legal advice* or other non-bank services, you may well come to regret it. For example, the banks all got into their own mutual funds late, and are not very good at it. Adam Mayers, in the *Toronto Star*, ex-amined the performance of the CIBC, which has 400,000 mutual-fund customers, and 11 mutual funds. Seven of the eleven ranked in the bot-tom half, or bottom quarter, of all similar mutual funds, and only one, a mortgage fund, ranked in the top 25 per cent.[36]

7. Split Your Cards and Accounts

Do not ever hold your credit card at a bank that has your savings in it. As we have seen, the bank has the right to go into any account, in case of a dispute, seize the funds, and settle with you later. Keep your card at one bank or trust company, and your money at another.

---

* Scotiabank wants me to subscribe to a legal-advice service for $25 a month; what would be the position, I wonder, if I signed up and then either wanted to sue, or was sued by, the bank?

8. Consider a Credit Union

With the gradual disappearance of independent trust companies, the only alternative to the banks among deposit-taking institutions will soon be credit unions. This may turn out to be good news, since most credit unions provide better services for less cost than the banks. Moreover, you get to share in the profits, which are paid out as dividends to the credit-union members. The catch is that not everyone is eligible to join a credit union, since they are often tied to employment or other criteria.

9. Try to Protect Your Privacy

The major Canadian banks adopted a privacy code in 1990, which gives the consumer the right to see and challenge whatever information the institution has on him or her. What you do not have, for practical purposes, is any right to prevent the bank from selling information about you to third parties. In most cases, you waive that right through the near-invisible small print at the bottom of, for example, a credit-card application. Douglas Goold, in *How to Get What You Want from Your Bank*, suggests that we may have reached the point where attempts to protect our privacy are pointless, in a computer age. Still, you can, and you should, complain about the careless bandying-about of personal information every time you hear about it. Goold cites a case in which the Royal Bank gave client information to the market-research firm it used to test the demand for products, and, when a complaint was lodged, the bank, in effect, shrugged its shoulders. However, a story on the subject in the *Globe and Mail* resulted in a torrent of complaints, and the bank ended the practice.[37]

10. Beware

My favourite institution, of the four banks and two trust companies where I currently have accounts, is the Laurentian Bank in Lindsay, Ontario. The personnel there are helpful, courteous, cheerful, and knowledgeable. This branch was formerly part of General Trust, and some of the staff have stayed on. General did a good job of training them, and the manager does a good job of keeping them friendly and effective. I suspect that I am the beneficiary of a happy accident, in that I can ask for guidance and get advice, rather than a sales pitch. For most Canadians, in most banks, accepting the suggestions of the personnel is like asking a car salesman whether this is really a good car.

Banks are not run by saints or supervised by angels; they are tough, self-centred, aggressive business enterprises. Do not accept that something is correct because your bank says so, and do not assume that your bank has your best interests at heart. What the banks have at heart is the same as any large corporation—growth, profits, and satisfied shareholders. The way to achieve this is to get as much money out of you as possible while delivering as few services to you as possible. Despite what the ads say, you cannot count on the Commerce, and the TD is not anxious to do it your way.

Caveat depositor.

Speak Up Now

The Bank Act is currently under review, and there will never be a better time to register your views about how our banking system operates.

Below are the addresses of a number of bodies and agencies which would like to hear from you about your experiences, good or bad, with Canadian banks, and about what changes you would like to see in the Bank Act.

1. The Task Force on Canadian Banking
This body has not established offices at this writing, but submissions will be forwarded if you send them to:

> The Task Force on Canadian Banking
> Office of the Secretary of State, Finance
> Ottawa, ON K1A 0G5

There will no doubt be a Web site for the group, once it is established, which you will be able to find through the main federal government information number, 1-800-667-3355.

2. The Senate Committee on Banking
The Senate
Ottawa, ON K1A 0A4

3. The Standing Committee on Industry
   House of Commons
   Ottawa, ON K1A 0A6
   (for business matters)

4. The House of Commons Finance Committee
   House of Commons
   Ottawa, ON K1A 0A6
   (for other banking matters)

5. Democracy Watch, the consumer watchdog group, collects information, statistics, and stories:

   Democracy Watch
   P.O. Box 821, Sta. B
   Ottawa, ON K1P 5P9

6. There is now a Canadian banking ombudsman, whom you can call, and the best of British luck to you, on matters relating to small business:

   R. Michael Lauber, Canadian Banking Ombudsman
   4950 Yonge Street, Suite 1602
   North York, ON M2N 6K1
   Call Centre 1-888-451-4519

7. Probably of more practical value is:

   The Banking Issues Committee of the Canadian Organization of
       Small Business
   c/o Susan Bellan, 39 Front St. East
   Toronto, ON M5E 1B3

8. The Canadian Bankers Association
   Suite 3000, Commerce Court West
   199 Bay Street
   Toronto, ON M5L 1G2

9. Office of the Superintendent of Financial Institutions
   Kent Square, 255 Albert Street
   Ottawa, ON K1A 0H2

10. Finally, each of the large banks has a Customer Service department, where you will be told to talk to your branch, but which will take note of your complaints.

These offices are regional, and the Canadian Banking Association, or your local bank, can give you the appropriate office to address. Why not write to the chief executive officer of the bank? And send a copy along to (1) the task force and (2) the House of Commons committee on either Industry or Finance.

The names you want for our seven largest banks are:

Bank of Montreal
Matthew Barrett, Chairman and Chief Executive Officer
129, rue St-Jacques ouest
Montréal, PQ H2Y 1L6

Canadian Imperial Bank of Commerce
Holger Kluge, President
Commerce Court
Toronto, ON M5L 1A2

National Bank
André Bérard, Chairman and Chief Executive Officer
National Bank Tower
600, rue de la Gauchetière ouest
Montréal, PQ H3B 4L2

Royal Bank
John E. Cleghorn, Chairman and Chief Executive Officer
Royal Bank of Canada
P.O. Box 6001
Montréal, PQ H3C 3A9

Scotiabank
Peter C. Godsoe, Chairman and Chief Executive Officer
Scotia Plaza
44 King Street West
Toronto, ON M5H 1H1

Toronto-Dominion Bank
Richard M. Thomson, Chairman and Chief Executive Officer
P.O. Box 1, Toronto-Dominion Centre
55 King Street West
Toronto, ON M5K 1A2

Laurentian Bank
Henri-Paul Rousseau, President and Chief Executive Officer
Tour Banque Laurentienne
1981, avenue McGill College
Montreal, PQ H3A 3K3

Appendix

Table 1
The Assets of Canadian Banks

Name of Bank	Assets in $ Million Canadian	% of All Canadian Bank Assets
Bank of Montreal	151,834	17.98
CIBC	179,244	21.22
Royal Bank	183,652	21.74
Scotiabank	147,189	17.43
Toronto-Dominion	108,806	12.88
Total Big Five	770,725	91.25
The other 57 banks	73,922	8.75
Total all Canadian banks	844,647	100.00

Sources: Annual reports of the Big Five banks; *Bank of Canada Review*, Summer 1995, p. S17

Table 2
Key Numbers on the Big Five Chartered Banks, 1991–1995*
(in alphabetical order)

I. Bank of Montreal

	1991	1992	1993	1994	1995
1. Assets					
($ Million)	94,118	104,591	113,387	122,234	151,834
2. Profit					
($ Million)	595	640	709	825	986
Return on Equity (%)	14.2	13.2	13.1	13.9	14.5
Return on Assets	0.63	0.61	0.63	0.68	0.68
3. Service Charges					
($ Million)	357	390	415	422	434
4. Shares					
Closing Share Price ($)	18.668	23.563	26.875	25.125	29.750
Earnings per Share ($)	2.31	2.38	2.59	3.01	3.45
Dividends Paid per Share ($)	1.06	1.06	1.11	1.18	1.29
Dividend-Payout Ratio (%)**	46.0	44.7	43.3	40.3	38.2
Price-to-Earnings Ratio (%)†	8.1	9.9	10.4	8.3	8.6
5. Employees					
Number of Branches	1,239	1,231	1,214	1,248	1,245
Employees††	32,130	32,126	32,067	34,769	33,341
Automatic Banking Machines	1,221	1,293	1,538	1,708	1,763

* All figures are from the banks' 1995 annual reports.

**"Dividend-Payout Ratio" refers to the amount of net profit actually paid out, including dividends on preferred shares, as a percentage of that earned.

†The "Price-to-Earnings Ratio" (P/E), a crucial market indicator, shows the share price compared with earnings; if you bought a share for $10, and the company earned $1 of income per share issued, the P/E is 10 (i.e., 10 to 1); this is not the same as the dividends, because the company will retain most of the earnings. Here, you will see that the bank paid out just over 38 cents out of every dollar of earnings as dividends in 1995, and kept the rest. Any share with a P/E of less than 10 to 1 is a good buy. Bank stocks are nearly always all good buys.

††The banks lump together full-time, part-time, part-day, contract, and casual employees with overtime hours for regular employees in something called "Full-time equivalent employees," so the number of full-time workers dropped is not so apparent. The B of M increased by 61 per cent in assets, and 65 per cent in profit, while adding 1,203 employees, or 4 per cent. Most banks, as you will see, cut employees.

II. Canadian Imperial Bank of Commerce

	1991	1992	1993	1994	1995
1. Assets					
($ Million)	121,025	132,212	141,299	151,033	179,244
2. Profit					
($ Million)	**811**	**12**	**730**	**890**	**1,015**
Return on Equity (%)	13.9	(2.0)	10.6	11.7	12.9
Return on Assets	0.68	0.01	0.53	0.60	0.64
3. Service Charges					
($ Million)	412	428	423	422	437
4. Shares					
Closing Share Price ($)	30.875	28.750	31.625	32.000	36.375
Earnings per Share ($)	3.93	(0.59)	2.99	3.52	4.18
Dividends Paid per Share ($)	1.32	1.32	1.32	1.32	1.48*
Dividend-Payout Ratio (%)	33.6	—	43.9	37.5	35.4
Price-to-Earnings Ratio (%)	7.9	—	10.6	9.1	8.7
5. Employees					
Number of Branches	1,529	1,515	1,453	1,428	1,390
Employees	n.a	42,584	41,322	40,618	39,329
Automated Banking Machines	2,405	2,596	2,754	2,887	2,990

*Something of the impregnability of the banks shows in this line; although the CIBC made only $12 million in 1992, the year of its disastrous real estate write-offs, the dividend remained constant, and so, relatively, did the share price.

III. Royal Bank

	1991	1992	1993	1994	1995
1. Assets					
($ Million)	132,352	138,293	164,941	173,079	183,652
2. Profit					
($ Million)	**983**	**107**	**300**	**1,169**	**1,262**
Return on Equity (%)	15.5	(0.3)	2.4	16.8	16.6
Return on Assets	0.76	0.08	0.21	0.70	0.73
3. Service Charges					
($ Million)	467	500	486	482	486
4. Shares					
Closing Share Price ($)	27.000	24.130	27.250	28.380	30.130
Earnings per Share ($)	2.92	(0.05)	0.46	3.19	3.49
Dividends Paid per Share ($)	1.16	1.16	1.16	1.16	1.18
Dividend-Payout Ratio (%)	40.0	—	—	36.4	33.8
Price-to-Earnings Ratio (%)	8.2	—	—	8.9	8.2
5. Employees					
Number of Branches	1,747	1,744	1,826	1,693	1,682
Employees	50,547	49,628	52,745	49,208	49,011
Automated Banking Machines	3,651	3,828	3,981	3,948	4,079

IV. Scotiabank

	1991	1992	1993	1994	1995
1. Assets					
($ Million)	88,155	97,377	106,510	132,928	147,189
2. Profit					
($ Million)	**633**	**676**	**714**	**482**	**876**
Return on Equity (%)	16.7	15.7	14.4	7.9	14.2
Return on Assets	0.72	0.72	0.71	0.40	0.64
3. Service Charges					
($ Million)	206	218	218	244	269
4. Shares					
Closing Share Price ($)	19.750	24.000	29.000	27.500	28.888
Earnings per Share ($)	2.81	2.94	2.98	1.76	3.38
Dividends Paid per Share ($)	1.00	1.04	1.12	1.16	1.24
Dividend-Payout Ratio (%)	35.6	35.3	37.5	65.8	36.7
Price-to-Earnings Ratio (%)	5.4	7.4	8.6	16.0	8.1
5. Employees					
Number of Branches	1,329	1,361	1,376	1,454	1,460
Employees	29,616	30,675	30,375	33,272	33,717
Automatic Banking Machines	1,070	1,190	1,280	1,381	1,429

V. Toronto-Dominion Bank

	1991	1992	1993	1994	1995
1. Assets					
($ Million)	68,905	74,133	85,011	99,759	108,806
2. Profit					
($ Million)	**497**	**408**	**275**	**683**	**794**
Return on Equity (%)	10.6	8.4	5.4	13.3	14.3
Return on Assets	0.72	0.58	0.34	0.72	0.76
3. Service Charges					
($ Million)	220	228	231	240	251
4. Shares					
Closing Share Price ($)	18.500	18.130	21.000	20.500	23.750
Earnings per Share ($)	1.51	1.25	0.82	2.14	2.51
Dividends Paid per Share ($)	0.76	0.76	0.76	0.79	0.88
Dividend-Payout Ratio (%)	50.5	60.9	93.0	37.0	35.1
Price-to-Earnings Ratio (%)	12.3	14.5	25.7	9.6	9.5
5. Employees					
Number of Branches	908	907	978	966	955
Employees	24,003	23,514	25,603	25,767	25,413
Green Machines	1,290	1,663	1,858	1,891	1,966

Table 3
Interest and Mortgage Rates

The Buying and Selling Prices of the Big Five Chartered Banks and Their Trust Companies

1. When they buy — Rates paid on savings accounts and term deposits, September 21, 1996

Institution	Daily Interest	1 Yr.	2 Yr.	3 Yr.	4 Yr.	5 Yr.
Bank of Montreal	1.75	4.0	4.5	5.25	5.50	6.12
CIBC	0.25	3.62	4.5	5.12	5.40	6.00
Royal	0.25	3.62	4.5	5.12	5.40	6.00
Scotiabank	0.50	3.62	4.5	5.12	5.40	5.85
TD	1.50	3.62	4.5	5.12	5.40	6.00
Montreal Trust	0.50	3.62	4.5	5.12	5.40	5.85
Royal Trust	0.25	3.62	4.5	5.12	5.40	6.00

Montreal Trust is owned by Scotiabank, Royal Trust by the Royal; their rates are the same. The Bank of Montreal and TD pay more on daily interest savings; there is no difference worth mentioning on any of the other deposits.

2. When they sell — Mortgage rates, September 21, 1996

Institution	Six mos.	1 Yr.	2 Yr.	3 Yr.	4 Yr.	5 Yr.
Bank of Montreal	6.62	6.87	6.75	7.37	7.7	7.95
CIBC	6.62	6.87	6.75	7.37	7.7	7.95
Royal	6.62	6.87	6.75	7.37	7.7	7.95
Scotiabank	6.62	6.87	6.75	7.37	7.7	7.95
TD	6.62	6.87	6.75	7.37	7.7	7.95
Montreal Trust	6.62	6.87	6.75	7.37	7.7	7.95
Royal Trust	6.62	6.87	6.75	7.37	7.7	7.95

Before the trusts were owned by the banks, their mortgage rates were lower than the bank rates by between one-quarter and one-half a point.

Table 4
Women as Directors and Officers of Schedule I Banks

Bank	Directors	Women Directors	Officers	Women Officers
Bank of Montreal	27	3	12	1
Canadian Western Bank	17	3	34	1
CIBC	36	6	73	8
National	31	4	22	1
Royal	35	2	44	2
Scotiabank	29	2	87	8
Toronto- Dominion	30	3	47	1
TOTALS	205	23	319	22

Women represent more than 50 per cent of bank customers and have, for more than a decade, represented more than 70 per cent of bank employees. They represent 11 per cent of directors and 7 per cent of bank officers.

Source: Annual reports of the banks.

Table 5
The Bank Rate and the Spread

Year	Bank Rate	Prime Rate	Savings	Spread
1979	11.25	12.00	9.50	2.50
1981	17.93	19.29	15.42	3.87
1983	9.55	11.17	6.85	4.32
1985	9.65	10.58	6.08	4.50
1987	8.40	9.52	4.81	4.71
1989	12.29	13.33	8.08	5.25
1990	13.05	14.06	8.77	5.29
1991	9.03	9.94	4.48	5.46
1992	6.78	7.48	2.27	4.51
1993	5.09	6.10	0.77	5.33
1994	7.43	8.00	0.50	7.50
1995	6.99	8.75	0.25	8.50
1996	4.75	6.25	0.25	6.00

This table measures the difference between what the banks give you for your savings, and what they charge their very best customers—the Prime Rate. In point of fact, most loans are made at at least one percentage point over Prime, so the banks' take is even larger than shown here.

Between 1979 and the end of 1995, the banks more than tripled their take from the customers, as the spread went from 2.5 to 8.5; it fell back slightly in 1996, and, on July 28, 1996, when the last line of this table was calculated, was at 6.0 per cent.

Table 6
Spheres of Influence:
Subsidiaries of the Big Five*

1. BANK OF MONTREAL

Subsidiary Name	Head Office	Book Value ($ Millions [Cdn.])
In Canada		
Bank of Montreal Investment Counsel Ltd.	Toronto	3
Bank of Montreal Investment Management Ltd.	Toronto	11
Bank of Montreal Investor Services Ltd.	Toronto	5
Bank of Montreal Mortgage Corp.	Calgary	828
Holding Company for:		
BMRI Realty Investments	Toronto	
Bank of Montreal Securities Canada Ltd.	Toronto	459
Holding Company for:		
The Nesbitt Burns Corporation Ltd. and subsidiaries	Montreal	
The Trust Company of Bank of Montreal	Toronto	13
In the United States		
Bankmount Financial Corp.	Wilmington, DE	2,550**
Holding Company for:		
BMO Financial	Wilmington, DE	
Harris Bankcorp Inc. and subsidiaries	Chicago	
Harris Bankmont Inc. and subsidiaries	Dover, DE	
Harris Futures Corporation	Wilmington, DE	
Nesbitt Burns Securities Inc.	Chicago	
HGC Bank	Chicago	

* The banks are required, under section 308(3) of the Bank Act, to disclose subsidiaries in which they own more than 50 per cent of the shares. This is only a small portion of their subsiaries.

** Bankmount Financial is the holding company for the Bank of Montreal's largest subsidiary, the Harris Bank of Chicago, which in turn has dozens of subsidiaries, including a trust. This figure, $2.55 billion, was the *purchase* price of the shares.

In other Countries

Bank of Montreal Asia Ltd.	Singapore	30
Bank of Montreal (Barbados) Ltd.	Bridgetown	315
Bank of Montreal Capital Markets (Holdings) Ltd.	London	15
Bank of Montreal Europe Ltd.	London	34
Concordia Insurance Corporation	Bridgetown	26
Concordia Life Assurance Corporation	Bridgetown	64
First Canadian Assessoria e Servicos Ltda.	Rio de Janeiro	

2. CANADIAN IMPERIAL BANK OF COMMERCE

Subsidiary Name	Head Office	Book Value ($ Millions [Cdn.])
In Canada		
CIBC Asset Trading Inc.	Toronto	
CIBC Mortgage Corporation	Toronto	133
CIBC Holdings Corporation	Toronto	487
Holding Company for:		
The CIBC Wood Gundy Corporation		
Holding Company for:		
Wood Gundy Inc.		
CIBC Insurance Management Company Ltd.		
Holding Company for:		
CIBC Life Insurance Company Ltd.		
CIBC General Group Insurance Company Ltd.		
The Personal Insurance Company of Canada		
CIBC Securities Inc.		
CIBC Investor Services Inc.		
FirstLine Trust Company		
The Dominion Realty Company Ltd.	Toronto	75
Holding Company for:		
CIBC Development Corporation		
167947 Canada Inc.	Toronto	47
Holding Company for:		
CIBC Trust Corporation		
Comcheq Services Ltd.	Winnipeg	49

Subsidiary Name	Head Office	Book Value ($ Millions [Cdn.])
CIBC Wood Gundy Capital (SFC) Inc.	Toronto	29
Holding Company for:		
Tillsmith Systems Inc.		
Bickford Enterprises		
1079879 Ontario Ltd.		
CIBC Equipment Finance Ltd.	Toronto	75
CIBC Finance Inc.	Toronto	90

In the United States

Canadian Imperial Holdings Inc.	Wilmington, DE	494
Holding Company for:		
Canadian Imperial Bank of Commerce (New York)		
CIBC Inc.		
Holding Company for:		
CIBC Capital Corporation		
CIBC WG Argosy Merchant Fund 1, L.L.C.		
CIBC WG Argosy Merchant Fund 2, L.L.C.		
CIBC Wood Gundy Inc.		
CIBC Wood Gundy Capital Corporation		
CIBC Leasing Inc.		
Holding Company for:		
CIBC Aviation Inc.		

In other Countries

Canadian Imperial Bank of Commerce (Suisse) SA	Geneva	47
C.H.O. Holdings Ltd.	St. Michael, Barbados	25
CIBC Asia Ltd.	Singapore	144
CIBC Australia Holdings Ltd.	Sydney	610
Holding Company for:		
CIBC Australia Ltd.		
Holding Company for:		
CIBC Australia Securities Ltd.		

Subsidiary Name	Head Office	Book Value ($ Millions [Cdn.])
Martin Corporation Service Pty. Ltd.		
CIBC Finanz AG	Zurich	4
CIBC Finanziaria S.p.A.	Milan	8
CIBC Euroleasing S.p.A.	Milan	
CIBC Holdings (Cayman) Ltd.	Grand Cayman	35
Holding Company for:		
Canadian Imperial Bank of Commerce Trust Company (Bahamas) Ltd.		
Canadian Imperial Fund Managers (Cayman) Ltd.		
CIBC Bank and Trust Company (Cayman) Ltd.		
Holding Company for:		
CIBC (Hong Kong) Ltd.		
CIBC Servicos Ltda.		
CIBC Bank and Trust Company (Channel Islands Ltd.)		
Holding Company for:		
CIBC Management Services (Guernsey) Ltd.		
CIBC Fund Managers (Guernsey) Ltd.		
CIBC Holdings GmbH	Frankfurt	5
Holding Company for:		
CIBC Verwaltungs AG		
CIBC Insurance (Barbados) Ltd.	Bridgetown	3
CIBC (U.K.) Holdings Ltd.	London	106
Holding Company for:		
CIBC Finance plc		
CIBC International Trust Ltd.		
CIBC Bank plc	London	15
CIBC West Indies Holdings Ltd.	Bridgetown	24
Holding Company for:		
CIBC Caribbean Ltd.		
Holding Company for:		
CIBC Trust and Merchant Bank (Barbados) Ltd.		
CIBC Jamaica Ltd.		
Holding Company for:		
CIBC Trust and Merchant Bank Jamaica Ltd.		

Subsidiary Name	Head Office	Book Value
		($ Millions [Cdn.])
CIBC Wood Gundy Finance Ltd.	Dublin	673
Holding Company for:		
CIBC Wood Gundy Ireland Ltd.		

3. ROYAL BANK OF CANADA

In Canada

Royal Bank Mortgage Corporation	Montreal	854
Royal Trust Corporation of Canada	Toronto	746
The Royal Trust Company	Montreal	147
RBC Insurance Holdings Inc.	Brampton, ON	51
Holding Company for:		
Voyageur Insurance Company		
Royal Bank Export Finance Co. Ltd.	Toronto	8
RT Investment Management Holdings Inc.	Toronto	20
Holding Company for:		
Royal Bank Investment Management Inc.		
RT Capital Management Inc.		
Royal Mutual Funds Inc.		
Royal Bank Action Direct Inc.	Richmond Hill	5
Royal Bank Holding Inc.	Toronto	7,203
Holding Company for:		
RBC Dominion Securities Ltd.		
Holding Company for:		
RBC Dominion Securities Inc.		
DS Marcil Partnership		
Royal Bank Realty Inc.	Montreal	
Royal Bank Capital Corporation	Toronto	

In the United States

RBC Dominion Securities Corporation*	New York	
RBC Holdings (U.S.A.) Inc.	New York	265

* This is a subsidiary of RBC Dominion Securities Inc. of Toronto.

Subsidiary Name	Head Office	Book Value ($ Millions [Cdn.])
In other Countries		
R.B.C. Holdings (Bahamas) Ltd.	Nassau	
Holding Company for:		
Finance Corporation of Bahamas Ltd.		
Royal Bank of Canada Trust Company (Bahamas) Ltd.		
Holding Company for:		
Multinational Services (Cayman) Ltd.	George Town	
Royal Bank of Canada (Asia) Ltd.	Singapore	
Investment Holdings (Cayman) Ltd.	George Town	
Holding Company for:		
Royal Bank of Canada (Barbados) Ltd.	Bridgetown	
Royal Bank of Canada Reinsurance (Cayman) Ltd.	George Town	
Holding Company for:		
Royal Bank of Canada Insurance Company Ltd.	Bridgetown	
Royal Bank of Canada Financial Corporation	Bridgetown	4
Atlantis Holdings Ltd.	Bridgetown	297
RBC Finance B.V.	Amsterdam	843
Holding Company for:		
Royal Bank of Canada (Suisse)	Geneva	
Royal Bank of Canada AG	Frankfurt	
RBC Holdings (Guernsey) Ltd.	Guernsey	
Holding Company for:		
Royal Bank of Canada (Channel Islands) Ltd.		
Royal Bank of Canada (Jersey) Ltd.	Jersey	
Royal Bank of Canada Holdings (U.K.) Ltd.	London	
Holding Company for:		
Chancellor Investments Ltd.		
Royal Bank of Canada Europe Ltd.		
Royal Bank of Canada (IOM) Ltd.	Isle of Man	
RBC Investment (Asia) Ltd.	Hong Kong	27
Royal Trust Bank (Asia) Ltd.	Singapore	

4. SCOTIABANK*

Subsidiary Name	Head Office	Book Value ($ Millions [Cdn.])
In Canada		
The Bank of Nova Scotia Properties Inc.	Toronto	
Holding Company for:		
Kings Place II Ltd.		
The Bank of Nova Scotia Trust Company	Toronto	16
Market Square Leaseholds Ltd.	Saint John	
Montreal Trustco Inc.	Montreal	1,044
Holding Company for:		
Montreal Trust Company		
Montreal Trust Company of Canada		
MontroServices Corporation		
Montrustco Associates Inc.		
RoyNat Inc.		
Holding Company for:		
RoyNat Management Inc.		
ScotiaMcLeod Corporation	Toronto	165
Holding Company for:		
ScotiaMcLeod Holdings Inc.		
Holding Company for:		
ScotiaMcLeod Inc.		
Holding Company for:		
ScotiaMcLeod Financial Services Inc.		
ScotiaMcLeod Financial Services (Ontario) Inc.		
Structures MBS Inc.		
Scotia Export Finance Corporation	Toronto	
Scotia Insurance Holdings Inc.	Toronto	15
Holding Company for:		
Scotia Life Insurance Company		
Scotia Investment Management Ltd.	Toronto	4
Scotia Mortgage Corporation	Scarborough	661

* Scotiabank is the only one of the Big Five that gives more information than the Bank Act demands, listing subsidiaries in which it holds less than 50 per cent.

Subsidiary Name	Head Office	Book Value ($ Millions [Cdn.])
Scotia Properties Quebec Inc.	Toronto	
Scotia Realty Ltd.	Toronto	39
Scotia Securities Inc.	Toronto	43
Holding Company for:		
Scotia Discount Brokerage Inc.		
Spring Garden Development Corporation	Halifax	
Tour Scotia Ltée	Montreal	

In the United States

The Bank of Nova Scotia Trust Company of New York	New York	2
ScotiaMcLeod U.S.A. Inc.*		

In other countries

BNS International (Hong Kong) Ltd.	Hong Kong	10
The Bank of Nova Scotia Asia Ltd.	Singapore	521
The Bank of Nova Scotia Berhad	Kuala Lumpur	59
The Bank of Nova Scotia International Ltd.	Nassau	1,833
Holding Company for:		
BNS International (Barbados) Ltd.	Warrens	
The Bank of Nova Scotia Channel Islands Ltd.	Jersey	
Holding Company for:		
Channel Islands Ltd.		
Holding Company for:		
The Bank of Nova Scotia Trust Company		
	Channel Islands Ltd.	
The Bank of Nova Scotia Trust Company (Bahamas) Ltd.	Nassau	
Holding Company for:		
The Bank of Nova Scotia Trust Company (Cayman) Ltd.	Grand Cayman	
Scotiatrust (Asia) Ltd.	Hong Kong	
Scotiabank (Ireland) Ltd.	Dublin	
Scotia Insurance (Barbados) Ltd.	Warrens	

* Subsidiary of ScotiaMcLeod Corporation of Toronto.

Subsidiary Name	Head Office	Book Value ($ Millions [Cdn.])
Scotia Realty Bahamas Ltd.	Nassau	
The Bank of Nova Scotia Jamaica Ltd.	Kingston	90
Holding Company for:		
Scotiabank Building Society		
Scotiabank Jamaica Trust & Merchant Bank Ltd.		
The West India Company of Merchant Bankers Ltd.		
The Bank of Nova Scotia Trust Company (Caribbean) Ltd.	Bridgetown	
Boracay Ltd.	Hong Kong	8
Caribbean Mercantile Bank	Grand Cayman	2
Corporacion Mercaban de Costa Rica, SA	San Jose	6
Holding Company for:		
Banco Mercantil de Costa Rica, SA		
Puesto de Bolsa Mercantil Valores, SA		
Nova Scotia Inversiones Limitada	Santiago	
ScotiaMcLeod (Hong Kong) Inc.*		
Scotia Realty Antilles N.V.	St. Maarten	3
Scotia Realty Cayman Ltd.	Grand Cayman	6
Scotiabank (Coatbridge Centre) Ltd.	Edinburgh	
Scotiabank de Puerto Rico	Hato Rey	137
Scotiabank (U.K.) Ltd.	London	82
Banco Quilmes	Buenos Aires	76
Banco Sud Americano	Santiago	39
The Bank of Nova Scotia Trinidad and Tobago Ltd.	Port of Spain	32
Grupo Financiero Inverlat, SA	Mexico City	6
Maduro & Curiel's Bank N.V.	Curaco	47
Solidbank Corporation	Manila	62

* Subsidiary of ScotiaMcLeod Corporation, Toronto.

5. TORONTO-DOMINION BANK

Subsidiary Name	Head Office	Book Value ($ Millions [Cdn.])
In Canada		
TD Capital Group Ltd.	Toronto	57
TD Mortgage Corporation	Toronto	438
Toronto Dominion Leasing Ltd.	Toronto	
Penlim Investments Ltd.	Toronto	
Toronto Dominion Place Ltd.	Toronto	20
TD Factors Ltd.	Toronto	
TD Evergreen Investment Services Inc.	Toronto	
Green Line Investor Services Inc.	Toronto	30
TD Pacific Mortgage Corporation	Toronto	102
Toronto Dominion Securities Inc.	Toronto	100
TD Trust Company	Toronto	15
TD Nordique Inc.	Toronto	
TD Finance Ltd.	Toronto	
Business Windows Inc.	Toronto	
Terbert Investment Properties Ltd.	Toronto	23
Lancaster Trading Inc.	Toronto	
Lancaster Investment Counsel Inc.	Toronto	
Toronto Dominion General Insurance Company	Toronto	10
Toronto Dominion Life Insurance Company	Toronto	10
In the United States		
Green Line Investor Services (USA) Inc.*	New York	
Webb International Minerals Inc.	Houston	
Toronto Dominion Holdings (U.S.A.) Inc.	Houston	490
Holding Company for:		
Toronto Dominion New York Inc.	New York	
The Toronto-Dominion Bank Trust Company	New York	
Toronto-Dominion Texas Inc.	Houston	

* Subsidiary of Green Line Investor Services of Toronto

247

Subsidiary Name	Head Office	Book Value
		($ Millions [Cdn.])
Toronto Dominion Investments Inc.	Houston	
Toronto Dominion Mortgage Company (U.S.A) Inc.	Houston	
Toronto Dominion Securities (USA) Inc.	New York	

In other countries

Toronto Dominion (South East Asia) Ltd.	Singapore	604
TD Reinsurance (Barbados) Inc.	Bridgetown	5
Toronto Dominion (Caribbean) N.V.	Bridgetown	181
Holding Company for:		
TD Trust (Bermuda) Ltd.	Hamilton	
Toronto Dominion Bank (Europe) Ltd.	London	33
TD Ireland	Shannon	200
Toronto Dominion Investments B.V.	Amsterdam	509
Holding Company for:		
Toronto Dominion Holdings (U.K.) Ltd.	London	
Toronto Dominion Finance (U.K.) Ltd.	London	
Toronto Dominion (United Kingdom) Ltd. London		
Toronto Dominion International Ltd.	London	
Toronto Dominion Investments Ltd.	London	
Toronto Dominion Australia Ltd.	Melbourne	
Holding Company for:		
Toronto Dominion Leasing (Australia) Ltd.		
Toronto Dominion Securities Pty. Ltd.		
Bannister Pty. Ltd.		

Table 7
How They Grew

Bank	Canadian Subsidiaries, 1987	Canadian Subsidiaries, 1996
Bank of Montreal	24	76
CIBC	26	62
Royal	33	138
Scotia	19	82
TD	30	50
TOTALS	132	408*

*Statistics Canada keeps track of who owns whom in the corporate world in a document issued annually, called *Inter-Corporate Ownership*. This table is constructed from the 1987 and 1996 volumes, which include *all* of the *Canadian* subsidiaries the researchers have been able to locate, not merely those the banks are required to report under the Bank Act. What it does not show is the foreign subsidiaries, since these do not show up in the reports the banks file with StatsCan, and are only partially shown in the annual reports. I have not named the hundreds of subsidiaries, since the purpose of this table is merely to give you some idea of the mushrooming growth of the empires after the Bank Act amendments removed the Four Pillars in 1987.

Table 8
Interest Charges and the National Debt, 1965–1995
(in $ billions)

	Federal Revenues	Program Spending	Interest Charges	Increase in Federal Debt*
1965–75	159	150	19	10
1975–82	289	312	56	79
1982–85	196	239	57	101
1985–94	956	944	314	302
1994–95	124	119	44	39
TOTALS	1,724	1,764	490	531

*To understand how the federal government could be more in debt during periods when it is taking in more in revenues than it is spending in programs, consider this example. You earn $30,000 a year, and spend, on all living costs, $27,000, leaving you savings of $3,000. However, interest charges on previous bank loans come to $5,000 during the year, so you have to borrow another $2,000 to meet these. Now, you owe $2,000 more than when you began. What is more, interest rates rise, so the interest charge next year will be on more money, and at a greater rate; every year this is compounded, so that, while you spend less than you earn on living, you get further and further in debt. The purpose of this table is to determine to what degree this happened to the federal government. You will see, for example, that between 1965 and 1975, the government received $159 billion in revenues, of which it spent $150 million on programs. This should have delivered a surplus of $9 billion. But the cost of financing the debt on the $16 billion owed when 1965 began, and which rose each year, came to $19 billion, so that, at the end of the decade, the debt was increased by $10 billion.

In 1965, the federal government owed $16 billion; at the end of fiscal year 1994, $547 billion, an increase of $531 billion. The bottom line of the table shows us that $490 billion of this, or 92.3 per cent, represented interest charges; the rest represented money spent on programs in excess of government revenues. Nearly all the damage was done in two periods, 1975–82, and 1982–85. At all other times, government expenditures were in the black, except for interest charges. A sophisticated study of this area was conducted by a Statistics Canada researcher, Hideo Mimota, and came to the same conclusion. The process by which it was pushed aside by federal bureaucrats and conventional economists is laid out in gripping detail in Linda McQuaig's *Shooting the Hippo*.

Source: *Canadian Global Almanac*, various years.

Table 9
Derivatives Exposure and Capital Bases of the Big Five Banks
(in $ billions)

	Derivatives (Notional Value)*	Credit Equivalent**	Shareholders' Equity
Bank of Montreal	666.8	12.2	7.0
CIBC	1,178.6	16.4	8.7
Royal Bank	1,337.8	16.7	9.0
Scotiabank	653.9	9.0	7.3
Toronto-Dominion	1,087.0	11.4	6.0
TOTALS	4,924.1	65.7	38.0

*The Big Five have derivative instruments whose notional value amounts to nearly $5 trillion; this does not mean this amount is at risk. The notional value is the amount of a contract in total. If you have an option to purchase $10 million worth of interest-rate swaps, the notional value is $10 million, but you will purchase the option for a fraction of that, and your risk is in the option cost, not the total.

**The banks are required to show the Credit Equivalent involved as part of their Off Balance Sheet transactions. You will see that the banks have considerably more on the table than their total shareholders' equity.

Table 10
Comparison of the Growth in Canada's Gross Domestic Product and Assets of the Chartered Banks
(in $ billions)

Year	GDP	Change from 1960 (%)	Chartered Bank Assets*	Change from 1960 (%)
1960	39.4	—	16.9	—
1970	89.1	126	46.3	174
1980	309.9	686	269.9	1,497
1990	669.5	1,599	406.8	2,307
1994	747.3	1,797	577.4	3,317

*Canadian chartered banks have constantly gained more than the general economy. Between 1990 and 1994, they grew by $170.6 billion, an increase of 42 per cent in that period alone.

Table 11
Chartered Banks' Income and Profit Growth, 1985–1994
(in $ millions)

	1985	1988	1991	1994
Interest Income	41,244	43,622	56,198	48,232
Interest Expense	30,703	29,727	39,351	28,167
Other Income	3,298	5,574	7,595	10,992
Non-Interest Expense	8,258	11,012	15,205	19,806
Net Income Before Tax	3,170	5,837	6,008	7,331
Provision for Credit Losses	(2,390)	(2,618)	(3,227)	(3,920)
Provision for Income Taxes	(951)	(2,371)	(2,139)	(2,893)
Net Income*	2,217	3,466	3,778	4,334
Growth % over 1985	—	56.3	70.4	95.5
GDP growth % over 1985	—	26.8	41.5	56.3
Consumer Price Index (1986 = 100)	96.0	108.6	126.2	130.7

*During the decade examined here, profits of Canadian chartered banks rose much faster than either the Gross Domestic Product or the Canadian Price Index, a clear indication that the banks are doing much better than the general economy. Note that the big jumps are in net interest income, despite the banks' claims that their margins have narrowed, and other income, which includes service fees.

Source: *Bank of Canada Review,* Winter 1995, Table K2. Gross Domestic Product Growth and CPI figures from *The Canadian Global Almanac,* 1996.

Notes

Introduction: The Birth of a Notion

1. Speech to the annual general meeting of the Canadian Life and Health Insurance Association, Ottawa, May 30, 1996.
2. Interview, Ottawa, May 31, 1996.
3. Press Release, June 19, 1996.
4. Walter, Stewart, *Towers of Gold, Feet of Clay: The Canadian Banks* (Toronto: Collins, 1982).
5. The Bank Act, section 2(1).
6. Ibid., section 173(1).
7. Canadian Bankers Association, *Bank Facts*, 1994, p. 1, hereinafter cited as *Bank Facts*.
8. H.H., Binhammer, *Money, Banking and the Canadian Financial System* (Toronto: Methuen, 1977), p. 140.
9. There is a detailed account of these goings-on in Linda McQuaig's excellent inquest into the Free Trade Agreement, *The Quick and the Dead* (Toronto: Viking, 1991), pp. 176ff. McQuaig doesn't think there was a deal, just palship between Prime Minister Brian Mulroney and Jim Robinson, the president of American Express: "Mulroney dealt with him as he'd always dealt with the rich and powerful: he gave them what they wanted."
10. Laurentian Bank of Canada, *148th Annual Report, 1994*, p. 2.

Chapter 1: Myths and Reality

1. All details of this case are from *Western Weekly Reports*, 1990, *Blanchard and Blanchard* v. *Bank of Montreal*, Judgement of Mr. Justice Batten, pp. 682ff.
2. *Globe and Mail*, February 4, 1982, p. 1.
3. Canadian Bankers Association, *Bank Facts, 1994*, p. 1.
4. Bank of Montreal, *178th Annual Report, 1995*, p. 15.
5. Ibid.

6. Toronto-Dominion Bank, *140th Annual Report, 1995*, p. 3.

7. Vita Health Co. (1985) Ltd. v. Toronto-Dominion Bank (1993), 89 Man. R. (2d) 86 (Man. Q. B.).

8. See Walter Stewart, *Too Big to Fail: Olympia & York, The Story Behind the Headlines* (Toronto, McClelland & Stewart, 1993).

9. Bertrand Marotte, in the *Toronto Star*, March 25, 1996, p. C4.

10. *Toronto Star*, January 25, 1996, p. E1.

11. *Toronto Star*, February 28, 1996, p. B1.

12. Ibid.

13. Ibid.

14. *Bank Facts*, p. 2.

15. Ibid., p.1.

16. Max Ward, *The Max Ward Story* (Toronto, McClelland & Stewart, 1991), p. 168.

17. *Bank Facts*, p. 3.

18. Ibid., various pages.

19. Bank of Montreal, *178th Annual Report, 1995*, p. 35.

20. *Building on Our Strengths and Investing in Our Future*, CIBC Annual Report, 1995, p. 27.

21. *Bank Facts*, p. 6.

22. Ibid., p.7.

23. Quoted in Stewart, *Too Big to Fail*, p. 320.

24. *Bank Facts*, p. 13.

25. Ibid., p. 8.

Chapter 2: The Invention of a Useful Fraud

1. Roger Orsingher, *Banks of the World* (London: Macmillan, 1967), pp. 4–5.

2. See Campbell R. McConnell, Stanley L. Brue, and William Henry Pope, *Economics: Principles, Problems, and Policies*, 5th Can. ed. (Toronto: McGraw-Hill Ryerson), 1990, pp. 676ff.

3. H.H. Binhammer, *Money, Banking and the Canadian Financial System* (Toronto: Methuen, 1977), p. 48.

4. Ibid.

5. John Kenneth Galbraith, *Money: Whence It Came, Where It Went* (New York: Bantam, 1979), p. 24.

6. Ibid.

7. A. Andreades, *History of the Bank of England, 1640–1903* (London: P.S. King, 1924), p. 17.

8. Orsingher, *Banks of the World*, p. 43.

9. Andreades, *History of the Bank of England*, p. 19.

10. Galbraith, *Money*, p. 39.

11. Governor and Company of the Bank of England, *A Brief History of the Bank of England* (London, 1992), p. 2.

12. John Giuseppi, *The Bank of England* (London: Evans Brothers, 1966), p. 26.

13. R.D. Richards, "The Bank of England and the South Sea Company," *Economic History*, Vol. 2, no. 7, pp. 348ff.

14. Governor and Company of the Bank of England, *A Brief History*, p. 4.

15. Elgin Groseclose, *Money and Man* (New York: Ungar, 1961), p. 129.

16. Ibid., p. 31.

17. "Paper money provided the sinews of war in the first five years of the Revolution and other incomes were secondary to it ... Indeed currency finance sustained the war": E. James Ferguson, *The Power of the Purse* (Chapel Hill: University of North Carolina Press, 1961), p. 44.

Chapter 3: Maple Leaf Rogues

1. Adam Smith, *Wealth of Nations* (New York: F.P. Collier & Son, 1937), p. 772.

2. Richard A. Lester, "Currency Issues to Overcome Depression in Pennsylvania, 1723 and 1729," *Journal of Political Economy*, June 1938, p. 324.

3. William Henry Pope, *All You MUST Know about Economics* (Toronto: Bergendal, 1996), p. 38.

4. B.E. Walker, *A History of Banking in Canada* (Toronto: Bank of Commerce, 1909), p. 5.

5. Ibid., p. 8.

6. Martin Mayer, *The Bankers* (New York: Weybright & Talley, 1974), p. 44.

7. Walker, *A History of Banking in Canada*, p. 10.

8. Ibid., p. 12.

9. Ibid., p. 17

10. Thomas Naylor, *The History of Canadian Business, 1867–1914* (Toronto: Lorimer, 1975), Vol. 1, p. 108.

11. Ibid., p. 22.

12. Walker, *A History of Banking in Canada*, p. 54.

13. Both these incidents are documented in the museum at the Bank of Canada in Ottawa.

14. Gustavus Myers, *A History of Canadian Wealth* (Toronto: James, Lewis & Samuel, 1972), Vol.1, pp. 183ff.

15. Adam Shortt, *History of Canadian Currency and Banking, 1600–1800* (Toronto: Canadian Bankers Association, n.d.), p. 687.

16. Myers, *A History of Canadian Wealth*, p. 207.

17. Ibid., p. 260.

18. Ibid., p. 162.

19. H.H. Binhammer, *Money, Banking and the Canadian Financial System* (Toronto: Methuen, 1977), pp. 66ff.

20. Adam Shortt, *History of Canadian Currency and Banking, 1600–1800*, p. 134.

21. Ibid, p. 69.
22. All of these are on display at the Bank of Canada currency museum in Ottawa.
23. William L. Marr and Donald G. Paterson, *Canada: An Economic History* (Toronto: Macmillan, 1980), p. 249.
24. Binhammer, *Money, Banking and the Canadian Financial System*, p. 70.
25. George Hague, General Manager of the Bank of Toronto, quoted in Naylor, *History of Canadian Business*, p. 75.
26. Naylor, *History of Canadian Business*, p. 75.
27. Ibid., p. 46.
28. Ibid., p. 104.
29. Ibid., p. 28.
30. Ibid.
31. Ibid., p. 103.
32. Ibid., p. 106.
33. Ibid.
34. Ibid.
35. The Bank of Nova Scotia, *Corporate Concentration and Banking in Canada*, 1976, p. 3.
36. John Kenneth Galbraith, *Money: Whence It Came, Where It Went*, (New York: Bantam, 1979), pp. 106ff.
37. Naylor, *History of Canadian Business*, pp. 136–37.
38. Ibid., p. 149.
39. Ibid.
40. Ibid, p. 120.
41. *Encyclopedia Canadiana*, Vol. 5, p. 140.
42. Binhammer, *Money, Banking and the Canadian Financial System*, pp.74–75.
43. William F. Hixson, *Triumph of the Bankers* (Westport, CT: Praeger, 1993), p. 179.
44. Marr and Paterson, *Canada: An Economic History*, p. 252.

Chapter 4: Pulverizing the Pillars

1. A typical headline appeared in the *Toronto Star*, April 12, 1996, p. E2— "Global mergers could force us to bigger banks." It contained this quote from an unnamed Canadian banker, "The Swiss, the Americans, and the Japanese are preparing to better compete in the global market, while we're always on the defensive at home for already being too big and powerful." Slice that how you will, it is a plea to lessen competition by merging banks.
2. Quoted in Thomas Naylor, *The History of Candian Business, 1867–1914* (Toronto: Lorimer, 1975), Vol. 1, p. 96.
3. Roy Baldwin and Leonard Waverman, *Report to the Department of Consumer and Corporate Affairs on the Interlocking Directorates among the Largest 260 Corporations in Canada* (Toronto: University of Toronto Press, 1971), p. 56.

4. Ibid.
5. *Report of the Royal Commission on Banking and Finance* (Ottawa: Queen's Printer, 1964), p. 564.
6. See Walter Stewart, *Towers of Gold, Feet of Clay: The Canadian Banks* (Toronto: Collins, 1982), p. 169.
7. *Statutes of Canada*, Chapter C-46 (Criminal Code), Section 347 (2).
8. H.H. Binhammer, *Money, Banking and the Canadian Financial System* (Toronto: Methuen, 1977), p. 137.
9. *Bank of Canada Review*, November 1981.
10. Binhammer, *Money, Banking and the Canadian Financial System*, pp. 136ff.
11. Quoted in Stewart, *Towers of Gold, Feet of Clay*, p. 171.
12. *Report of the Royal Commission on Corporate Concentration* (Ottawa: Ministry of Supply and Services, 1978), p. 244.
13. *Canadian Banking Legislation, Proposals Issued on Behalf of the Government of Canada*, (Ottawa: Ministry of Supply and Services, 1976).
14. *Vancouver Sun*, April 2, 1980, p. 1.
15. Quoted in Stewart, *Towers of Gold, Feet of Clay*, p. 178.
16. Ibid., p. 179.
17. *Senate Banking Committee, Proceedings*, 1-11-1978.
18. *Summary of Banking Legislation* (Ottawa: Department of Finance, 1978).
19. Michael Babad and Catherine Mulroney, *Pillars: The Coming Crisis in Canada's Financial Industry* (Toronto: Stoddart, 1993).
20. Michael Bliss, writing in the *Report on Business*, March 29, 1991, p. 27: "Intelligent regulatory decontrol could have prevented most of the mess."
21. Babad and Mulroney, *Pillars*, p. 10.
22. Ibid., p. 12.
23. Ibid., p. 17.
24. *Inter-Corporate Ownership*, Statistics Canada, 1996, p. 37.
25. Badad and Mulroney, *Pillars*, p. 120.
26. Ibid., p. 82.
27. Ibid., p. 83.
28. *Toronto Star*, April 5, 1995, p. C1.
29. *Globe and Mail*, November 6, 1995, p. B1.
30. *Globe and Mail*, February 8, 1996, p. B1.
31. *Canadian Banker Magazine*, November-December 1995, p. 17.
32. Ibid., p. 19.
33. The memo bobbed up during court proceedings, and was reported in the *Toronto Star* on April 11, 1996, pp. E1 and E8.
34. Ibid. A 1990 report prepared for the Gardens showed that the renewal of broadcast agreements promised "significant upside potential" for the shares. The independent evaluators brought in by the estate to appraise the value of these shares did not know about this, but, court documents showed, the bank did.

35. Ibid., p. E1.
36. Badad and Mulroney, *Pillars*, p. 30.

Chapter 5: Multiplying Money

1. W.T.G. Hackett, *A Background to Banking Theory* (Toronto: Canadian Bankers Association, 1945), p. 54.
2. William Henry Pope, *All You MUST Know about Economics*, (Toronto: Bergendal, 1996), p. 44.
3. Walter Stewart, *Towers of Gold, Feet of Clay: The Canadian Banks*, (Toronto: Collins, 1982), p. 224.
4. J.A. Galbraith, *Canadian Banking* (Toronto: Ryerson, 1970), p. 70.
5. *ER*, formerly *Economic Reform*, the magazine of the Committee for Monetary and Economic Reform (COMER), reprinted the exchange in its February 1996 issue. Also to be found in Pope, *All You MUST Know about Economics*, pp. 45–46.
6. Pope, *All You MUST Know about Economics*, p. 46.
7. *ER*, February 1996.
8. William F. Hixson, "Exploding a Disingenous Myth," in *ER*, February 1996, p. 8.
9. Ibid.
10. Pope, *All You MUST Know about Economics*, pp. 46ff.
11. Ibid., p. 47.
12. Ibid., p. 49.
13. Quoted in William F. Hixson, *A Matter of Interest: Reexamining Money, Debt, and Real Economic Growth* (Westport, CT: Praeger, 1992), p. 98.
14. Ruben C. Bellan, "Getting the Economy off the Ground," *ER*, March 1996, p. 6.
15. William F. Hixson, "Getting Banking Straight," *Economic Reform*, August 1995, p. 8.

Chapter 6: The Buck Starts Here: The Bank of Canada

1. A detailed study of the campaign, complete with quotations from the parliamentary committee that studied it, is contained in William Krehm's *A Power Unto Itself: The Bank of Canada* (Toronto: Stoddart, 1993). Krehm didn't think much of the proposal, or the Bank.
2. Letter, Jordan Grant to Paul A. Samuelson, November 18, 1993.
3. Letter, Paul A. Samuelson to Jordan Grant, November 19, 1993.
4. Ibid., p. 2.
5. *Financial Post*, November 25, 1993, p. 5.
6. Interview, Jordan Grant, April 9, 1996.
7. David Crane in the *Toronto Star*, September 19, 1996, p. E2.
8. Bank of Canada, *Annual Report, 1995*, p. 10.
9. Interview, May 31, 1996.

10. Ibid.
11. Douglas H. Fullerton, *Graham Towers and His Times*, (Toronto: McClelland & Stewart, 1986), p. 59.
12. Michael Babad, and Catherine Mulroney, *Where the Buck Stops: The Dollar, Democracy and the Bank of Canada* (Toronto: Stoddart, 1995), p. 11.
13. Robert MacIntosh, *Different Drummers: Banking and Politics in Canada* (Toronto: Macmillan, 1991), p. 6.
14. George S. Watts, *The Bank of Canada: Origins and Early History* (Ottawa: Carleton University Press, 1933), p. 13.
15. *Financial Post*, November 24, 1934, p. 8.
16. Watts, *The Bank of Canada*, p. 31.
17. Ibid.
18. Ibid, p. 15.
19. Fullerton, *Graham Towers*, pp. 55–56.
20. Babad and Mulroney, *Where the Buck Stops*, p. 34.
21. William Henry Pope, *All You MUST Know about Economics* (Toronto: Bergendal, 1996), pp. 50-51.
22. Ibid.
23. Thomas K. Rymes, "On the Coyne–Rasminksy Directive and Responsibility for Monetary Policy in Canada," in *Varieties of Monetary Reforms,* ed. Pierre L. Siklos (Boston: Kluwer Academic, 1994), p. 352.
24. Peter C. Newman, *Renegade in Power: The Diefenbaker Years* (Toronto: McClelland & Stewart, 1963), p. 296.
25. Babad and Mulroney, *Where the Buck Stops*, p. 99.
26 H.H. Binhammer, *Money, Banking and the Canadian Financial System* (Toronto: Methuen 1977), pp. 232–33.
27. *House of Commons Debates*, 1956, p. 7351.
28. Newman, *Renegade in Power*, p. 302.
29 Quoted in ibid., p. 295.
30. Ibid., p. 319.
31. Babad and Mulroney, *Where the Buck Stops*, p. 148.
32. Rymes, "On the Coyne–Rasminsky Directive," p. 361.
33. Walter Stewart, *Towers of Gold, Feet of Clay: The Canadian Banks* (Toronto: Collins, 1982), pp. 148–49.
34. Quoted in Babad and Mulroney, *Where the Buck Stops*, p. 185.
35. Campbell R. McConnell, Stanley L. Brue, and William Henry Pope, *Economics: Principles, Problems, and Policies*, 5th Can. ed. (Toronto: McGraw–Hill Ryerson, 1990), pp. 729–53.
36. Quoted in Pope, *All You MUST Know about Economics*, p. 30.
37. Arthur W. Donner and Douglas D. Peters, *The Monetarist Counter-Revolution* (Toronto: Canadian Institute for Economic Policy, 1979).
38. Pope, *All You MUST Know about Economics*, p. 52.

39 *Bank of Canada Review*, October 1975, p. 28.

40. Quoted in Donner and Peters, *Monetarist Counter-Revolution*, p. 11.

41. Marjorie Deane and Robert Pringle, *The Central Banks* (London: Hamish Hamilton, 1994), p. 101.

42. William Greider, *Secrets of the Temple, How the Federal Reserve Runs the Country* (New York: Simon & Schuster, 1987), pp. 116ff.

43. Ibid., p. 447.

44. *Bank of Canada Review*, January 1982.

45. Stewart, *Towers of Gold, Feet of Clay*, Table 3(a), p. 371.

46. Babad and Mulroney, *Where the Buck Stops*, p. 181.

47. Clarence L. Barber, "Monetary and Fiscal Policy in the 1980s," in *False Promises: The Failure of Conservative Economics*, ed. Gideon Rosenbluth and Robert C. Allen (Vancouver: New Start, 1992), p. 101.

48. *Financial Post*, February 2, 1988, p. 1.

49. See Linda McQuaig, *Shooting the Hippo* (Toronto: Viking, 1995), pp. 122ff.

50. Ibid., p. 152.

51. *Globe and Mail*, July 25, 1988, p. B1.

52. *Toronto Star*, June 29, 1995, p. B2.

53. *Ottawa Citizen*, June 29, 1995.

Chapter 7: The Gnomes of Basel Unleash the Banks

1. Ruth Dudley Edwards, *The Pursuit of Reason* (London: Hamish Hamilton, 1993), p. 637.

2. Carroll Quigley, *Tragedy and Hope: A History of the World in Our Time* (New York: Macmillan, 1966), p. 326.

3. Ibid., p. 237.

4. Marjorie Deane and Robert Pringle, *The Central Banks* (London: Hamish Hamilton, 1994), p. 58.

5. Governor and Company of the Bank of England, *A Brief History of the Bank of England* (London, 1992), p. 8.

6. Ibid.

7. Martin Mayer, *The Bankers* (New York: Weybright & Talley, 1974), pp. 30ff.

8. Ibid. Mayer, puts it this way: "Because the banks live by making loans and investments, they will tend to add new demand deposits to the money supply to the maximum permitted by their reserve position. In the Depression, this did not work so well, because interest rates were so low the banks were willing to let their reserves sit rather than run any risk at all. These days, the member banks as a group are loaned to the gunwales and have no excess reserves" (p. 34).

9. Deane and Pringle, *The Central Banks*, p. 6.

10. Ibid., p. 237.

11. Bank for International Settlements, *Annual Report, 1994*.

12. Ibid.

13. Deane and Pringle, *The Central Banks*, p. 10.
14. George S.Watts, *The Bank of Canada: Origins and Early History* (Ottawa: Carleton University Press, 1933), p. 9.
15. Deane and Pringle, *The Central Banks*, p. 276.
16. Ibid.
17. William Krehm, *A Power Unto Itself: The Bank of Canada* (Toronto: Stoddart, 1993), p. 19.
18. Bank for International Settlements, *Annual Report, 1994*.
19. Deane and Pringle, *The Central Banks*, p. 156.
20. Ibid., p. 157.
21. Ibid., p. 162,
22. CIBC, *Annual Report, 1995*, p. 44.
23. *Wall Street Journal*, October 24, 1994, p. 1.
24. Department of Finance, *New Directions for the Financial Sector* (Ottawa, 1986), p. 12.
25. Mayer, *The Bankers*, p. 93.
26. Department of Finance, *New Directions for the Financial Sector*.
27. Discussion Paper nos. 1, 2, and 3, *Implementation of Monetary Policy in the Absence of Reserve Requirements* (Ottawa: Bank of Canada, 1987–1991).
28. The Bank Act, section 457(4).
29. *Wall Street Journal*, November 4, 1991.
30. *Economic Reform*, December 1992, p. 3.
31. Kerry Sufrin and Barbara Amsden, "The Real Meaning of Reserve Reform," *Canadian Banker*, January/February 1992, pp. 14–18.
32. Ibid., p.18.
33. *Bank of Canada Review*, Table C1 and Weekly Financial Statistics, April 8, 1996.
34. *Bank of Canada Review*, various issues, Table C1.
35. *Bank of Canada Review*, Summer 1995, Table G5.
36. *Economic Reform*, March 1995, p. 2.
37. Jordan Grant, *Cost to Taxpayers of the Decrease in the Bank of Canada's Holdings of Federal Debt* (Toronto: Bank of Canada for Canadians Coalition, 1996), table.

Chapter 8: The Largest, Established, Permanent Floating Crap Game

1. CIBC, *Annual Report, 1996*, p 42.
2. From a report prepared by the U.S. Comptroller of the Currency, Eugene Ludwig, and quoted in *Economic Reform*, May 1994, p. 7.
3. *Scientific American*, January 1995, p. 28.
4. Ibid.

5. *Fortune*, July 25, 1994, p. 107.
6. *New York Times*, November 27, 1995, p. 3.
7. Nick Leeson, *Rogue Trader*, (London: Little, Brown, 1996), p. 262.
8. Ibid., pp. 253ff.
9. Reuters Newswire, July 19, 1995.
10. Quoted in *The National Times*, March 1995, p. 56.
11. *Scientific American*, January 1995, p. 280
12. *Globe and Mail*, April 15, 1994, p. B3.
13. *Globe and Mail*, May 12, 1995, p. B1.
14. *Economic Reform*, April 1994, p. 3.
15. *Economic Reform*, May 1994, p. 7
16. *Wall Street Journal*, February 28, 1994, p. 1.
17. *Business Week*, August 11, 1993, p. 39.
18. *Fortune*, July 25, 1994, p. 108.
19. *Wall Street Journal* March 3, 1995, p. 1.
20. *Wall Street Journal*, March 28, 1996, p. 11.
21. Ibid.
22. Ibid.

Chapter 9: Puff the Magic Watchdog

1. Interview, Ottawa, May 31, 1996.
2. Alix Granger, *Don't Bank on It* (Toronto: Doubleday, 1981), p. 23.
3. Office of the Superintendent of Financial Institutions, *Annual Report*, 1995, p. 3.
4. Canada Deposit Insurance Corporation, *Protecting Your Deposits* (Ottawa, March 1996), p. 2.
5. House of Commons, *Report of the Proceedings of the Standing Committee on Finance, Trade and Economic Affairs*, March 16, 1972, p. 3:15.
6. Walter Stewart, *Towers of Gold, Feet of Clay: The Canadian Banks* (Toronto: Collins, 1982), p. 108.
7. *Toronto Star*, May 12, 1977, p. B1.
8. Stewart, *Towers of Gold, Feet of Clay*, p. 110.
9. *Report of the Inquiry into the Collapse of CCB and Northland Bank* (Ottawa: Supply and Services Canada, 1987), p. 12.
10. A number of books have been written about this farrago of fraud, the best of which is Terence Corcoran and Laura Reid's *Private Money, Public Greed* (Toronto: Collins, 1984).
11. Estey Report, p. 12.
12. Arthur Johnson, *Breaking the Banks* (Toronto: Lester & Orpen Denys, 1986), p. 244.
13. Ibid., p. 212.
14. *Canadian News Facts*, September 1–15, 1985, p. 3310.
15. Estey Report, p. 502.

16. Ibid.
17. Ibid., p. 501.
18. Ibid., p. 17.
19. Ibid., p. 5.
20. Ibid., p. 502.
21. Ibid., p. 5.
22. Ibid., p. 7
23. *Maclean's*, December 1, 1986, p. 36.
24. Estey Report, p. 530.
25. Johnson, *Breaking the Banks*, p. 245.
26. *Financial Post*, November 3–5, 1990, p. 1.
27. *Annual Report of the Inspector General of Financial Institutions*, 1994, p. 1.
28. Ibid., p. 13.
29. James Ring Adams and Douglas Franz, *A Full Service Bank: How BCCI Stole Billions Around the World* (New York: Pocket, 1992), p. 348.
30. Ibid., p. 11.
31. Ibid., p. 226.
32. *New York Times*, December 18, 1987, p. A1.
33. Adams and Franz, *A Full Service Bank*, p. 134.
34. Ibid., p. 292.
35. *The Times*, July 21, 1991, p. A1.
36. *Financial Times*, July 24, 1991, p. 1.
37. *The Times*, May 23, 1991, p. 4A.
38. *Washington Post*, August 6, 1991, p. 1.
39. *Globe and Mail*, September 27, 1993, p. B3.
40. *Financial Post*, April 22, 1991, p. 3.
41. Ibid.
42. *Financial Post*, April 20–21, 1991, p. 1.
43. Patricia Best and Ann Shortell, *A Matter of Trust: Power and Privilege in Canada's Trust Companies* (Toronto: Viking, 1985), p. 53.
44. Ibid., p. 58.
45. *The Economist*, July 10, 1993, p. 75.
46. Ibid.
47. Ibid.
48. *Toronto Star*, September 2, 1993, p. C3.
49 *Toronto Star*, January 4, 1994, p. A12.
50. Ibid.
51. He wrote a column on the subject in the *Toronto Star*, January 20, 1994, p. A23.
52. The figures were given in a speech John Palmer, the superintendent of the OSFI, made to a joint session of the Canadian and Empire Clubs in Toronto, April 4, 1995.

53. See *Minutes of Proceedings*, the Standing Committee on Finance, August 15, 1995, testimony of the Honourable Doug Peters, Secretary of State (International Financial Institutions).

54. OSFI, *Annual Report, 1994*, p. 3.

55. Testimony of John Palmer, Superintendent of the OSFI, Standing Committee on Finance, *Minutes of Proceedings*, p. 35.

56. Ibid., p. 37.

57. Interview, Ottawa, May 31, 1996.

58. *Toronto Star*, July 31, 1995, p. E6.

59. *Toronto Star*, April 8, 1995, p. B1.

Chapter 10: Giving the Business to Small Business

1. *Bank of Nova Scotia* v. *Dunphy Leasing Enterprises Ltd.*, Alberta Court of Queen's Bench, Judicial District of Calgary, Judgement of Mr. Justice Power, March 26, 1990. Alberta Court of Appeal (1991), 120 A.R. 241, 8 W.A.C. 241, 83 Alta. L.R. (2d) 289, (1992), 1 W.W.R. 557. *Dunphy Leasing Enterprises Ltd.*, *S&D Rent-a-Car Ltd.* and *106315 Canada Inc.* v *The Bank of Nova Scotia*, 1 S.C.R. 552, Supreme Court of Canada, March 18, 1994.

2. Interview, Ottawa, May 31, 1996.

3. This is the estimate that was released by the office of the new bank business ombudsman in June 1996.

4. Democracy Watch, *Bulletin*, November 1995.

5. Susan Bellan, *Small Business and the Big Banks* (Toronto: Lorimer, 1995), p. 25.

6. Ibid., pp. 63ff.

7. Letter, January 29, 1992, from the Royal Bank to Amy Brooks.

8. *Taking Care of Small Business*, Report of the Standing Committee on Industry (Ottawa: Minister of Supply and Services Canada, October 1994), p. 15.

9. Interview, Toronto, May 14, 1996.

10. Bellan, *Small Business and the Big Banks*, p. 74.

11. *Toronto Star*, October 4, 1995, p. E7.

12. *Toronto Star*, November 5, 1995, p. B1.

13. *Toronto Star*, August 21, 1995, p. B2.

14. Ibid.

15. Bellan, *Small Business and the Big Banks*, p. 28.

16. Interview, Ottawa, May 29, 1996.

17. *Taking Care of Small Business*, p. 20.

18. Telephone interviews, with machines, and one person named Marc, July 30, 1996.

19. *Overview of the Canadian Banking Ombudsman Service*, pamphlet of the Canadian Banking Ombudsman, May 6, 1996, p. 2.

20. Interview, Ottawa, May 30, 1996.

21. *Taking Care of Small Business*, p. 17.
22. Ibid., p. 16.
23. Based on figures from the *Bank of Canada Review*, various years, in a table provided in Bellan, *Small Business and Big Banks*, p. 23.
24. *Report of the Standing Committee*, p. 18.
25. Ibid., p. 17.
26. *Globe and Mail*, April 26, 1995, p. B1.
27. Standing Committee on Industry, *Performance Benchmarks for Small Business Financing by Banks: A Progress Report*, October 1995.
28. Canadian Bankers Association, "Proposed Performance Benchmarks for Banks," April 25, 1995.
29. Standing Committee on Industry, *Performance Benchmarks*, p. 13.
30. *Report on Business Magazine*, June 1996, p. 30.

Chapter 11: Service with a Snarl

1. *Toronto Star*, April 26, 1996, p. A1.
2. Ibid.
3. Ibid.
4. It would earn 75 cents in the first year, and lose $11.40 in service charges; you end up with $289.35. And so on, until it is entirely gone.
5. *Economic Reform*, June 1994, p. 8.
6. Douglas Goold, *How to Get What You Want from Your Bank* (Toronto: Macfarlane, Walter & Ross, 1994), p. 163.
7. Ibid., p. 166.
8. Ibid.
9. *Toronto Star*, January 12, 1996, p. E1.
10. CIBC, *Annual Report, 1995*, p. 27.
11. *Toronto Star*, December 9, 1995, p. E1.
12. Calculated from the banks' annual reports; the CPI figure is from the 1996 *Canadian Global Almanac*, p. 189.
13. Canadian Press, August 1, 1996.
14. *Toronto Star*, September 19, 1995, p. C3.
15. *Toronto Star*, December 30, 1995, p. D2.
16. Royal Bank, *Pricing Options*, November 1, 1995. The Royal V.I.P. service is "a comprehensive package including unlimited transactions, a Royal Credit Line, Royal Direct Enhanced Service, a Visa gold card, and other account services."
17. *Toronto Star*, April 20, 1996, p. A20.
18. *Toronto Star*, May 22, 1996, p. C2.
19. *Toronto Star*, April 16, 1996, p. D1.
20. Ibid.
21. Office of the Superintendent of Bankruptcies, *Annual Report, 1995*, p. 3.

22. Cpl. Michael Duncan, "Partners in Crime Prevention," in *Canadian Banker*, November–December 1995, p. 25.
23. Ibid., p. 26.
24. *ScotiaGold Visa Cardmember Agreement*, 1993, p. 1.
25. Ibid.
26. This wording is from the MasterCard Agreement, which spells this part of the deal out in greater detail than Visa's.
27. Figures supplied by the Interac Association, telephone call, June 17, 1996.
28. Goold, *How to Get What You Want from Your Bank*, p. 76.
29. *Toronto Star*, June 12, 1996, p. C2.
30. *Toronto Star*, November 1, 1995, p. B9.
31. Goold, *How to Get What You Want from Your Bank*, p. 210.
32. Scotiabank Visa application form, 1994.
33. *Globe and Mail*, February 6, 1996, p. B4.

Chapter 12: Last One Out of the Vault, Turn Out the Lights

1. *Toronto Star*, May 16, 1995, p. D3.
2. White Paper, Department of Finance, 1997 *Review of Financial Sector Legislation: Proposals for Changes, Ottawa*: June 1996, p. 7.
3. Canadian Bankers Association, *Bank Facts*, p. 1.
4 *Globe and Mail*, June 24, 1996, p. B4.
5. White Paper, p. 8.
6. *Toronto Star*, May 13, 1996, p. B3.
7. *Toronto Star*, June 29, 1996, p. B3.
8. *Toronto Star*, July 26, 1996, p. B3.
9. Ibid.
10 *Journal of Commerce*, June 17, 1980.
11. Moody's *Bank & Finance Manual*, 1995, p. A2.
12. *Toronto Star*, June 17, 1996, p. C4.
13. Calculated from the annual reports.
14. *Toronto Star*, June 29, 1996, p. B3.
15. Quoted in the *Globe and Mail*, February 17, 1996, p. B7.
16. *Wall Street Journal*, December 20, 1995, p. B8.
17. Interview, May 31, 1996.
18. Interview, Ottawa, May 29, 1996.
19. White Paper, p. 13.
20. Telephone interview, May 23, 1996.
21. Interview, Toronto, April 9, 1996.
22. *Toronto Star*, March 24, 1996, p. D4.
23. Walter Stewart, *Towers of Gold, Feet of Clay: The Canadian Banks* (Toronto: Collins, 1982), p. 146.

Notes

24. H. Scott Gordon, "The Bank of Canada in a System of Responsible Government," in *Canadian Banking and Monetary Policy*, 2nd ed., (Toronto: McGraw-Hill Ryerson, 1972).

25. BDO Dunwoody Chartered Accountants, *Ontario Budget Report*, May 7, 1996, p. 3.

26. Susan Bellan, *Small Business and the Big Banks* (Toronto: Lorimer, 1995), p. 98.

27. Ibid., p. 99.

28. Susan Bellan, "Some Suggestions on Benchmarks for Banks re Increasing Loans to Small Business," March 22, 1995.

29. Ibid., p. 1.

30. Ibid.

31. Bellan, *Small Business and the Big Banks*, p. 95.

32. White Paper, p. 10.

33. *Toronto Star*, June 3, 1996, p. B3.

34. Ibid.

35. H.H. Binhammer, *Money, Banking and the Canadian Financial System* (Toronto: Methuen, 1977), p. 70.

36. *Toronto Star*, September 21, 1996, p. E2.

37. Douglas Goold, *How to Get What You Want from Your Bank* (Toronto: Macfarlane, Walter & Ross, 1994), p. 216.

Glossary

affinity card: A credit card tied to a merchant, university, charitable organization, or manufacturer, which sets aside a small percentage (usually 1 per cent) of the amount spent for the benefit of either the cardholder or an institution.

asset: Anything that has monetary value. Buildings and accounts receivable, even goodwill, are assets for any corporation. Because of the business it is in, a bank's main assets are the loans it has out to customers, since they represent money owed to the bank.

automatic banking machines (ABMs): Those twenty-four-hour-a-day machines that dispense money, accept deposits, and attempt to replace tellers. The Americans call them "ATMs," for "Automatic Teller Machines," but we know better. They don't replace tellers; they just make us do the work, and then charge us for the privilege.

Bank Act: The law under which Canadian banks operate. It was enacted in 1881, with a proviso that it be renewed once every ten years. What with one thing and another, that hasn't worked out, but it is still the technical requirement, and what this means is that, if the law is not renewed, or another law passed saying, Hold my coat, I'm coming, by the due date, the banks would be out of business.

Bank for International Settlements (BIS): The central bank of central banks, and a clearing and settlement agent for international financial transactions. It also acts as a lobby for central banks, and carries out research into international banking developments. Most of the shares are owned by central banks.

bank money: "Promise to pay" money, as opposed to legal tender. A cheque is bank money; refusal to accept a cheque does not invalidate a contract, whereas refusal to accept *bank notes* does.

bank notes: The real thing, money issued by the Bank of Canada and graced with the signature of the governor and deputy governor, as well as a picture of the Queen; a.k.a. legal tender. If I owe you ten dollars, and offer you two fives, a ten, or any other combination of legal tender, and you refuse it, the debt is discharged, whereas, if I offer you an IOU, or a cheque, and you refuse, the debt still exists.

Bank of Canada: The central bank, which is wholly owned by the government of Canada, acts as the government's fiscal agent, helps to carry out the government's borrowing program, provides banking services for the government and for the banks, and issues *bank notes*. It has a legal responsibility "generally to promote the economic and financial welfare of the Dominion," which it ignores, as well as a responsibility to implement monetary policy, which it has translated into a need to provide price stability, at whatever cost.

Bank Rate: The rate at which the Bank of Canada lends money to any private bank or other large financial institution. More importantly, the Bank Rate signals to the commercial banks the direction in which the B of C wants rates to go. Until February 22, 1996, the Bank Rate was set by a public auction at 0.25 per cent above the average yield on the weekly sale of ninety-one-day Treasury bills by the Bank of Canada. It is now set within a range of 0.5 per cent on the B of C's "target" for overnight loans to financial institutions. That is, the central bank decides whether it thinks the rate should be moved up or down, and, if so, changes the rate at which it charges overnight loans to the banks for clearing purposes, according to whether it sees the need for higher or lower interest rates. The advantage, according to the Bank, is that the change provides a clearer signal to the commercial banks as to the direction in which rates ought to go. The disadvantage is that only very short-term rates can be influenced; the Bank has, in effect, given up on exercising control over longer-term rates. However—and it is no small point—the political advantage is that the government can forswear all responsibility for interest rates, which are set, out of the rude public gaze, by a process few understand.

Big Five Banks: They are, in order of asset size, the Royal Bank of Canada, the Canadian Imperial Bank of Commerce, the Bank of Montreal, the Scotiabank, and the Toronto-Dominion Bank. They hold more than 90 per cent of the assets, and make a commensurate amount of the profit, of the entire banking system.

call loan: See *demand note.*

Canada Deposit Insurance Corporation (CDIC): A Crown corporation established in 1967 "to provide insurance against the loss of all or part of deposits," up to a maximum set by law, and currently at $60,000 per depositor, including interest and principal. Deposits are not insured separately in each branch; a depositor with $80,000 in two different branches of one bank would collect only

$60,000 in the event of the failure of that bank. However, joint deposits, deposits held in trust, and deposits held in registered retirement savings plans (RRSPs) or registered retirement income funds (RRIFs) are insured separately up to the same maximums. That is, a joint deposit of $120,000 held by two people in a bank that failed would be insured to a total of $60,000. You could, in theory, have coverage of $60,000 on a personal deposit, your share of $60,000 on a joint deposit, $60,000 in trust funds, and the same again in an RRSP and a RRIF. *Term deposits* are covered only if the term is no less than five years. Money orders, drafts, certified cheques, and traveller's cheques issued by any CDIC member are covered. However, foreign-currency deposits; debentures; bonds; Treasury bills; and investments in stocks, mortgages, and mutual funds are not covered. The insurance is financed by a small fee on all deposits.

Canadian Bankers Association: The professional industry association and lobby for Canada's banks. It is overwhelmingly dominated by the *Big Five*.

Canadian Payments Association: The group, made up of some financial institutions and the *Bank of Canada*, which operates the national clearing system for payments. A cheque deposited in one bank but drawn on another will be routed through the clearing system as a credit to the first bank and a debit to the second. Every day, the pluses and minuses among all the member institutions are totalled, and funds are transferred accordingly. Annually, 2.2 billion items, including cheques, Interac payments, direct deposit of pay, direct withdrawal of payments such as those for mortgages, money orders, Canada Savings Bonds, traveller's cheques, and bill payments are sorted out through the system. The annual total runs at more than $18 trillion.

capital-to-assets ratio: See *monetary mutiplier*.

chartered bank: Canadian banks can operate federally only by means of a charter, in addition to the normal articles of incorporation. In the past, charters were issued by Parliament, and each new bank's creation required the passage of an enabling act by both Houses of Parliament. Under the 1980 Bank Act amendments, a charter may be issued by letters patent; in effect, by the minister of finance acting on the advice of the *Office of the Superintendent of Financial Institutions*.

consultation process: The process through which a government accedes to the demands of various lobbying groups, and then insists that it was heeding the requests of the public.

consumer rate: The rate at which consumer loans are charged. It may be as much as 5 per cent above the *Prime Rate*.

credit card: One of those little slips of plastic that allows you to postpone payment. Visa and MasterCard are the dominant cards in Canada, but there are dozens of others, including department store credit cards. The trick is to pay off the balance by the due date, which is usually seventeen days after the statement was mailed, and three weeks after it was drawn up. Interest rates on unpaid balances are much, much higher than on ordinary bank loans, and the bank collects, as well, from the merchant.

credit risk: The risk that the other party to a transaction will not be able to fulfil its obligations, leaving the original party to bear the freight. Banks refer to the "credit risk exposure" or "credit risk equivalent" (same animal) resulting from *derivatives* trading as the current replacement value of derivatives contracts "with positive market values" plus the estimated future values of the same contracts; that is, the loss the bank would face if the deal went entirely sour. Compare with *liquidity risk* and *market risk*.

debit card: A card that allows the cost of a purchase to be deducted directly and instantly from a bank account and credited to a merchant or other vendor, at great convenience, and at considerable cost to the customer.

demand deposit: A deposit in a bank or *near-bank* that may be withdrawn by the customer at any time. The opposite of a *notice deposit*.

demand note: A call loan, that is, a loan on which the bank may demand payment in full at any time. Most business loans in Canada, but not elsewhere, are demand notes, which explains why most bankers look less worried than most business persons.

deposit-taking institution: Any institution which accepts deposits from the public, and holds them. The list includes banks, trusts, mortgage loan companies, credit unions and *caisses populaires*, government savings offices, and even some insurance firms.

derivatives: Financial instruments that derive from other financial instruments. An option is a derivative of a stock. Futures are derivatives of sales contracts, stocks, bonds, stock price indices, or anything else you care to name.

dividend: The distribution of *earnings* from a corporate treasury. Dividends are not the same as earnings, since a corporation will distribute only a portion of its earnings as dividends, keeping the rest for expansion or other purposes. Some corporations pay dividends even when there are no earnings, to keep the price of the stock up. There is very little direct relationship between earnings and dividends in Canadian bank stocks. A dividend is shown as the amount paid out for each authorized share in the company, so that a dividend of fifty cents would mean that the corporation was unbuckling its wallet to the tune of half a dollar per share, and a shareholder with 100 shares would collect fifty dollars. This would show in the annual report as "dividends per share."

earnings: A bit tricky, this one. The difference between what a company takes in and what it spends during a given period of time is its earnings, except that, due to the miracle of modern accounting, a company may show earnings when it is just about to fall over a cliff, or, indeed, is half-way down. Nonetheless, a company's profit, if any, is usually expressed as "earnings per share," annually, which is the calculated net income divided by the number of shares outstanding. If a loss, it is shown in parentheses. Note that earnings per share are not the same as dividends per share, since some of the earnings will be retained.

Electronic Funds Transfer (EFT): The system that allows funds to be transferred electronically instead of by cash or cheque.

equity: Usually, "shareholder's equity," the ownership interest possessed by the shareholders in a corporation, as expressed in common and preferred shares. The key distinction is between a corporation's equity, expressing ownership, and bonds, debentures, or mortgages, expressing debt.

exposure: The degree to which a lending institution is exposed on a doubtful loan. If Company A has a debt of $100 million to a banking syndicate, and Bank B has advanced $10 million of that loan, Bank B's exposure is $10 million.

fiduciary agent: Someone who can act in the position of a legal trustee. A major difference between banks and trust companies is that trusts can act as fiduciary agents—in handling estates, for example—and banks cannot. Since the trust companies are now almost all owned by the banks, this is not as important a consideration as it once was.

financial intermediation: Borrowing from Peter to lend, at a higher rate, to Paul. This was once the major occupation of the banks, and remains an important part of their work.

fiscal policy: Tax policy, as opposed to monetary policy.

Four Pillars: They were: banks, securities dealers, trust companies, and insurance firms.

fungibility: Interchangeability. A bank note is "fungible" if it is acceptable as legal tender, and can be exchanged for another note of stated value.

futures contract: An agreement to buy or sell a specified quantity of shares, or a commodity, or other financial instrument, on or before a named future date and at a named price. The contract obligates the buyer to buy and the seller to sell, unless the contract itself has been sold, the contracted amount of whatever is covered by the settlement date on the contract. The contrast is with an *option*, which the buyer may choose to exercise, or not, by the named date.

goldsmith-bankers: The early bankers who converted coins and acted as treasurers and, indeed, as goldsmiths.

hedge: A deal made to protect the future value of financial instruments, usually by betting both sides. That is, if the Canadian dollar is at 76 cents, its future value could be protected by a corporation that had a good deal of foreign-exchange contracts by buying financial instruments or *derivatives* based on a future value of anywhere from 70 cents to 90 cents. In poker, we call this "coppering your bet." Same game.

Interac: The shared network of *ABMs*, which allows customers to access their accounts from any ABM, regardless of which financial institution owns the machine, at, naturally, a higher price than access to your own bank through your own bank's machine.

liability: Demands against a corporation's *assets*, including loans owing, accounts payable, and depreciation. Just as a bank's major assets are its loans, its major liabilities are its deposits, since these represent sums owed to customers. In a corporation's balance sheets, assets and liabilities always balance, not because the corporation has no real worth, but because its net worth is treated as a neutral item for accounting purposes.

liquidity risk: The risk that there will be a sudden demand for legal tender to replace all the bank-created money.

market risk: The risk of market volatility upsetting the arrangements, by, for example, a sudden change in interest rates, so that financial instruments which had a positive value suddenly become wallpaper. The holder of a low-interest-rate bond faces a sudden plunge in its value when interest rates soar, because other bonds are now worth more.

monetarism: The touching belief that the key to determining economic activity is the supply and velocity of money—that is, the amount of money available in the system at any one time, and the number of times the same dollar is spent within a period. If these are controlled, the theory holds, the economy will automatically produce full employment at stable prices. And babies are born under cabbages.

monetary multiplier: The ratio between money actually employed and the multiplier effect available because the same money can be used over and over. In Canadian banks, this figure, also referred to as the "capital-to-assets ratio," was, until recently, about 32 to 1. It now ranges as high as 100 to 1.

money supply: There are three main versions of the money supply, M1, M2, and M3, with some subdivisions. M1, also known as the "narrowly defined" money supply, means all cash outside the chartered banks plus demand (personal and personal chequing) deposits. M1-b refers to this figure plus chequable savings deposits;

this figure is sometimes used because it corresponds with the U.S. version of M1. M2 means M1-b plus non-chequable savings deposits, personal *term deposits*, and some corporate *demand deposits*. M3 means M2 plus all corporate term deposits and foreign-currency deposits. Each M, as the numbers mount, contains its predecessors. The total measured money supply consists of M-3 plus government of Canada deposits in chartered banks. What is left out of the measurement are all credit and debit cards, plus any accounting for the "velocity" of money—which renders the whole process of trying to control the money supply through this system pretty nearly pointless, although it does keep bank economists busy.

near-bank: Any non-bank *deposit-taking institution*, viz., trust companies, mortgage loan companies, credit unions, and *caisses populaires*.

notice deposit: A deposit on which the holder is required to give notice before collecting. In law, a savings account is a notice deposit, and a bank may require up to ten days' notice for a withdrawal. The opposite of a *demand deposit*. See also *term deposit*.

notional value: The total value of the underlying instrument in a *derivatives* contract. If you have an *option* to purchase interest-rate swaps totalling $10 million, the notional value is $10 million, but you will purchase the option for a fraction of that, and your risk is in the option cost, not the total.

Office of the Superintendent of Financial Institutions (OSFI): The federal government body responsible for the supervision and oversight of all federally chartered or licensed financial institutions, including banks; insurance, trust, loan, and investment companies; cooperative credit associations; and fraternal benefit societies. In the past, banks were monitored, to the degree that they were monitored, by the inspector general of banks, but, with the collapse of the *Four Pillars*, the duties of the office were greatly expanded (and the staff very little expanded) to cover all the bases, more or less.

oligopoly: When a relatively few firms dominate the market for a good or service, those firms constitute an oligopoly; viz., the *Big Five* Canadians banks, the Big Three—autos—or the Seven Sisters—oil. A *monopoly* is an oligopoly squared, a situation where only one firm produces a product for which there is no close substitute, and a *monopsony* occurs when there is only one buyer for a product or service. The latter two terms are not used in the book, but I thought you might be interested.

option: The right, but not the obligation, to buy or sell securities, commodities, or other financial instruments within a given time at a given price. If the option is not exercised, it expires, and the holder loses the premium he or she put up for the option. The contrast is with a *futures contract*, in which the holder is obliged to complete the transaction.

outside director: A member of a corporate board who is not an employee of that company. On bank boards, the outside directors are normally executives of customer companies.

payout ratio: The amount of money paid out to shareholders expressed as a ratio of *earnings*. A corporation earning $1 million which pays out $500,000 has a payout ratio of 50 per cent.

Prime Rate: The rate at which loans will be granted to a *deposit-taking institution*'s most credit-worthy customers on secured loans. It is normally about one and a half points above the *Bank Rate*, so that if the Bank Rate is 6 per cent, the banks will, in unison, set their Primes at 7.5.

real interest: The difference between the inflation rate and the current interest rate. If inflation is at 10 per cent and interest paid generally is 13, the real interest rate is 3 per cent. Note that, if inflation is running at 2 per cent and interest rates at 6 per cent, the real interest rate is higher than when the figures were 10 and 13. Historically, Canadian real interest rates have run about three points above inflation, at 3 per cent.

reserves: In Canada, until 1994, there were always two kinds of reserves. "Primary reserves" were the amounts banks were required to keep on deposit with the Bank of Canada, without interest, in proportion to their liabilities (deposits). These no longer exist, and have been replaced by capital reserve ratios. "Secondary reserves" were based on a combination of Canadian and foreign-currency deposits held by the banks. These could be held within the bank, or on deposit with the Bank of Canada, where they paid interest. They are now mainly held within the chartered banks, and represent a reserve available to meet demands for cash.

return on assets: A measure of the proportion of profit a corporation makes compared with the total *assets* on its books. In banks, because the main assets consist of loans, this figure is always low, and a much better measure of a bank's profitability is its *return on equity*.

return on equity: A comparison between a corporation's annual profits and the value of shares outstanding.

Schedule I and Schedule II banks: Widely held Canadian banks—those in which no one owner holds more than 10 per cent of the shares, are Schedule I; foreign-owned, and closely held banks are Schedule II. In effect, all the big banks are Schedule I.

secured loan: A loan against which the borrower pledges *assets* as a promise of repayment, with the lender having the right to seize and sell the assets in the event of non-payment.

service charges: The fees a bank chooses to levy on any particular facet of its services.

spread: The difference between what a *deposit-taking institution* pays for money and what it gets for it. If the *Prime Rate* is 7 per cent and the bank is paying 0.25 per cent on savings accounts, the spread on Prime is 6.75 per cent. If the bank is paying 4.25 per cent on one-year certificates of deposit, and lending money to consumers at 8.25 per cent, the consumer rate spread is 4.00 per cent. Banks normally show only the aggregate of all their spreads, but the major newspapers usually carry tables once a week from which spreads can be calculated by, for example, comparing the five-year certificate of deposit rate with a five-year mortgage.

swaps, or, formally, **interest rate swaps:** *Derivatives* based on guessing which way interest rates are likely to go in the future, and turning this into a hedge, or bet. Company A thinks rates will go up, and Company B thinks they will go down; they engage in a wholly fictional transaction involving a loan by each party to the other of, say, $100 million. If interest rates go up, the party that bet that way collects the difference between the current yield and the new one, and, if they go down, the other side collects the difference.

term deposit: Money deposited with an institution for a fixed period of time, anywhere from twenty-nine days to five years or more. The difference between a term deposit and a *notice deposit* is that in the case of the former, the time-period is fixed; with the latter, a set period of notice is required, but the money may be left on deposit for an indefinite term. Certificates of deposit, used in most registered retirement savings plans, are term deposits.

Treasury bills: Interest-bearing government IOUs, sold in batches worth $1 million to chartered banks and other large financial institutions, for investment and resale to the public. They have maturities of 91 days, 182 days, and 364 days, and are sold to the banks by electronic auction by the *Bank of Canada*, at a discount. It is this discount that determines their value. A $1-million, 364-day Treasury bill, sold for $943,550, would return 6 per cent in interest. Ordinary citizens can buy T-bills, in denominations as low as $1,000, by paying a small premium to the selling institution.

trust company: These corporations, mostly provincially incorporated, act as executors, trustees, and administrators, as well as performing such bank-like functions as handling savings accounts, cashing cheques, and selling RRSPs. Until recently, they could not engage in business financing, but today the line between banks and trusts is all but eliminated, except for the trustee functions of the trusts (i.e., handling estates).

White Paper: A government document outlining proposals for legislation. A Green Paper normally opens a topic for discussion but does not lay down any government positions, whereas a White Paper gives an indication of the direction the government proposes to take, and invites discussion and debate, which may or may not be heeded.

Index